Delia Smith
The Biography

Alison Bowyer is a show business journalist who was worked for national newspapers for 17 years. She started working in Fleet Street at the age of 19, as a reporter for the *Sunday Mirror* and the *Mail on Sunday*. She later joined the staff of the *Sun* as a features writer before going freelance in 1990.

She is a regular contributor to national newspapers and magazines, writing about some of the biggest names in show business.

Alison has also written biographies of Dawn French, Noel Edmonds and Graham Norton.

Delia Smith

The Biography

ALISON BOWYER

André Deutsch

First published by Andre Deutsch Limited, 1999

This paperback edition first published
by Andre Deutsch, 2002
20 Mortimer Street
London
W1T 3JW

A catalogue record for this book is available from the British Library.

ISBN: 0 233 05080 9

Typeset by E-Type, Liverpool
Printed and bound in Great Britain

Contents

Acknowledgements

The author wishes to thank: Paul Scott, Judith Chilcote, Fiona Knight, Andy, Andrew Atherley, Glyn Smith, Professor Lionel Evans, Ken Toye, Alan King, Norman Hollands, Egon Ronay, Antony Worrall Thompson, Prue Leith, Tom Jaine, Denise Hatfield, Bexley Local Studies and Archives Centre, Caroline Hawkins, Frances Whitaker, Paul Cort-Wright, Betty Bealy, and everyone who helped with the book. Thanks also to Chester for his companionship.

1

'Delia Power'

During his first year in office, Prime Minister Tony Blair wanted to make Delia Smith a life peer. He offered Delia, a lifetime Labour voter, one of the highest honours the country could bestow on her: the chance to become Baroness Delia Smith.

She turned him down.

According to her good friend, the cookery writer Prue Leith, Delia felt she could do more good by continuing with her recipe books and television series than by devoting her time to politics. After mulling it over carefully, she quietly said no. As far as she was concerned, that was the end of the matter.

Even Prue, her friend for more than twenty years, did not hear about it from Delia herself. It was Delia's husband, Michael Wynn Jones, who proudly revealed that his wife had been offered a peerage. 'Mike told me Delia was asked if she would be a working peer,' Prue explains. 'They thought she would be wonderfully useful, which of course she would be. I've never heard of anyone turning down a peerage but Delia did. She thought long and hard about it and decided she could do more good by sitting in her farmhouse kitchen and writing *How to Cook*.

'She thought she would be more useful, and reach more people, if she got on with writing her cookery books and doing her television series, rather than be Baroness Delia Smith. She would never do something that she didn't do wholeheartedly. She felt she couldn't give it her all and so she said no. But I hope to God that they ask her again. I think Michael would have loved her to do it and she certainly deserves it.'

It's a sentiment many would share and no doubt Delia would make an excellent working peer. For during her three-decade reign as undisputed Queen of the Kitchen she has proved that she is capable of anything she puts her mind to. 'She's a legend in her own lunchtime,' says chef Antony Worrall Thompson. 'She's amazing – she could be Prime Minister really.'

Britain's favourite cook has sold more than 10 million books and there is scarcely a food-loving home in Britain that doesn't possess at least one Delia Smith book, Number 10 included. It comes as little surprise to realize that the Prime Minister is a fan of hers too, and that, like the rest of us, he and Cherie probably use her recipes when they cook for their friends. Delia's appeal is universal. Her recipes are accessible to everybody, be they first-time cooks or professional chefs, students or prime ministers.

Despite proclaiming that she isn't a great cook and has no wish to be, she none the less has the power to influence Britain's eating habits. Her appeal lies in her confident, no-nonsense approach to cooking and her calm persona. Her aim has been to teach people the basics, and to prove to her fans 'what I can cook, anyone can cook'. She has done much to demystify and de-snob the aura that surrounds food in this country, and with Delia the nation's amateur cooks know they are in safe hands.

Her word is culinary law. If Delia says we need it in our kitchens then we want it; be it glucose, limes, cranberries or a particular frying pan. And with the launch of her most recent book and TV series, *How to Cook*, she appears more popular than ever. Indeed, the magazine *Management Today* recently included her in their list of Britain's 'Fifty Most Powerful Women'. Her inclusion in the list is not to be wondered at, the only surprise being that she should come in at only number thirty-one. For of the thirty women who preceded her on the list, people outside the world of big business and finance would know scarcely half a dozen. Everyone, on the other hand, is well aware who Delia is.

Some chefs and foodies have no time for her particular approach to cooking, dismissing her work as 'boring' and her appeal 'confined to hopeless young marrieds', but to an extent they are missing the point. 'Delia teaches people to cook as a lesson rather than entertainment,' her friend Alberto Camisa points out. 'With other shows you see on television you might pick up an idea but you don't actually learn anything. You can look at Delia's dishes, you can understand what is going on, you can go into the kitchen and you can do it. With the other TV cooks it's more entertainment with food than cooking.'

Antony Worrall Thompson, himself one of our more flamboyant TV chefs, agrees: 'Delia talks in a fairly bland, unaffected way on television and nobody is looking at her character and quirks like they do with us; they are looking at someone who is giving them a pure lesson. She hasn't got airs and graces, she hasn't got any pretensions; she's just Delia and I think that's what's good about her.

'As far as I'm concerned she's brilliant. Chefs may kick up a fuss about her but they don't have to buy her books and they don't have to watch her television programmes. She gives the British public a huge amount of confidence because her recipes are simple to follow and they work. And anything to get the British back in the kitchen has to be a good thing.'

He admits cheekily, 'I have always called her the Volvo of cooking because she's safe and everything can be trusted about

3

her, which can't be said about a lot of other chefs' cookbooks. A lot of them remain unread on the coffee table but the thing about Delia's books is that they get nice greasy thumbprints because they are used. I've got all her books and I refer to them for basic knowledge occasionally. If someone wants a really simple recipe you see what Delia is doing and it gives you inspiration.'

Even Egon Ronay, who famously described Delia's approach as 'the missionary position of cooking', acknowledges her appeal. 'I think she's unique and her importance cannot be over-estimated,' he says. 'Her personality on television inspires confidence because she is so much like any ordinary member of the public. There are no airs about her or gimmicks. She talks very plainly, like one person to another, and that in itself is an unconscious art. People say nasty things about her, but I think it's mainly jealousy and envy that causes most of the problems. After all, how many cookery writers became millionaires out of books?'

Delia is indeed very wealthy; estimates have placed her as the 916th richest person in the country, a position she shared jointly with Diana Princess of Wales, and she is calculated to be worth £24 million. Not bad for the daughter of an ironmonger who left school without a single qualification to her name.

So how did she do it, and what is her secret? Lionel Evans, an academic and chef, has the distinction of being the man who taught Delia Smith how to cook. The two have been friends ever since she fell in love with his omelette soufflé flambé back in the early 1960s and begged him to show her how to make it. Known to his friends as Leo, he has kept a proud and watchful eye on Delia's career ever since and believes the key to her appeal lies in her very ordinariness. 'She is fundamentally an ordinary person and this is one of the basic secrets of Delia,' he says.

'One of the reasons why she is so successful in teaching the ordinary housewife is that she herself is not brilliant. She knows what it is to have to almost struggle to understand something and so is aware of being able to explain something in terms that people can understand. She is bright and she can learn well, but she is not brilliant and consequently she can relate to 70 per cent of the population. And she has a totally regionless accent; it's not quite Estuary English, it's slightly London suburbia affected. It's an almost unidentifiable classless voice which appeals across the board.'

It was not just her position in the richest women list that Delia shared with the late Princess of Wales. Like Diana, Delia has attained the kind of iconic status where her surname has become virtually redundant. And, like all icons, she exerts enormous influence over her fans. With the Princess it was primarily her hair and clothes that women sought to imitate, with Delia it is her prowess in the kitchen that millions wish to copy. If Delia tells people to make something with fresh herbs instead of dried, or advises us to invest in some good-quality baking trays, we jolly well do what she says.

Trend-watchers have even coined a phrase for it: 'Delia Power'. Comparatively expensive items, such as limes, capers and fresh coriander, soared in sales when Delia mentioned them in her best-selling *Summer Collection* book and television series in 1993. Shallot sales rose by an incredible 2000 per cent when she used them in one of her recipes, and she was single-handedly responsible for the Great Cranberry Crisis of 1995 when she mentioned the hitherto little-heard-of berry in her *Winter Collection* book and caused a worldwide shortage. More recently she has done the same for eggs. Sales increased by 1.3 million a day after a basket of white eggs appeared on the front cover of *How to Cook*.

And Delia Power doesn't just extend to food. The fortunes of entire companies have been saved after a single recommendation from Delia. Nick White, who runs Lune Metal Products, had been planning to scrap production of a humble omelette pan because of poor sales and had even laid off ten of his staff. That is until Delia used and fell in love with the eight-inch pan on her *How to Cook* BBC television series and sang its praises to five million viewers. It was, she said, 'a little gem, which will serve you for a lifetime of happy omelette making'. Before long sales of the £10.95 pan had leapt from 200 a year to 90,000 in four months and Mr White's family business in Morecambe, Lancashire, had to recruit fifteen extra staff. 'That pan has been part of our range ever since I started working for the company in 1959 but no one had ever shown much interest in it before,' he says in astonishment.

Delia's power lies in her influence over that mighty army of people – consumers. And it is this that has the big supermarket chains eating out of her hand. For many years she has been a paid consultant to Sainsbury's and the company she runs with her husband publishes *Sainsbury's The Magazine*, the glossy publication sold exclusively through Sainsbury's stores. David Benady, deputy editor of *Marketing Week* magazine, explains why Delia is so important to the supermarket: 'From Sainsbury's point of view it is important to have someone like her on board because they are trying to point their customers in the direction of high-margin products such as fresh food, rather than tinned or frozen goods.

'Supermarkets make more money out of selling fresh fruit and veg and expensive ingredients like herbs and fancy olive oil. If they can get someone who can speak to the people on their level it can act as a key to get people to trade up to those more high-margin products.'

Food importer Alberto Camisa, her friend for thirty years, has good reason to be grateful to Delia. His business gets a plug in the back of her *How to Cook* book, which in financial terms is advertising money can't buy. 'Delia has increased our business dramatically,' he admits. 'We've set up a mail-order service which is basically run for her customers and we've even set up our own website. She said it would be good for the book and good for us. It's basically two friends working things out between us. We're very grateful to Delia.'

But Alberto, who also supplies Sainsbury's with twenty lines of upmarket Italian products for their Special Selection range, stresses that Delia won't compromise herself. 'If she doesn't like something she won't do it,' he says. 'There's no way you can persuade her. I've shown her several types of olive oil, one of which I thought was absolutely brilliant, but she didn't like it and she took another one. She won't be pushed into recommending something if it's not good, or if she doesn't believe in it. But if it is something she likes and believes in there is no reason for her not to mention it to her friends, who are her readers basically.

'You wouldn't tell your friend, "Go and get an omelette pan", you'd tell them, "Get the one I've got because it works", and that's the way she does everything. She treats her readers as her friends, so if she recommends an item it's because she believes in it. If we had something that wasn't very good she would never mention it. It wouldn't matter what we did, she wouldn't recommend it just because we were friends.'

Friendship is also the reason that six pages of Delia's recommendations appear in the catalogue of cookware suppliers Lakeland Ltd, says director Michelle Kershaw. 'Delia is a great friend of ours. She's been a fan of Lakeland for ten years and she asks us to put things in because she can't recommend products unless there is somewhere for her readers or viewers to buy them,' she explains. 'She knows that she is going to get bombarded with letters if there isn't a source of supply for her products so we do her a favour really by putting them in our catalogue.

'A couple of years ago it was the pestle and mortar that everyone wanted and now it's the vanilla extract that she's been using in her television series. But they don't all sell and I can't say many of the others are flying out of the building. It is still the old favourites that sell well: the simple things like the wooden turning fork and spoon and the £1.95 spatula that Delia has been using for years.'

At first glance one could be forgiven for assuming that Delia is engaging in a commercial transaction to advertise the three dozen products that get her seal of approval in the catalogue. Hailed as Delia's 'tools of the trade', many of them have an individual dedication by Delia and it is obvious that she is giving them her unqualified endorsement. Cynics may wonder what is in it for Delia. She says she is doing the public a favour: 'I have a philosophy: If things are clever and good they shouldn't be exclusive but available to everybody. Why should luxury or rare ingredients just belong to the glitzy, groovy people who shop on the Fulham Road?'

Lakeland says Delia is not paid by them to push items in the catalogue. 'She doesn't get paid a bean for recommending products,' says Michelle Kershaw. 'In the early days she wrote recipes for the catalogue, which we obviously paid her for, but that was different; that's her work. Some companies send her products and ask her to recommend them but we would never dream of doing that. We know her too well; she just wouldn't do it. It's up to her what she chooses. She insists on paying for everything she orders from us. We wouldn't mind giving her the odd freebie but she insists on paying because she's very straight.'

More than anything else it is her connection with Sainsbury's that is the cause of so much talk and speculation within the cookery industry. 'There is loads of gossip about whether she is being paid to promote products,' admits Antony Worrall Thompson. As a presenter on the BBC consumer show *Food and Drink*, Worrall Thompson and his colleagues are forbidden from doing lucrative advertising work. But the BBC appears unruffled by Delia's close affiliation with Sainsbury's, even permitting her to include a list of Sainsbury's superstores at the back of her BBC *Winter Collection* book.

'Anything Delia pushes sells and there is a certain wry smile on certain people's faces how she manages to do that,' says Worrall Thompson. 'Obviously there's a bit of incest there with the Sainsbury's magazine being run by her husband, but if someone's not slapping her down, if the BBC are endorsing it when they are very strict with myself and others, then good luck to her. She's a businesswoman, and why people can't consider chefs as being business people I don't know.'

Of course the BBC would no sooner wish to alienate Delia than it would scrap the licence fee. The powers-that-be see her as one of the jewels in its crown and during her twenty-seven-year television career she has stayed the course while other 'celebrity' chefs have come and gone. BBC employees criticize Delia at their peril. 'I'm not frightened of Delia but I know that you've got a catch-22 situation because if you attack Delia too much and you work with the BBC, then things come round in a horrific circle,' reveals Worrall Thompson. 'Delia is selling the most books for the Beeb, her programmes are one of the biggest cookery programmes – although *Food and Drink* is actually still ahead of Delia – and her influence is enormous. I talk about a rimming tool for squeezing juice and sales will go up, but if Delia was to mention it they wouldn't be able to keep up with production.'

Food writer Tom Jaine, a former editor of *The Good Food Guide*, admits to being somewhat nonplussed by the whole concept of Delia Power. 'The remarkable thing about the Delia phenomenon is not so much Delia as the phenomenon itself,' he says. 'And what is fascinating is not her but the reverence with which she is treated. Although Delia is remarkable and she's done a good job, she's not that remarkable. There have always been successful cookery writers; it's the way we perceive them that changes.

'There are people like Agnes Marshall at the end of the last century, who had stunning book sales. I think we perceive this phenomenon as something quite amazing, but it isn't quite so amazing as we think. In the nineteenth century Mrs Beeton was phenomenally successful and Fanny Farmer was big in America. And in the 1950s Fanny Craddock was a big star. I think what is fascinating is our approach to Delia, not Delia herself. Why are so many column inches devoted to the fact that she sells a lot of books?'

If Jaine appears sceptical of the hype that surrounds Delia he is in good company. Her critics, among them celebrity chef Gary Rhodes, complain that 'people don't need to be shown what boiling water looks like' and accuse her of being 'a force for dullness in British cooking'. But Delia has the last laugh as her books race up the bestseller list and stay there. She is rarely seen to retaliate, perhaps safe in the knowledge that she was around long before many of today's famous chefs, and is likely to remain a household name when they are forgotten.

Antony Worrall Thompson believes Delia fulfils an important role. 'When you are as fanatical about cooking as I am you try to see why other people are doing things right and why they sell so many books,' he says. 'The answer is that you make it such basic language that everyone can understand. Step-by-step cookery is vitally important to people who don't know how to cook, and we have to accept that two generations of mums really haven't been in the kitchen and haven't been handing down knowledge. Cookery is no longer in the school curriculum, so nobody is learning how to cook. Delia has filled that vital gap and we definitely need her. Otherwise a few years down the line we're going to end up with nobody knowing how to cook.'

For someone providing such a service, Delia none the less evokes more than her fair share of bitchiness from her peers. At a food industry awards ceremony there were boos when her name was read out, and some chefs treat her almost with disdain.

'It smacks of jealousy to me,' says Worrall Thompson. 'There's an awful lot of bitchiness in our industry and she hasn't become part of it because she knows her market and she keeps herself to herself. She doesn't mix in chefs' circles, which is fine. To me, she doesn't show any sort of feeling about the food but I think that's a problem of not being able to express it more than anything else. I'm sure there is passion there because she wouldn't have got where she is without it.

'I don't think she'll ever be remembered in the same breath as Elizabeth David or Jane Grigson, but she will be remembered as a woman who had amazing vision about what people want. Elizabeth David and Jane Grigson were purists; they analysed food and got to the heart of food. Delia is more like a production line, churning out very good honest food without any major feeling. None of her recipes hasn't been done before really, all she does is put them into a painting-by-numbers format.'

Prue Leith shares some of these sentiments: 'For years I've found restaurant chefs being grand about Delia, saying, "Oh my dear she's just got on to crab and avocado – we were doing that fifteen years ago," But the brilliant thing about Delia is she always knows when the public is ready for something. It's not the most fashionable, state-of-the-art restaurant food; it's what

Mrs Jones in Huddersfield is ready for, and I think that's been her genius. That's why she's sold 10 millions books and is much beloved by the public in a way that fancy chefs aren't.

'Chefs are, by and large, incredibly opinionated and a lot of them aren't very well read. They think that the only take on cooking is their take, which is restaurant food for expensive people. Whereas what is actually far more important is home food for not very expensive people. And Delia has always had this carefully in mind. She isn't trying to appeal to their customers, who are sailing down the Waitrose aisles picking out the very best of everything. The public trusts her and they believe her. I'm exactly the same: the only cookbooks I ever buy are Delia's.'

TV chef Rick Stein admits he finds the concept of Delia Power 'frightening'. 'As soon as Delia mentions something on television, sales rocket,' he says incredulously. 'It's in the realms of fantasy. If someone like Evelyn Waugh had written a story about a cook changing the nation's perception of omelette pans, you'd think he was exaggerating.'

2

War Baby

Delia Ann Smith was a war baby, born on 18 June 1941. Her parents had been married only six months before, on 6 December 1940 in a wartime ceremony at the tiny parish church at White Waltham, near Maidenhead in Berkshire. Harold Bartlett Smith, the son of a carpenter from the North East, was a twenty-year-old air craftsman and wireless operator stationed with the Royal Air Force nearby and Etty Jones Lewis, also aged twenty, was the daughter of an engineer from Llwyngwril, a farming village in mid-Wales.

'It was a very small wedding because Harold was in the Air Force,' recalls Etty's sister Gladys Evans. Gladys was close to her sister and made the journey from her home in Wales to be a witness at the wedding. She was the only member of Etty's family there. Etty's father, David Lewis, had died from pneumonia when she was five, leaving her mother Sarah with three young children to bring up. Etty's younger brother Rene was sent away to live with his grandparents, while Etty and Gladys remained with their mother. Sarah subsequently married a local man called William Pugh and had five more children: daughters Eirwen and Doreen and sons Griffith, Harold and Ronald.

At the beginning of the 1940s, becoming pregnant outside

wedlock was still very much a social stigma. During the Second World War unplanned pregnancies became more common as young couples, not knowing what the future held, snatched moments together before being parted by the war. But, none the less, it was still considered shameful to walk up the aisle 'in the family way'. This 'shame' might have been why Etty's mother didn't attend her daughter's wedding. But in fact there was a much more practical reason why she didn't make the journey from Wales: she couldn't afford the train fare. Sarah and William Pugh had a big family to feed and clothe and money was tight. 'We didn't go to the wedding because my mother couldn't afford the cost of the journey,' explains Renee Lewis. 'And the war made travelling difficult so only Gladys was there.'

By the time Delia was born, Harold's work with the RAF had taken him and Etty from Berkshire to Pulborough, in West Sussex, where numerous aerodromes had been set up to fight the war from the South Coast. Delia, however, was actually born more than twenty miles away in Woking, Surrey at the Wynberg Emergency Maternity Hospital, as during the war years it wasn't unusual for expectant mothers to be sent to hospitals some distance from where they lived.

The war in Europe dominated the news throughout 1941 and the final months of her pregnancy were a worrying time for Delia's mother. London and the South-East were the main target of the German Luftwaffe's night-time raids. In London 500 planes dropped 100,000 bombs in one all-night attack, among the heaviest of the war. The raid left 1,400 dead and Etty Smith must have wondered what kind of world she was bringing a child into.

Delia was born into a period of austerity. The conflict was costing Britain £11 million a day and income tax was raised to a record 50 per cent. Rationing of food, clothing and coal was widespread and the government issued an official recipe for 'Blitz Broth'. For the first time in history women were being called on to fill the jobs left by men who had gone off to war, and also to work in the munitions factories. As a married woman with a young child, Etty was exempt from war work but, as wireless operators, Harold Smith and his colleagues had an important role to play. The month Delia was born the RAF revealed that 'radio location' had been Britain's key weapon against German bombers.

Like other married men, Harold – by now a sergeant – was granted permission to 'live out' and he and Etty rented Hillside, a house situated in the small farming hamlet of North Heath, four miles from Pulborough. It was a peaceful place, set among pretty rolling hills and farm fields. But in 1943, when Delia was two, a bomb was dropped on the infant school adjacent to Delia's house. The teacher heard the bomb coming and had the sense to order the children under their desks and fortunately no one was hurt. But the windows were all blown in and the event sent a shudder through every parent in the village.

When the war ended, Harold was demobbed from the RAF and the family moved to Bexleyheath, a suburban town on the London–Kent border. Prior to the early 1930s Bexleyheath had been a rural area, well-known for its market gardens. But in the early 1930s it changed almost beyond recognition. All the privately owned estates were sold off and the developers moved in. Once green fields and woods were torn up by bull-dozers and row on row of new brick houses built in their place. Between 1933 and 1939 the whole of Bexleyheath was completely covered with new houses, changing the topography of the area for ever. The building firm Ideal Homes put up most of the new dwellings and by the end of the 1930s the area bore no resemblance to how it had been at the beginning of the decade.

During the war stray V1 bombs destroyed many of the new houses as the town was sufficiently close to London, and also near the Royal Arsenal at Woolwich. These were rebuilt after the war as part of a nationwide redevelopment programme. By the time the Smith family moved to the area in the mid-1940s Bexleyheath had developed into pretty much the town it is today. It has changed comparatively little since Delia lived there all those years ago. It is still a predominantly middle-class town in the commuter belt with many of its residents white-collar workers engaged in the retail business, either in the town or in London. Although in recent years the town veered towards a hung council, for many years it was staunchly Conservative.

Keen for a quieter life, Harold took up a position as manager of Straws, a small ironmongers shop on The Broadway, and spent his spare time tending his allotment. Etty was a house-wife, although she later on worked part-time at Smiths, the pharmacy next door to Straws. The family lived at 90 Belvedere Road, Bexleyheath, a modest semi-detached Victorian home on three storeys. Delia's grandparents, Marshall and Ellen Smith, lived next door at 92.

Food was always taken seriously in both houses. Delia's grandfather kept chickens on his allotment, ensuring a ready supply of eggs, and the vegetables grown by him and Delia's father meant that the family never went without. Ellen Smith was a very good cook and Etty's mother Sarah had also handed down a love of cooking to her daughter. Hence Delia was intro-duced to good food at an early age and grew up surrounded by women who enjoyed cooking and took pride in their culinary skills. 'Her mother's priority was always good cooking,' says Delia's husband Michael. 'She took great pride in the food she prepared. She was the one who set the standards for Delia.'

In her *Winter Collection* book Delia fondly recalls the teatimes of her childhood. 'I well remember both my grandmother and mother having weekly "baking days", an entire day spent in the kitchen producing cakes, apple pies and all sorts of tarts,' she wrote. 'All of these would be cooled, then stored in large, airtight tins and each day at teatime out would come something like a piece of jam sponge, an almond or jam tart or some fluffy butterfly cakes.'

Perhaps only too well aware of the attraction of ready-made cakes and biscuits for the modern mum, Delia appeared wistful about the idyllic-sounding baking days of yesteryear and urged her readers to step back in time once in a while. 'Now this tradition has died out; we count calories one minute and eat snack bars the next,' she lamented. 'I want to indulge a little in the pleasures of my childhood and suggest that, although batch-baking might be ruled out by the pressures of our modern lives, you can still take just one free Saturday afternoon, closet yourself in the kitchen and immerse yourself in some very rewarding home baking. If there's no rush and no pressure it can actually be very relaxing – put on some music, listen to the radio, or just be silent with your thoughts. Then watch the smiles of pleasure as the house is filled with a delicious aroma and everyone gets a teatime treat.'

Her enthusiasm and passion for those baking days are such that one can almost smell the aroma of freshly cooked cakes. Delia inherited her love of food from her mother and Etty remains a source of inspiration to Delia, so much so that she even includes her recipes in her books. Delia's fruit cake is in fact Etty's own recipe and she also came up with the idea for the mouth-watering coconut lime cake that appears in Delia's *Summer Collection* book.

Holidays in Wales, spent visiting Etty's family, also stimulated Delia's interest in food. As a small child, her step-grandfather William Pugh would take her out on early-morning mushroom-gathering expeditions in the mountains. Delia has shared these moments from her childhood with her readers, tales which appear to evoke an idyllic, carefree existence. 'He seemed able to spot a field mushroom from dozens of yards away, and I would run and pick them – some small, round and delicate with pink gills, others large and flat and velvet-brown,' she wrote nostalgically in her bestselling *Complete Cookery Course.* 'Back at home they would sizzle in bacon fat for breakfast, with plenty of bread to mop up the last traces of juice. They were the best mushrooms I've ever tasted.'

In 1946, at the age of five, Delia began her education. She was enrolled as a pupil at Upland Infant School, a Victorian building in Church Road, Bexleyheath. Over-subscribed and under-staffed, it offered hardly the best academic start in life. Teachers struggled to cope with intolerably large classes and there was a high turnover of staff who couldn't stand the strain of trying to teach so many children. While many new homes had been built in the area there were no new schools to take the youngsters who lived in them. Uplands was swamped by children and, at its largest, it had 500 pupils in nine classes.

Fellow pupil Linda Knight remembers Delia as being 'quite vivacious' and Denise Morris, now Denise Hatfield, became a friend of Delia's. She knew Delia for more than eleven years and inadvertently revealed a fact that Delia has managed to keep secret the whole of her adult life – the fact that she is a redhead. 'She was quite attractive but the thing I remember most about Delia is her hair, which was a lovely colour – the colour of a red-setter dog,' she says. 'And you couldn't put a pin between her freckles; she was that freckled.'

But, like many redheads, Delia hated her auburn hair with a passion and as soon as she was old enough to do what she wanted she dyed it a dark chestnut brown. She hasn't been her natural colour for almost forty years. She couldn't do anything about the freckles that she loathed just as much and has had to learn to live with them. 'It seems a shame that she dyed her hair because it wasn't a horrible red, it was a really lovely colour,' says Denise. 'But she can't have liked it if she's been dying it all these years.'

Delia was in Denise's class at infant school and the two girls went through junior school together. Denise lived around the corner from Delia in Oldfield Road and after school she and Delia would often walk up to The Broadway to see Delia's father in the ironmonger's shop, or play with their friends Judy French and Jennifer Nelson. However, perhaps surprisingly, Denise doesn't recall ever being invited in for one of Delia's mother's famous teatime spreads. 'I don't think we went in to Delia's house much, although she did come to mine,' she says. 'The other girls in the road were in and out of each other's houses all the time, but I got the impression that Delia's family didn't invite other people in.'

This apparent failure by her parents to welcome her school pals is starkly at odds with the idyllic picture Delia paints in many of her books. 'I will always cherish fond memories of my mother's and my grandmother's cooking trays piled high with freshly baked mince pies on Christmas Eve, ready to be packed into tins and brought out whenever friends popped in for Christmas drinks,' she wrote in her Christmas book.' But if friends were asked in to 90 Belvedere Road they must have been adult friends of Harold's and Etty's because Delia's pals were not invited. Excluding Delia's schoolchums didn't exactly help their daughter to make friends, and she was considered to be somewhat 'aloof' from the other children.

From an early age Delia stood out from the other children in the Belvedere Road area, which was a working-class area. Her parents had brought her up to speak properly and Etty was meticulous about her daughter's hair and clothes. Better spoken than many of her contemporaries, she received unwelcome attention from the other children who singled her out for bouts of teasing. 'She always talked nicely and was well turned out,' recalls Denise. 'But I suppose we thought Delia was a bit on the snobby side, and to be quite honest, she probably got teased behind her back. She never talked about her parents that much when we were out but I think they were quite strict.'

Her parents were traditional Welsh Methodists and, according to Leo Evans, the man who later became her mentor, as she grew older Delia didn't have a happy home life. 'Non conformist people tend to be a bit strict and puritanical and that may have made for unhappiness at home,' he reveals.

Delia's mother was a woman who was not afraid to speak her mind. 'Etty is rather small but she is quite definite in her approach to life,' says Delia's friend Father James Walsh. 'She's not afraid of standing up and saying what she thinks, but at the same time she is very kind. She's got a heart of gold and she'll do anything for anyone. I suppose deep down Delia is like her in temperament, but Etty is more forthright than Delia; I think she is perhaps closer to her Welsh roots.'

Religion was an important part of Delia's life from a very young age. Etty taught her daughter to pray every night and there was a picture of the Good Shepherd at the end of Delia's bed. Today Delia is said to have a four-foot high Crucifix on the wall above her bed. She attended a Methodist Sunday school and her Brownie group was attached to the Congregational Church. It was a subject she loved and perhaps one that offered her an escape from the reality of her often unhappy life. Reading the uplifting stories of faith and hope were a form of escape for the young Delia, a vision of what was beyond her existence in a boring post-war town.

She excelled at religious studies, but in virtually all other aspects of her education she was a flop. 'I loved all the Bible stories,' she reveals. 'It was something I had an instinct for, and one of the few things I was good at. I was always asked to read at Easter and carol services. I'd always be the first choice to read the Scriptures.' A spiritual child, she loved to hear about the story of Christ and daydream about what it would be like to meet Jesus' disciples. 'How I would have loved to have been present when Paul was preaching,' she wrote in *A Feast for Lent*. 'I would have loved to have seen the look in his eyes, the expression on his face, and heard the sound of his voice!'

While in reality she had few friends in Bexleyheath, in her escapist world of the Bible Delia felt safe and secure. Those early Bible classes were the only lessons Delia looked forward to. They awoke a spirituality inside the quiet, rather distant, youngster. Delia, who had always felt something of an outsider, found that religion gave her a sense of belonging. The stories of miracles and great deeds became key to the fantasy world she created. The words she read in the Bible seemed to make sense to her and perhaps helped transport her away from her feelings of failure and rejection. For a girl who realized that the only ambition anyone held for her was that she should get a job in a shop, religion provided an escape from her feelings of worthlessness.

Christmas was a particularly special time for Delia because to her it didn't simply represent presents and a holiday from school. She recalls the awe she felt at that magical time. 'I still remember, as a small child, on Christmas Eve when everyone else seemed preoccupied, stealing away to the room where the Christmas tree was,' she recalls. 'I would turn out the room lights and just sit staring at the tree shimmering and sparkling with jewelled lights, letting my eyes feast on the beauty of it all.'

She was also instilled with a love of nature at a young age, perhaps inspired by her holidays in the scenic Welsh mountains around her grandparents' home. 'Ever since I was a small child I have felt a sense of magic in the changing seasons,' she waxed lyrical in her *Winter Collection* book. 'Winter has every bit as much charm as the other seasons for me: the dazzling splendour of autumnal colour and Keats's as yet unmatched description of mists and mellow fruitfulness, the stark emptiness of bare branches against the winter skies, and always the very special pale winter light.'

And in her book *A Journey into God*, she wrote, 'I recall my grandmother, who had no particular religious belief herself, gazing reflectively at a lilac tree in full bloom highlighted by the sun. "If they looked at that," she said, "how could anyone say there isn't a God?" ' She also told how her grandmother appeared to have psychic powers. 'Some people have quite natural psychic gifts,' she wrote. 'My grandmother, with her Celtic perceptiveness, would suddenly announce that we should "expect visitors", and sure enough visitors arrived!'

Throughout her childhood Delia's big dream was always to live in the country. She no doubt would have approved of Bexleyheath the way it was before the developers moved in. By the time she came to live there, there was scarcely a patch of green in sight. Delia vowed that one day she would have enough money to be able to live where she wanted to: in the country, surrounded by open fields. She says, 'I love the countryside. Right from a child I always wanted to live in the country and when I started work I was always saving so I could live in the country.'

So strong was this desire to live somewhere green and pleasant, that even at the tender age of eleven she already had a clear vision of how she wanted her life to be. She was asked to write an essay about how she saw her future and what she wrote must have appeared as hopeful fantasy to her teacher, given Delia's all too evident academic shortcomings. But it was to prove prophetic. 'With amazing foresight, I dreamed of being a writer living in a cottage deep in the country,' she says. 'As I recall. I got one thing wrong in that I described a field of cows, and they have not materialized yet.'

For Delia, who failed her 11-plus, even to contemplate becoming a writer showed an enormous faith that things would somehow work out. And it must have been faith rather than confidence that convinced her of this because Delia always suffered from a lack of self-confidence. Failing her exam and being sent to Bexleyheath School, a secondary modern with a poor academic record, was a huge knock to the young Delia and crushed what little self-confidence she had. She was effectively confined to the academic scrap heap and would leave school without a single qualification to her name.

This early failure must at times have appeared to Delia to be a sign of things to come. As she progressed through her teens she could see the future that people expected for her laid out before her eyes: an undemanding job in a shop, and then marriage to a local boy and a home in Bexleyheath.

It was certainly what her teachers had in mind for her. And to make doubly sure that Delia harboured no false hopes about her future, her headmistress laid it down for her plainly. Almost fifty years on, Delia still remembers the lecture that she received from her headmistress when she failed the 11-plus. 'She said to me, "If you'd worked a bit harder and passed that exam, you could have been a secretary," ' she recalls. 'When I was at school, being a secretary was the top job. If you were a secretary you were really something, otherwise you went to work in a shop.'

Her headmistress's ill-judged words had a profound effect on Delia, and it is clear that her remarks still rankle, even after all this time. Her all-too-apparent shortcomings caused Delia a great deal of unhappiness when she was young. 'I was dreadful at school and that was quite painful,' she has admitted. 'I never passed an exam. I might have ended up as a domestic science teacher, but without qualifications I couldn't get into college.' What makes this especially sad is the fact that Delia desperately wanted to learn. 'I have an innate love of words: poetry, literature, any form of communication through words fascinates me,' she says. To have such a passion and be unable to express it must have been cruelly frustrating for her.

But, says former pupil Pat Header, Delia was by no means the only girl to leave Bexleyheath Secondary without qualifications. 'It was a large school, with a large catchment area and we all left at fifteen without qualifications,' she explains. 'There weren't any qualifications to be had from school at that time.' Delia's brother Glyn, who was born ten days before her eighth birthday, fared better educationally. He won a scholarship to the prestigious Dulwich College but today denies that he was the cleverer of the two. 'My sister was the brainy one of the family,' he says emphatically. 'She's made the money, not me.'

Despite the family tradition of cooking and baking, Delia didn't excel at home economics either. In fact surprisingly for the daughter of such a keen cook, by the time she was twenty-one she could scarcely boil an egg. When the school held a cake-making competition it wasn't she who won it, but her classmate Shirley Charman.

Shirley recalls: 'We had a cake competition when we were thirteen or fourteen and I won it out of six hundred girls. I think it sticks in Delia's mind because when she was on the children's television programme *Multi-Coloured Swap Shop* years later my daughters told me she mentioned my cake. It was quite an outstanding cake for the period: square with quite intricate trellis work. Now you could do it easily, but then it was hard and I think Delia was quite impressed with all this – she must have been because according to the girls she talked about it on the show.'

Shirley was in the school choir with Delia and the two of

them used to stay behind after school to practise their singing. She remembers her as being very ordinary. 'There was nothing outstanding about Delia, apart from her freckles,' she says. 'She was full of freckles. I seem to remember that she spoke a bit posher than anybody else; she was a bit snobby.' Her former classmate's words say it all: finding her guilty of speaking too nicely for her own good, Delia was looked upon almost suspiciously by her contemporaries. She was too different from the other girls for her own good. She was not one of them.

At the secondary school Delia was put into the top set which meant that she was separated during lessons from her friend Denise. 'We were streamed and I was in B and she was in A,' explains Denise. But the two met up during the breaks and, being typical teenagers, to break the monotony they would ogle the boys from the school next door. It was all rather touchingly innocent. 'We were an all-girls school, so apart from looking out the windows watching the boys come out at playtime, we didn't have much to do with boys,' says Denise. 'I don't remember Delia ever having a boyfriend though and I don't know where her interest in football has come from as she was the opposite of a tomboy.'

Delia left school in the summer of 1957 as British teenagers danced to a daring new music: rock and roll. The American Bill Haley arrived in England with his Comets to a hero's welcome and hits of the year were his 'Love Letters in the Sand' and Elvis 'the Pelvis' Presley's 'All Shook Up'. In July Stirling Moss won the British Grand Prix, the first Briton to do so since 1923, and Chelsea Football Club were causing a stir with their brilliant new star, seventeen-year-old Jimmy Greaves.

It was a time when a feel-good factor pervaded the nation and Prime Minister Harold Macmillan memorably told the country, 'You've never had it so good.' There was full employment and excellent job prospects and despite the fact that Delia had no qualifications, there were still plenty of opportunities to be had. But Delia was already yearning for a life far away from Bexleyheath. Denise Hatfield reveals how, when they left school, both she and Delia wanted to become hairdressers. But, unlike her friend, Delia would not settle for a job in a local salon. She set her sights on the altogether far more glamorous and exciting world of hairdressing onboard cruise ships.

Despite what people expected of her, Delia's ambition was certainly not to marry a local boy and settle for life in a back-water. She considered Bexleyheath to be provincial and dull and intended to travel and see the world. A job hairdressing on a liner would provide her ticket to freedom. 'She came round and told me she didn't want to get a job locally,' says Denise. 'She wanted to work in London and then get into hairdressing on the cruise liners and see the world. So she went up to town to start her apprenticeship and I did mine locally.'

Denise was somewhat mystified as to why her friend was so keen to leave the area. As an expanding suburb twenty miles from London, Bexleyheath boasted good job opportunities and while it was hardly Las Vegas, the town had a respectable nightlife, even by teenage standards. There were certainly far worse places to live and Denise failed to understand Delia's reasons for wanting to get away.

What she didn't realize, and what Delia confided to no one, was that her home life was desperately unhappy. Contrary to the idyllic-sounding stories of mushroom hunts and home-made cakes that she chooses to tell her readers, the reality was far from perfect. In her books, Delia has been able to create an idealistic childhood for herself. To the outsider it appears almost perfect, like something from the pages of an Enid Blyton novel. But the apparent scenes of domestic bliss that Delia writes about are at odds with the turmoil that enveloped her when her parents' marriage broke up.

In truth her childhood must have seemed far from idyllic. Writing now about her early days a note of wishful thinking can be detected. Is Delia perhaps seeing those early days through rose-tinted glasses, or has she chosen – like most people – to remember only the good bits, blanking out the bad? Either way, when her parents' rocky marriage finally disintegrated she and her brother Glyn found themselves the unhappy victims of a broken home.

The break-up coincided with Delia reaching puberty, a difficult enough time for any teenage girl, and one that requires careful handling. But at the very moment she needed stability to help her cope with her changing hormones, her family life was turned upside-down. Everything that she had trusted and depended on collapsed around her and Delia despaired.

Her father Harold moved out of the family home, and Delia and Glyn were left alone with their mother. While Etty effectively became a single parent, Delia and Glyn had to try and adjust to their father no longer being around. But after a while Harold announced that he wanted the children to come and stay with him and the youngsters left their mother to move in with him.

It was a desperately unhappy situation that caused yet more upheaval. It was hard on them all. Harold missed the children when they weren't with him; Etty was distraught when Delia and Glyn weren't living at home with her, and the children missed their mother and father when they were with the other parent. It was a no-win situation for all concerned. During one particularly difficult and highly-emotional period the brother and sister were shunted back and forth between their parents. It was a bewildering and confusing time, but, says her brother, Delia bottled her emotions up. 'I don't know how Delia coped with it all,' he admits. 'We didn't really talk about it much. I was only about six or seven. We were living with my mum and then

Delia and I had to go and stay with my father for a while. We lived with my father then we went back to my mum.'

Perhaps because of the age gap between them, Delia didn't feel she could talk to her brother about the misery she felt. Although he was going through the same trauma as her, he was still only a kid and, as such, couldn't be counted on to be any real help. Nor could she talk to her parents about her unhappiness because they were too wrapped up in their own problems to be able to deal with Delia's sadness as well. She might have been expected to confide in friends of her own age, but Delia told no one. She kept her own counsel and never mentioned that her parents had separated.

Even her friend Denise Hatfield didn't realize that Delia's parents had divorced until years later. 'She never spoke to me about it,' she says. 'Delia didn't speak about her parents much at all. She was keen to go to London to do her hairdressing apprenticeship, but I thought that was because there were more opportunities there.'

Her parents' separation marked a turning point in Delia's life. She became increasingly eager to get away from home, and the emotional baggage that went with it, and make a new life for herself. Struggling to cope with the emotional injury that Harold and Etty had caused her, Delia realized that she had only herself to rely on. It was strangely comforting. She recognized that she didn't have to make do with what life had given her: she could go out there and change things.

That was the reason Delia was so keen to leave the area and make a fresh start: she wanted to reinvent herself. Getting rid of her red hair was just part of that reinvention. Delia cut the ties with her past with almost ruthless ease. The day Delia told Denise that she wanted to work in town was practically the last her friend saw of her. 'Once she started work in London I probably saw her a couple of times but then we lost contact,' says

Denise. 'We would have been about sixteen and she didn't really come back much after that. No one ever saw her around and we thought that she wanted to mix in different circles. I wasn't surprised when we lost contact because she always wanted higher things.'

In London Delia started to mix with an altogether more glamorous crowd and going back home to Bexleyheath served only to remind her what a failure the old Delia had been. She didn't want to bump into the teachers who had considered her so stupid. Even the house she grew up in was a constant reminder of her shortcomings because it was just down the road from her old school.

Significantly, Delia's entry in the directory *Who's Who* omits all details of her education and where she grew up. It is almost as if she has erased her past and is further evidence of her determination to break away from it. As far as she was concerned, those early days in Bexleyheath ceased to exist and once her career took off she never looked back.

Her new life socializing with well-educated literary and media types from the world of television and publishing was a million miles away from Bexleyheath. Having made the break, Delia showed no inclination to keep in touch with the people she had known then and has appeared to shun all attempts by them to make contact. Denise, who still lives happily in Bexleyheath, says sadly, 'I don't think Delia likes to admit she lived here to be quite honest. Speaking to people locally, we all get the impression that she is not that keen on people knowing that she came from Bexleyheath. I think she considered herself to be a bit cut above us.

'A few years ago it was the Junior School's centenary and one of the old teachers told me that they wrote to Delia and asked her if she would either come to the school or participate in something to celebrate. But they didn't receive any acknowledgement whatsoever; it appeared that she didn't want to know. And our friend Judy French sent Delia a letter and a photograph of her family a few years ago but she had no response from Delia.

'I didn't see her for years and then all of a sudden she started popping up on telly. She hasn't altered much to look at, apart from her hair colouring. You can't take anything away from her; she has done very, very well. We used to laugh at her but I suppose she's having the last laugh.'

Having been so cruelly mocked and teased at school, Delia could perhaps be forgiven for not wanting to be involved in her old school's celebrations. But it is, none the less, further evidence that she has put her time in Bexleyheath firmly behind her. She isn't the first celebrity to discover that their new life left them with nothing in common with the people they grew up with. But in Delia's case it even extends to her own brother who at one point she would not see for more than ten years. And she never felt the same way about either of her parents after they broke up. Everything had changed and there could be no going back for any of them.

Leo Evans, whom Delia met soon after leaving home, says that Delia didn't appear to be close to her parents at that time in her life. Leo taught Delia to cook and for many years he was her mentor. 'I think she had difficulty in her relationship with both her parents, which is why she left home,' he explains. 'They were rather aloof, and there is a slightly 'keep your distance' aspect to Delia as well. I don't think it's a bad thing but it's there none the less. I would say that once her career took off she wasn't really close to either of her parents; that would be my assessment. I got the impression that her brother was a bit of a cipher – a nonentity – who wasn't very big or significant in her life and I think Delia wanted to make a career and a life for herself.'

The wariness that Delia unknowingly but instinctively gave off may have been a defensive mechanism from a young woman frightened of getting hurt. Her brother describes how Delia was a sensitive child, but admits that they were never close: 'She was quite shy and didn't have much self-confidence when she was young. We weren't alike in that respect; I wasn't exactly extrovert but I went to one of the best schools.

'When she moved out I missed her to an extent. But I was only quite young and I don't recall much about her. She came home now and again to see our mum. I think Delia and my father got on alright but by then my father had left home. I was never that involved because we were so different in age. We weren't really close at that time.'

Delia is famously guarded about her private life and has never spoken about her relationship with her parents or brother. Friends and relatives are given strict instructions not to talk about her and the only insight she has ever offered into her childhood can perhaps be gleaned from something she wrote in her religious book, *A Journey into God*. In it, she writes about the concept of God as father and the reader is left with the impression that, for Delia, God has become a surrogate father who has provided her with things her own father could not. Her heartfelt words provide an interesting glimpse into her relationship with her own father: 'In our journey of prayer it is normal and natural to be uncomprehending in the face of the mysterious truths of God, but we are not left absolutely in the dark, we are at least given these simple human images to reflect on. Of course there can be a problem here if my own personal experience of a father's love is flawed and inadequate, but in prayer I can at least begin to grasp how it is meant to be and even more than that, prayer puts me on the receiving end of a father's perfect and absolute love, where I can begin to experience perhaps for the first time what providence, protection, foresight and loving discipline are really about. The relationship we are invited to share is a close and familiar one, and our part in this relationship is to respond and learn to entrust ourselves to this divine fatherhood, in other words to become in spirit like a little child relating to a very loving daddy.'

Leo Evans believes her parents' strict Methodist faith may have been a cause of friction between them and Delia. 'Originally she was a non-conformist and that may have been one of the rubs in her home life,' he says. And in her book, Delia hints at the kind of fearful God that she was brought up to be afraid of. 'I suppose we all have recourse from time to time to one of the false gods we encountered earlier: perhaps before this mine had been the god who "waits for us to make mistakes",' she wrote. 'But now I had discovered the real God by discovering the real Jesus, the man who understands human frailty from within.'

Speaking about her lack of confidence, something that began in her childhood and persists to this day, Delia says: 'I don't like the way I look. In general I have a very poor self-image.' When she appeared on *Swap Shop* she opened her heart to the children who rang into the show and told them how nobody had ever rated her when she was young. In a rare moment of complete frankness, Delia's obvious anger at being written off as a child came tumbling out. She was the no-hoper people thought would never amount to anything, but she had showed them and here she was on television, a star. The torrent of bitterness released seemed out of place on a children's Saturday morning programme, but something in that child's innocent question tapped into the burning resentment that was obviously still there just below the surface all those years on.

It had been the feeling that she was somehow lacking that attracted her to religion. 'People like me are unsure of themselves to such an extent that they need something that other people don't need,' she said recently. 'I'd say it's born of people who in some way feel slightly inadequate.' Religion provided a substitute for family and friends and gave her a sense of belonging to something. Being part of a faith and belonging to a church fulfilled her emotional needs as well as her spiritual ones. For the first time Delia, always been the outsider, truly felt that she belonged.

When she first left school Delia worked for a time in a travel agency, answering the telephone, and then got a job in a hairdressers. She left home for good soon afterwards. She arrived in London at the start of the Swinging Sixties, a decade when anything was possible. The next ten years would prove to be the most interesting and important of her entire life. Fame and fortune, and the excitement that went with them, lay just around the corner.

3

The Singing Chef

To Delia, London, with its pace and energy, seemed to be a million miles away from the suburbs of Bexleyheath instead of fifteen. As a child she had harboured dreams of living in the country, but as a teenager she was attracted to the bright lights of the metropolis. Like thousands of other young people who descended on the capital in the 1960s, Delia was keen to find excitement. It was the decade when the city was considered by the rest of the world to be the most vibrant and happening place on earth. The King's Road, Carnaby Street, Mary Quant and Vidal Sassoon were names that conjured up images of trendy young things dressed in mini skirts and drainpipe trousers.

It was a decade in which attitudes changed dramatically. In 1960, when Delia was nineteen and had just left home, 'Swinging London' was only just starting to swing. Young people were beginning to find their voice for the first time, something that sent tremors of fear through the Establishment. In the Commons, MPs gave an unopposed second reading to a bill to curb Teddy Boys and at the Old Bailey Penguin Books was prosecuted for daring to publish the 'obscene' book *Lady Chatterley's Lover*.

In the year Delia arrived in London, teenagers were dancing to hits such as 'Cathy's Clown' and 'The Girl of My Best Friend'; the famous bands of the 1960s, The Beatles and the Rolling Stones, had yet to emerge. At the cinema, filmgoers trembled in their seats as the Alfred Hitchcock classic *Psycho*, starring Anthony Perkins and Janet Leigh, opened to rave reviews. And movie fans mourned the death of Clark Gable from a heart attack at the age of just fifty-nine. The year saw two major royal events: the birth of Prince Andrew in February 1960 and the marriage of his twenty-nine-year-old aunt Princess Margaret to Antony Armstrong-Jones.

At the start of Delia's working life, things hadn't looked terribly promising on the job front. Both the travel agency and the shop, seemed to be dead-end jobs with no prospects and she wanted to do something more creative. But once she arrived in London opportunities abounded. It was a time when youth was everything and if you were between eighteen and twenty you got the job. Delia landed a hairdressing position at one of the West End salons and one of the first things she did was dye her hated red hair brown. The money she got as a junior stylist was poor but one of the perks of the job was having your hair done for free by one of the other crimpers. Delia had hers cut into a fashionable Mary Quant-style bob, which was the trendiest hairstyle of the day and perfectly suited her elfin features.

After a short spell spent commuting back to Bexleyheath at night, she rented a small bed-sit and worked hard to support herself. Working in a bustling West End salon gave her the opportunity to meet people and she enjoyed her job at the salon. Indeed, were it not for a chance encounter she might have happily settled for a career in hairdressing.

One evening in 1962, when she had been working in London for just over two years, she stumbled on a place that would change the course of her life. Out for a meal with three friends, she walked through the doors of The Singing Chef restaurant in Connaught Street in the West End little realizing that the evening would turn out to be one of the most significant of her life. Leo Evans, who was cooking at the busy French restaurant that evening, remembers the night well and recalls how Delia caught his eye.

'The men were "terribly-terribly" Kensington types, what you would now call Hooray Henrys, and one of them was in the record business,' he says. 'They had two young women with them, one of whom looked like she had just come straight out of Vidal Sassoon's salon with her hair and make-up and everything.' The glossy haired young woman was Delia and, although he didn't know it at the time, Leo Evans was about to find himself a much needed washer-upper.

When the party had finished their starter and main course they ordered the dessert speciality of the house. It sounded innocent enough: an omelette soufflé flambé, but with one mouthful Delia's fate was sealed. 'The omelette soufflé flambé was my signature dish,' explains Leo. 'A puff omelette, flavoured with lemon and orange and brought out to the table flaming in brandy. I served it and one of the women said, "Do you know, I would do absolutely *anything* to be able to make something like that. I think it's absolutely marvellous. I am interested in cooking and I'd just do *anything* that anyone said."

'I went back to the table a little later and asked her if she really meant what she'd said. She said she did so I told her we had a vacancy for a part-time washer-up. I said, "You can start on Monday and if you survive the work as a washer-up after a few weeks you can be the kitchen assistant." The woman was Delia and that's how it started.'

Delia found herself in an extraordinary place. The Singing Chef was owned by Ken Toye who was, inevitably, a chef who sang. Whenever it was a customer's birthday or wedding anniversary, the lights would be dimmed and Ken Toye would appear from the kitchen and sing them a song. It was an eccentric establishment to say the least. Alan King, one of Delia's fellow washer-uppers, explains the attraction the restaurant held for him and dozens of other young people who begged to be allowed to scrub pans there. 'I fell in there by accident, as most of us did,' he says. 'I called round one evening to meet my girlfriend Joan, who was working there as a waitress, and I was furtively hanging around outside when this short, dumpy guy called Leo Evans came out and asked me what I was doing.

'I said, "Nothing, I am actually waiting for my girlfriend", and he said, "Well, don't hang around out here, come in." I thought it was nice of him and I knew from the moment I walked over the doorstep that my whole life was going to change. And it did. From that second onward. It was like finding Aladdin's cave; it really was extraordinary. The place had the same effect on lots of people; it changed people.'

A sense that The Singing Chef was not an ordinary restaurant was reinforced when he noticed that two of the 'waitresses' were in fact well-known top models. 'The night I walked in Celia Hammond and Jean Shrimpton were working there as waitresses,' Alan recalls. 'I thought, "This is different." There was a whole clique of people who worked there to earn a bit of extra money and got hooked on it because it was wonderful to be there.

'Before I realized what I was doing my sleeves were rolled up and I was scrubbing the biggest pots I'd ever set eyes on in a sink that wasn't even big enough to get them in; it was like the washbasin you get in a downstairs loo. The conditions were appalling but the most wonderful smells and creations were coming out of the kitchen. Leo said, "You will stay and have dinner, won't you?" and, before I'd realized, he'd got me to voluntarily beg him to come back the next day and wash up.'

And that is how it was for Delia too. To Ken Toye and Leo Evans, the staff were not there to be shouted at and abused, as in some 'celebrity' restaurant kitchens, but were welcomed into The Singing Chef and became part of a select clique. 'We've always made friends with the people we've worked with,' explains Ken. 'They become part of the family. Delia would come on in the early evening at about five-thirty and wash pans until twelve or one in the morning. She'd bring a huge pair of rubber gloves with her because she didn't want to ruin her hands. I'll always remember that: she had the humblest job in the world then but she was obviously going to rise above it.'

The washing up was an important job, says Ken, and was taken very seriously. 'If anyone is decent they learn by the washing up,' he explains. 'It's a great teacher. It's the hardest work you can think of; it's like working in a coal mine, only at the oven face. Delia would be the only washer-upper on that night and there would be a continuous stream of diners. And in those days of course we didn't have dishwashing machines, just deep sinks.'

When the hard work was finally over and the last plate had been washed and dried it would usually be well past midnight. But instead of returning home Delia would sit down and relax around the table with Leo and Ken and the other staff for a meal. It was something Ken Toye insisted on. 'We'd all sit down and have something to eat; that was one of our traditions,' he says. After Delia had eaten, Alan King would walk her home and, after a few short hours sleep, she would get up to do her day job. She was burning the candle at both ends but loved going to The Singing Chef so much that before long it would be her hairdressing job that took second place in her priorities.

Both Ken Toye and Leo Evans were impressed with her work

ethic but, as Alan King recalls, he and Delia didn't really look on their roles at the restaurant as being *work*. He explains, 'I remember very vividly that my life then was made up of happy days and not-so-happy days. The happy days were the days when I finished my day job, jumped in a cab and rushed over to Connaught Street and washed up. Whoever was doing the washing-up had to buy a jug of beer from the pub over the road for the kitchen staff. People did this very voluntarily; in effect we were paying to work!'

Delia viewed her job at The Singing Chef more as a training course than a job and Ken Toye's cousin Barbara Toye remembers Delia's surprise when she discovered she would be paid for working there. She recalls, 'When I gave Delia her wages at the end of her first night she looked at me in absolute genuine surprise and said, "Oh, do I get paid as well?" She thought she was going to work for nothing and learn the trade of cooking.'

Delia also took turns at waitressing, and serving on tables at the restaurant gave her a valuable insight into people's attitude to food which would prove useful later on. In the early 1960s, eating out in restaurants had yet to become a leisure pursuit and even for those who did dine out the kind of food on offer was incredibly limited. When Italians started coming to Britain at about this time and opened restaurants they found that people simply had no concept of their food whatsoever. When listing spaghetti dishes on their menus they would often have to insert in brackets 'not from a tin' to avoid confusing their customers, and diners complained that their pasta hadn't been cooked properly and was hard, when it had been prepared *al dente* in the traditional Italian style. Olive oil was something that was sold in small bottles in chemist shops.

Prawn cocktail was considered daring and sophisticated when it first emerged on restaurant menus, and Chinese and Indian food, where it was available, was viewed with suspicion. Even French food, the fashionable cuisine at the time, was a source of apprehension for many diners. 'Serving taught me a lot,' Delia admits. 'I found that people were basically afraid of what they thought was exotic food. The menu was in French and a lot of people didn't understand it. They didn't know how to eat an artichoke and they were full of shyness and embarrassment, so I used to explain what to do.' Delia's sensible and friendly approach, a marked contrast to the snooty-nosed waiters who staffed many French restaurants, must have appeared as a godsend to her customers.

When he first met Delia, Ken remembers being struck by her calm aura. 'Delia was very quiet, but I thought she was assured,' he says. 'She sat very quiet and still and she had that quality that some people have – a poise. I know that she didn't do very well at school. I've met tons of people who are very gifted but school just doesn't suit them. Shyness is a great problem; you get left behind and that would be my guess as to what happened with Delia – she got pushed aside at school. But she was very determined: I got the impression of a girl who had finally found her niche in life and was absolutely determined to make a go of it.'

When Ken went to France for two years to do a degree at a university in Aix-en-Provence, Leo Evans ran the restaurant. 'Leo took Delia under his wing and wrote and told me how she always brought a notebook with her to make a note of things,' recalls Ken. In contrast to the way her school teachers had perceived her, Leo found Delia to be an able pupil and within only two or three weeks she was promoted to kitchen assistant, which was in effect assistant chef.

'Delia was a quick and good learner; very able,' he says. 'Because she had trained as a hairdresser she had manual dexterity and an ability to see a pattern. She could follow a method, and learned quite quickly. After a while I would say to her, "We are going to have beef goulash tonight," and she would know the recipe, know the method and she would make it.'

Throughout her career, Delia's particular style has been to take her reader or viewer by the hand and lead them every step of the way through her recipes. It is how Leo Evans taught her nearly forty years ago. 'She learned that way and she teaches that way,' he says. 'I was very patient with her and because of her dexterity she learned very effectively. I'm a great believer in teaching and explaining and not keeping secrets. With a dish like the omelette soufflé flambé, for example, it is all a question of technique and if you get it wrong it can end up as lemon-flavoured scrambled eggs. I'm very happy to give people specific instruction and co-operation and I did teach Delia to make it. I taught her quite a few dishes.'

One of the first things she learned how to make at The Singing Chef was roast duck with sour cherry sauce, which remains one of her favourite dishes. She included the recipe in her *Winter Collection* book, describing it as 'quite nostalgic'.

Under Leo's expert tuition, Delia discovered that she wasn't as hopeless as her teachers had led her to believe. For virtually the first time in her life she discovered she was actually good at something. 'If she knew she could do something she was very competent and confident about doing it,' says Leo. 'I can't remember her making any mistakes and the only time I can remember shouting at her was when I had taught her how to make boeuf bourginon.

'Within fifteen minutes she had opened the oven door twice to look at it. I shouted to her, "It's not going to change for two hours; all you are doing is letting flavour out and dropping the temperature, leave it alone!" I think that was the only time I spoke sharply to her.' Delia was quick to learn from this too and years later Leo gave a wry smile when he watched her on television, telling her viewers, 'Once you have made this and put it in the oven, leave it alone.'

Just as Delia has done for readers of her 1998 recipe book *How to Cook*, Leo started by teaching her the basics. 'The first thing I taught her was how to make an omelette because in many ways it epitomizes French cooking; you've got to be fast, you've got to control heat and you've got to do it at the moment it's necessary and serve it immediately,' he says. Omelettes of any kind were Leo's speciality and some of his passion for them must have rubbed off on Delia, for in one of her early books she admitted to being 'obsessed with eggs'.

Eggs were also the subject of an amusing episode at the restaurant when Delia was waiting on tables one evening. Fanny Craddock, the most famous television cook of her day, was a regular diner at The Singing Chef while Delia was work-ing there and could often be a difficult customer. During the 1950s and 1960s millions of people watched her cookery programme *Kitchen Magic*, in which she would prepare food while dressed in elaborate Norman Hartnell ballgowns, diamonds and thick make-up. She was a formidable character who became more famous for the ear-bashings she gave her downtrodden husband Johnnie than for her recipes. 'More wine, Johnnie! More butter! Don't stint!' she would bark to her amiable-looking co-presenter, cum dogsbody.

She was the country's favourite battle-axe and she revelled in it. 'I have always been extremely rude,' she once boasted, 'And I have always got exactly what I wanted.' She and Leo Evans had crossed spoons on more than one occasion, and Delia and the other staff always perked up when she came in because they knew they would be in for a spot of entertaining theatre.

'Fanny and Johnnie were drinkers and she was a poseur *par excellence*,' explains Leo. 'I had several run-ins with her but she wasn't too tricky after I had one spat with her. She had been on television a couple of nights before, really selling silver-plated copper omelette pans. We got talking and she said, "You can't make omelettes decently without the right sort of pan, it's got to be silver-plated copper." I told her that if you know how to make an omelette you can make one in a biscuit-tin lid.' She said, "Oh no you can't", and I said, "Oh yes you can" – it was like a pantomime.

'Anyway, I went away and cooked her an omelette in a biscuit-tin lid and we had no more trouble from Fanny Craddock after that!' Indeed, Mrs Craddock later said, 'Who, so far, has debunked the old wives' tale that perfect French omelettes must be made in perfect French omelette pans? No one. Yet any frying pan can be used if heated slowly and then rubbed with a small piece of pork fat just before tossing in the butter.'

Before long, Delia was holding down not two but three jobs. Her job as a hairdresser had led to other openings and she was also working as a stylist in a photographic studio and as a make-up artist for a company making television commercials. According to Barbara Toye, The Singing Chef had one of the most qualified staff in London. 'We all held down other jobs as well as working in the restaurant,' she explains. 'Leo was the Professor of Metallurgy at the City University; Ken was a teacher; I was a qualified dental nurse and a professional singer and Alan and Delia were both hairdressers.'

Alan King remembers Delia dashing around from one work venue to another, juggling her various jobs. 'In the daytime she was working around the corner in Carlton Studios, in the mews off Connaught Square, setting up shots for food shoots,' he recalls. 'And in the evenings she and I would alternate as assistant chef at the restaurant. It was great fun and we were learning as we went along.'

They considered themselves fortunate to have got a job at The Singing Chef because places were in hot demand. 'People were fighting for work,' explains Alan. 'They would ask Leo if they could have an evening's work and Leo would say, "I can fit you in in three weeks' time on a Wednesday." Delia was very good, obviously, because if you weren't any good you didn't get in because there was such competition for places. One knew at the time that she was going places because she seemed to be much more commercially aware than us, as she has since proved. I remember when she later got her job on the *Daily Mirror* magazine and had stopped working at the restaurant regularly we would say, "My god, this is our Delia doing this." She went on and she never looked back.'

Alan, on the other hand, couldn't bear to tear himself away from the restaurant. 'I loved the place so much I ended up owning it,' he says. 'When Ken sold up I took over. It was such a marvellous place and it was the age of the wonderful amateur. It all came from Ken originally and then from Leo. Being a professor, Leo was someone to be slightly feared as well as held in awe. He was very domineering but he was an absolutely brilliant teacher. He could fire you up and teach you things you didn't even know how to pronounce. He was extraordinary. We never ran out of washer-uppers because he would just ring someone who was getting bad marks and say, "Right you, down the restaurant – you're washing up." '

Leo explains how Delia's work experience at the restaurant stood her in good stead when disaster struck during a photo shoot she was involved in. 'She was working on a TV set for a food commercial and somebody dropped the pie they had to photograph,' he recalls. 'Everyone was horrified but Delia said, "I can make that", and went away and made it. Word got round and when people asked later on if she was capable of doing a TV programme, somebody said, "Yes, she will be OK." '

Working in a trendy London salon and meeting actresses and models in the photographic studios ensured that Delia was well up on the latest looks. She enthusiastically followed the fashions of the day and was into the Beatles and Mary Quant. 'Delia was a bright young thing who wore mini skirts,' recalls Joan King, while Barbara Toye remembers Delia buying a white PVC raincoat, one of the most essential fashion items of the 1960s. 'Delia had that slightly asymmetrical bob that Mary Quant made famous and it always suited her,' says Barbara. 'I was so envious of her because she was the only person I knew with such a trendy haircut.' The Mary Quant angle stuck. 'When she first became famous, somebody said of her that she was the Mary Quant of cooking,' recalls Leo Evans.

Although Delia was several years younger, Barbara and Delia struck up a friendship while they were working at the restaurant together. 'She was such a likeable person, and we used to giggle and have fun together,' Barbara recalls. 'I think Delia was living in Kent at that stage, so if she had a photo shoot in the West End the next day I used to let her sleep over in my room above the restaurant. There was a double bed, which I occupied, and a single bed which I let Delia sleep in. So I can actually say I have slept with Delia Smith!'

Ken Toye recalls how Delia developed a love of football when England was playing in the World Cup in 1966 – something else that has stayed with her and become a life-long passion. 'She loved football and she used to go off as a supporter with her scarf and her hat when she was poor,' he says. 'She was a pretty and attractive girl, with nice colouring and very deep brown hair. She looked very much as she does today really. She hasn't changed much, she's still the little Delia that I knew.'

But Ken also observed a more introspective, slightly sadder side to Delia at that time. 'I suspect she could have been lonely,' he says. 'She made friends with the boys in the kitchen and with Leo but she wasn't thrusting herself forward to be a friend, to be interesting. She was just prepared to stay in the background and be one who listens.'

On her nights off, Delia would often babysit for Leo Evans's children, David and Frances. She was a strict babysitter. 'Lots of babysitters would be persuaded to play games with them and we'd come home after an evening out to find the kids still up,' explains Leo. 'But Delia would say, "I was told you had to go to bed at eight o'clock, so you go to bed at eight o'clock." ' Both of them say that Delia was the strictest babysitter they ever had. David is now a chef and as a one-upmanship thing often says to people, 'Well, of course, Delia Smith was my babysitter!'

Delia has often remarked how grateful she is that she never learned home economics. 'I was lucky that I didn't go to cook- ery school and learn so much about making clever things like classic butter sauces that I forgot people need to know how to make good gravy,' she says. Ken Toye can see her logic. 'If she had done home economics it may have ruined her, she might not have got anywhere,' he reasons. 'I'm always a great believer that things come out well in the end.'

Delia has fond memories of her time at The Singing Chef. Ken Toye says: 'Years later she told me that she thought we did her good. She said, "I had so much fun and I laughed so much that I thought I'd like to be in this business." And that's the bit I like. OK, she learned some bits and pieces with us, but the important thing was she enjoyed it and I think that shows in what she does now.'

Almost forty years on, Delia looks back on her days as washer-upper at The Singing Chef with a certain degree of awe. In November 1984, to celebrate selling her 2 millionth book, Delia gave a special party at Miller Howe, her friend

Delia Smith

John Tovey's restaurant in the Lake District. She took over the entire hotel for a weekend and invited all the people who had been involved in her career.

Ken Toye and Leo Evans were there, along with dozens of other people who had featured prominently in her life. 'I was actually the guest of honour,' says Leo proudly. 'I sat next to her at the formal dinner and gave the speech and toast to her. Afterwards she said to my wife, "Do you know, I sometimes wonder what would have happened if I hadn't survived the washing up." She told her, "You cannot believe what it was like. There was this small kitchen, hot, busy and with no dish-washing machines. There was a serving hatch where all the dirty crockery would be placed. I'd wash it all up, breathe a sigh and then lift the hatch and it would be full of dirty crockery again." '

When she had been cooking at The Singing Chef for a few years, Delia told Leo Evans that she was keen to expand her knowledge. Happy to help his protégée, Leo got her a job working in the kitchen at Madame Maurer's, one of the best restaurants in London. 'Delia wanted more experience so I spoke to Madame Maurer and she took her on as an assistant,' he explains. 'Her restaurant was in Greek Street, Soho and it was very well known and featured in all the good-food guides of the day. Lots of Royal Ballet and University of London people frequented it.

'Madame Maurer was an Alsace woman whose family came to Britain in the First World War but she retained the German/Alsace style of cooking and served masses of whipped cream with everything. On Delia's first day she said to her, "You vill whip ze cream", and gave her a large balloon whisk and a huge bowl. Delia had to sit and whisk it by hand because Madame claimed the texture wasn't right if you used a machine. Delia recounted this to me, rolling her eyes. She

48

seemed to be unlucky in her first experience working anywhere; she had to cope with the washing up at The Singing Chef and then beat about half a gallon of cream by hand at Madame Maurer's!'

4

A Higher Love

Sixties London might have been one of the most exciting places in the world, but for a shy teenager from small-town suburbia it could also be the loneliest. When she first left home, Delia had few friends in the capital and spent much of her time alone as the city buzzed around her.

But in the spring of 1961 she was to meet the man who would become the most pivotal figure in her life so far. Not only would Delia fall in love for the first time, but the ultimately doomed relationship would have a profound and lasting effect on her. Because of her love for one man the whole course of her life was inexorably changed.

Delia has never revealed the identity of her first love. The intensely private, some would say secretive, woman has always deflected questions about him, determined that her first, lost love should never be unmasked. But his name was Louis Alexander and he was a Catholic missionary. He was a strikingly handsome young man, with dark hair and features inherited from his Indian father. Although he was the same age as Delia, in worldly terms he was many years her senior.

The son of an Indian doctor and his Austrian wife, Louis had had a cosmopolitan upbringing and as a result was far more

Delia Smith

sophisticated than the average twenty-year-old. He was well
travelled, having been brought up in Switzerland and Mexico,
and had been educated for a time in California where he'd stud-
ied law. He had a taste for the finer things in life, including good
food and wine, and Delia thought he was the most exciting man
she had ever met.

They met when she was just nineteen and fell madly in love.
Delia was somewhat in awe of this charming man of the world.
She was a rather shy, unassuming girl from Bexleyheath who
was happy to stay in the background, watching and listening
while others took centre stage. Meanwhile, Louis was a bon
viveur who held court wherever he went and drew admiring
glances from Delia's rivals for his attentions.

But despite the cultural differences and their distinctly different lives so far, the couple seemed made for each other. This was
no nine-day wonder, not a casual, fun fling between two people
barely out of their teens looking for a no-strings relationship.
When they had been dating for a while they talked of marriage
and becoming engaged. It was a love affair in the most romantic sense, with the shy, unconfident Delia completely captivated
by handsome, charismatic Louis.

Through him, she glimpsed a world so completely different
from her own that it was almost like meeting someone from a
novel. Louis was also a committed Catholic, something that
Delia found intriguing and which added an extra dimension to
his attraction for her. To Delia, Catholicism was full of romance:
saints and sinners and martyrs. Louis opened the door for her
into a new world of religion that would become the biggest
single influence on her life.

Louis's faith was the most important thing to him and under
his careful tutelage Delia too would embrace religion and
become a Roman Catholic. But her joy at finding God would be
bittersweet as Louis's religious beliefs ultimately came between

them. In a decision that would break both their hearts, Louis would choose God over Delia and decide to enter the priesthood.

But when he first met Delia, he wasn't entertaining ideas of a life exclusively devoted to God. In the autumn of 1961, a few months after they had started going out together, he entered the University of London to do a diploma in international relations, a course that would lead to a Bachelor of Arts. Unlike Delia, whom Ken Toye had guessed to be somewhat lonely when she first arrived in London, Louis was outgoing and had lots of friends.

Father Maurice McGill, who knew him when he became a student with a group of missionary brothers, recalls how he was the life and soul of the party. 'Louis had so many friends and so many contacts it seemed as though he met half of London,' he says. 'He was certainly very sophisticated and well educated; very much the kind of person who went out and searched for himself, and found for himself.'

This sociability was partly born out of necessity. 'His mother died when he quite young and he had nobody really to look after him,' explains Father McGill. 'His mother had died before he came to London and I think his contact with his dad wasn't so brilliant. In fact his dad went back to live in India quite soon afterwards and I think Louis probably looked after himself.'

It was Louis who introduced Delia to the pleasures of eating out and he often took her to restaurants where they would dine on seemingly exotic dishes such as spaghetti bolognese and coq au vin. 'We went to one place and ordered scampi cocktail and half a bottle of sweet wine and thought we were really fancy,' Delia once said. But, more importantly, he provided the impetus for her to learn how to cook. If she hadn't met him she might arguably have never switched from hairdressing to cooking and might still be cutting hair for a living. For despite her mother and grandmothers being such keen cooks, by the time she was twenty-one Delia scarcely knew how to boil an egg.

It was discovering that Louis's ex-girlfriend had been a good cook that changed things for Delia. It transpired that her predecessor wasn't only a good cook, she was a cordon-bleu cook, and Delia was left feeling desperately lacking. It wasn't the first time in her life that she had felt inferior to other girls, but this time she decided to do something about it. Spurred on by jealousy of the mysterious-but-talented ex, Delia vowed to become just as good a cook as her, if not better. Delia has never talked about Louis in interviews except to say, almost in passing, how jealousy of his former girlfriend gave her the impetus to learn how to cook.

'The boy I was going out with had a previous girlfriend who was a cordon-bleu cook and he kept going on about her,' she once said. 'I was always hearing about her great pigeon en croute and so on, and I was rather peeved. I had hardly boiled an egg before so I decided I'd better learn something quickly. That's how my career started – out of pique.' Her boss Ken Toye remembers Delia's determination to outshine Louis's previous girlfriend. 'Delia said, "I won't let this beat me, I'm going to win this battle," ' he says.

As well as sparking her interest in cookery, Louis was also instrumental in Delia getting her job at The Singing Chef. 'He was a regular customer and I got to know him quite well,' says Ken Toye. 'He was a very interesting young man who was trying to do good things. There was something special about him. He was a lovely, smashing lad – a very bright, imposing character even though he was very young. Because we knew him we were happy to employ Delia. It was like she had come recommended.'

Delia and Louis were together for several years. She introduced him to her family, and her younger brother Glyn recalls meeting him on several occasions, liking him enormously. Alan King, who worked with her at The Singing Chef, recounts how Delia would sometimes ask to use his flat to entertain Louis. 'She used to borrow my place, which was in Bell Street, just up the road from the restaurant, because it was close,' he says. 'She used to go round there and cook her boyfriend dinner. He was slightly older than I was and I remember thinking that he seemed to have his life sorted. He had a car and he used to terrify the living daylights out of me when he gave me lifts home because he drove so fast.'

During their time off, Louis, a keen photographer, would take reams of photographs of Delia and captured her transformation from shy teenager to confident young woman. They would also discuss religion and Delia became increasingly fascinated by how important her fiancé's faith was to him. He went regularly to Mass and, intriguingly for Delia, showed every sign of enjoying it. To Delia, who had always suffered from poor self-esteem and a feeling of worthlessness, seeing Louis so obviously fulfilled by his religion had a big effect on her.

She began to wonder if it might do the same for her too. 'I became fascinated by the idea of religion because I definitely felt something was missing in my life,' she says. 'But I also thought, "Oh God, not a Catholic. All they do is produce hundreds of children so that there are lots more Catholics." '

Louis, keen to foster Delia's obvious interest in the faith, lent her the autobiography of St Thérèse of Lisieux, the French Carmelite nun who died when she was only twenty-four. Her moving story had a profound effect on Delia, as it has had on millions of Catholics all over the world, and by the time she had finished reading it she had changed her mind. Delia later described the work as 'my own most treasured spiritual book'.

St Thérèse was born Thérèse Martin in Alençon, France in 1873. In 1888, at the age of fifteen, she entered the Carmelite convent at Lisieux. Thérèse's mission was 'to make God loved as I love him, to teach souls my little way – the way of spiritual childhood, the way of trust and absolute surrender'. She died aged just twenty-four of tuberculosis and was canonized the following year. Reading her words, Delia felt an immediate affinity with the nun's description of her relationship with God. 'I started going to Mass and taking instruction – it just seemed right,' she said.

It meant a great deal to Louis that his fiancée wanted to convert to Catholicism and he took Delia along to the London church where he worshipped. The first time Delia ever went to Mass was with Louis and she found it an uplifting, if bewildering, experience. 'It was all in Latin and I didn't understand a word of it, but I knew there was something really going on there,' she says. This introduction to Catholicism clearly struck a chord with Delia, who realized that she wasn't the only person who had faults or doubted themselves. 'It was full of fallible and weak people, people with flaws, and I loved it,' she recalls.

She became a Catholic in 1963 at the age of twenty-two. 'I think it is the most important thing to me,' she said recently. 'I can't say I've ever had a vibrant faith all the way through, but I've never lost it. I'm very lucky that I've got a clear view.'

But her lack of confidence was evident even in her approach to her faith – something that ought to have brought her pleasure and happiness. She began to worry that she might not be praying enough, or that she wasn't as close to God as other people were. The pain this caused her is evident. 'When some claim to have privileged information and special access to God denied to the rest, it can make others feel second-class in their own search for God,' she later wrote in her book, *A Journey into God*. 'I speak with feeling on this point, for there was a stage in my life when – although I knew deep down that no one is more special to

God than anyone else – I began to feel that, since others seemed to be so persuasive about their "special experiences", there must be something wrong with me and the barrenness of my prayer.'

Delia's conversion to Catholicism was something that was deeply personal to her and Louis and, at that time in her life, she did not speak about it in general conversation. Indeed, people who knew and worked with her when she was in her early twenties were surprised to discover years later how strongly she felt about Catholicism. 'Delia's now well-known religious convictions were not so obviously fervent then,' says Barbara Toye. 'That obviously came later. She didn't particularly talk about religion or religious things when I knew her.'

Her religion is something that has lasted throughout her life, but her relationship with the man who inspired it sadly did not. 'I remember that they were either engaged, or about to get engaged,' says Alan's ex-wife Joan King. 'But then it all went wrong.' Delia hinted at a possible reason for the break-up in a casual throwaway remark she once made. 'He had a different girlfriend every week,' she said.

Famously secretive about her private life, she has always shied away from discussing her relationship with Louis in any detail. In interviews she sticks to the same few facts: that he was a Catholic, a bit of a 'Jack the Lad', and had an ex-girlfriend who had been a cordon-bleu cook. Above and beyond that the story – and his identity – has been a closed book. 'I soon forgot about the boyfriend because I became so wrapped up in learning recipes and cooking techniques,' she has said, perhaps in an attempt to deflect interest away from her private life and back on to the safer subject of cookery.

But the truth is far sadder and more complicated than that. In July 1964, when he had been going out with Delia for more than three years, Louis decided that he wanted to become more involved with religion. He had met some people from a Roman Catholic missionary society and applied to join them. The Mill Hill Fathers, a North London-based organization, trained priests, brothers and lay people to work overseas, promoting the Roman Catholic Church. Louis had long felt a calling to help people and he was also keen to spread the word of Catholicism. Having been brought up in different countries, he had a natural wanderlust and it was unusual for him to have stayed in one place for so long. He had been in London for four years and, perhaps inevitably, began to get itchy feet.

To Delia's dismay, Louis announced that he was going to study philosophy at the Mill Hill Fathers' college in the Netherlands. He was away in the Netherlands from September 1964 to June 1966 while Delia remained in London, learning the culinary ropes at The Singing Chef. They were in touch throughout this period and their relationship might well have survived the two-year separation. But while he was abroad, Louis, after much soul searching, realized that he wanted to devote himself wholly to God. He broke the bombshell news to Delia that he had decided to train for the priesthood.

For him it wasn't enough to love God and do good works; he wanted to dedicate his entire life to God, and that meant giving up Delia. He decided he would never marry and would take a vow of celibacy as laid down in Catholic law. Theirs is a story that wouldn't have been out of place in the pages of Colleen McCullough's best-selling novel *The Thorn Birds*, about a priest torn between his love of God and his love of a woman. The irony of the situation didn't escape Delia: through Louis she had found God, but because of God she had lost Louis.

In the summer of 1966, as England celebrated winning the World Cup, Louis arrived back in London. He enrolled at St Joe's College in Mill Hill to study theology and prepare for the priesthood. His decision was to leave lasting scars on Delia. She was left devastated by his decision to end their relationship in favour of the Church.

Louis threw himself into training to be a priest for three years, desperate to put Delia firmly out of his mind. But the painful soul-searching didn't stop there. In an ironic twist of fate, and despite having given up the woman he loved, Louis never actually became a priest after all. He started to have serious doubts whether he had made the right decision and as the day drew nearer when he would have to make his final vows, he realized he didn't want to go through with it.

Father McGill recalls: 'Louis was here from September 1966 until some time in 1969, studying for the priesthood. But for some reason he decided to take time out and went to study at the London School of Economics. During his time there he must have decided not to continue training for the priesthood.'

But by the time that Louis realized that a life of piety wasn't for him it was too late for him and Delia. She had met someone else and there was no way back for the couple. In early 1972 he went to the church of St Martin-in-the-Fields in Trafalgar Square where he ran The Centre, a place for lonely young Londoners to go to meet people. He ran the meeting place throughout the early 1970s and is still involved in missionary work today.

He and Delia kept in touch intermittently over the years but he has now not seen or spoken to her for more than fifteen years. Speaking about her for the first time, he explains how close their bond was. 'Delia is someone who was very close to me, and to whom I was very close for a very long time,' he admits. 'Her spiritual development was very important to her, to me and to us. I was part of a group of people who were very involved in her becoming a Catholic. We knew each other extremely well. It was quite a big thing; I didn't just meet her on the top of the 53 bus one evening.'

Louis, who is now married, reveals how he still treasures the photographs that he took of his young love almost forty years ago. 'I knew Delia over a period of several years and I have got a whole stack of photographs of her in her teens and twenties,' he says. 'I am a keen photographer and the pictures show her aged nineteen, twenty and twenty-one.

'To tell you the truth I haven't had any real contact with Delia for many years. I met her once or twice going into church and we spoke briefly but we have had no contact for a long time. We've both got our own lives now. She's become very famous and that's terrific. She's done wonderfully well and I'm very pleased for her. As far as I'm concerned, Delia and I knew each other, we were great friends, we had a great time and that was it. There's no rancour, disappointment or hurt or anything like that. The past is the past. I'm very happy to leave it like that.'

Louis and his wife Victoria live in London, where they help couples who are having marital trouble, with the aid of counselling and religion. 'We're both involved in marriage evangelism at the moment and have been for many years,' explains his wife. 'We work with an ecumenical Christian community, so Louis is still involved in missionary work, depending on what your definition of missionary work is. He is still a committed Christian and still very much involved in his faith.'

Louis was the first of only two men Delia has ever loved. She lost Louis, her first love, to his religion but she would not remain broken-hearted for long. The great love of her life was waiting in the wings ready to sweep her off her feet. Significantly, her next lover would prove to be a man with his feet firmly set on the ground. Unlike Louis, he would not give up the woman he loved in the pursuit of God, but would snap her up and keep her for himself.

5

Smith and Jones

Later on in the 1960s, Delia branched out into yet another direction when she answered an advertisement to be a live-in cook for a Harley Street doctor and his family. Professor Simon Yudkin was a paediatrician at a London hospital and Delia was hired to prepare meals for him and his wife Cicely and their son John.

By coincidence, Barbara Toye, with whom Delia had worked at The Singing Chef in the early 1960s, was working at the dental surgery underneath Professor Yudkin's flat at 118 Harley Street and was delighted when their paths crossed again. 'The dentist I worked for said that an attractive young woman called Delia had moved in upstairs,' recalls Barbara. 'I wondered whether it was "my" Delia and sure enough it was. It was really lovely to see her again because I had always liked her enormously. I remember thinking that she had landed on her feet with that job and I was really pleased for her.'

Delia enjoyed working for the Yudkins and found that her job gave her scope to try out different recipes. Whenever the couple held dinner parties, Delia would experiment with new dishes in addition to the ones that she had been taught by Leo Evans and Madame Maurer. Professor Yudkin and his wife were willing and enthusiastic guinea-pigs for her new creations, doubtless never realizing that their keen young chef would become one of Britain's most famous cooks.

French food was the fashion at the time and Delia cut her culinary teeth on dishes such as boeuf bourgignon, coq au vin, ratatouille, and crêpes Suzette. They were what she had been taught how to make at The Singing Chef but she was keen to find out more about traditional English recipes too. This was more easily said than done because the popularity of British food was at one of its lowest ebbs. It was spoken about almost derisively and people genuinely considered that when it came to cooking, the French wiped the floor with us.

Chef Gary Rhodes, an ardent advocate of traditional British cooking, believes that it is the very simplicity of British food that has often been its downfall. In his book *Rhodes Around Britain*, he argues that the only difference between the French and the British is that the French have never forgotten their traditions. 'So what happened to us?' he says. 'Was it that the traditions weren't strong or numerous enough? Or that we just didn't have the passion for cooking that we associate with the French and Italians? Probably, on reflection, a combination of all these.

'British cookery had always been simple – with wonderful ingredients like our own beef, which didn't need anything more fancy than just roasting. The British always wanted everything to taste of exactly what it was, so there were no rich comple-mentary sauces, or tricky combinations of foods. It was a ques-tion of featuring the main ingredient and achieving the very best taste with it. Perhaps when nothing much had changed for hundreds of years, the passion for the dish and for the art was lost.'

Back in 1968, when Gary was still at junior school and had yet to ponder the whys and wherefores of British food, Delia too was intrigued by why our native cuisine got such a bad press. An avid reader of cookery books, she began to wonder why everyone thought English food was so awful. She read somewhere that in the eighteenth century the British ate better than anyone else in Europe and this further sparked her curiosity. She bought a ticket for the Reading Room in the British Museum and in her spare time began researching the history of English cuisine. Poring over the dusty old volumes for hours at a time, she unearthed a whole series of delicious-sounding recipes from the eighteenth century.

She tried out some of them out on Simon and Cecily Yudkin and, encouraged by their praise, began to think about compiling them into a book. 'It doesn't sound much now,' she explains. 'But in the sixties it was unheard of. Somehow, because of the war, British cooking stopped. Everyone had forgotten just how good it was.' One of the first recipes that she tried was eighteenth-century creamed apple flan. She liked it so much that she later included it in her huge-selling *Complete Cookery Course*.

'This recipe is a nostalgic one for me as it's one of the first I tried after some research at the British Museum and it prompted me to do a whole lot more!' she confessed to her readers. So inspired was she by the research she began while working in Harley Street, that Delia started to think of writing about food as a career.

When she later became famous, Delia would come to be known as 'The Mrs Beeton of Our Age', after the phenomenally successful nineteenth century cook. Isabella Beeton was the best-known cook of the Victorian age and her *Book of Household Management* is the most famous cookery book of all time. First published in 1861, it combined recipes for every type of cooking, together with practical guidance for running a household and advice in matters of etiquette. It became the Victorian woman's bible and has been reprinted over and over again. It is still in demand today and can be found in most bookshops, sitting alongside Delia's books.

Delia's sensible, no-nonsense approach and the way she has championed home cooking have led to obvious parallels between her and Mrs Beeton, but Mrs Beeton was never an influence on Delia. Like many others before and since, Delia had been seduced by the colourful Mediterranean recipes of Elizabeth David. Acknowledged to be one of the twentieth century's greatest food writers, Elizabeth David is credited with changing the way the British thought about and prepared food. Her nine books, written with wit and brilliance, helped to educate the taste buds of the post-war generation. Insisting on authentic recipes and fresh ingredients, she showed that food didn't have to be complicated to be good.

Her now-classic recipe book, *A Book of Mediterranean Food*, published in 1950, introduced Britons to the ingredients of a sunnier world: olive oil, garlic, aubergine and basil. Years later Delia would feature these same ingredients in many of her recipes, most notably in her best-selling *Summer Collection* book. David's cookery books celebrated the smell and taste of the ingredients they featured and, above all, she highlighted the concept that food reflects a way of life and should be a source of joy. Subsequent books on French and Italian cooking followed, and her *English Bread and Yeast Cookery* became the bible of the Real Bread movement.

In an early interview, Delia told how Elizabeth David had influenced and inspired her. 'I was brought up on the finest English cooking and later graduated to a diligent study of the works of Elizabeth David, who seemed to epitomize my own instincts for simplicity and purity matched with inventiveness,' she said, rather stiltedly.

But not everyone is a fan of Elizabeth David. Tom Jaine, former editor of the food lover's bible *The Good Food Guide*, makes an interesting point about the way both she and Delia are revered. 'My current view of Elizabeth David is that obviously she was a great woman et cetera, et cetera, but the interesting thing about Elizabeth David is not her. If you were to move to the planet Mars with a copy of her book in your knapsack and read it, you would not be gobsmacked by the sheer genius of it. It's good, but it's not genius stuff. There's no point trying to compare it to John Donne or something like that.

'What is really interesting about Elizabeth David is our perception of her; in other words the interest moves to us and not to the person. And what is fascinating is not her but the reverence in which she is held. The same is true of Delia now.'

In recent years some foodies have even controversially suggested that Elizabeth David was actually responsible for killing off decent British food by championing French and Italian cooking. They argue that she was singing the praises of foreign cuisine immediately after the Second World War at a time when our national produce was bound to be substandard. It's a theory that Delia finds herself agreeing with. 'I think in some ways that's right,' she says. 'That's probably what started me off – that feeling: why should everything be French? But Elizabeth David also wrote a wonderful book on bread and about salt, spices and aromatics in English cookery, so the point is exaggerated.'

Even back in the late 1960s, Delia was shrewd enough to realize that Elizabeth David wasn't for everyone. David's fans were generally middle-class people who already had an interest and experience in food and could afford to travel. She appealed to people at the more sophisticated end of the recipe market while, at the other end, magazines such as *Good Housekeeping* offered economical but often dull recipes to the housewives of Britain. There was virtually nothing in the middle.

'In those days you had only the two extremes of Robert

Carrier at one end and the recipes in *Family Circle* magazine,'
Delia explains. 'Nobody was interested in English cooking. The
colour supplements were keen on food, but that was very
upmarket and very French. Dinner-party books were two a
penny – it was everyday eating that had to be improved.'
Always looking for opportunities to expand her knowledge and
experience, Delia cleverly spotted a gap in the market and was
keen to put pen to paper. What she didn't know was how she
should go about getting started. All that was about to change,
however, as she was just about to meet the person who would
kick-start her writing career and start her on the road to fame.

During her time with them, Delia had become extremely fond
of the Yudkin family and was devastated when Simon Yudkin
died unexpectedly when she had been working for them for
only a short while. With his premature death, Delia's job came
to an end. She remained in touch with his widow Cicely until
her death many years later and is still in contact with the
Yudkins' son John, who is now a Professor of Diabetes. Without
the Harley Street job, Delia was glad that she had kept up her
other jobs – especially as she now had to find herself somewhere to live.

As well as cooking for the Yudkins and continuing to help out
occasionally at The Singing Chef, Delia was still working as a
food stylist on photographic shoots. Preparing the food ready
for the commercial photographers, Delia learned the tricks of
the trade. Somebody crouching underneath the table with a
lighted cigarette in their hand could create 'steam', and glycerine was routinely used to make strawberries glisten attractively.
'In the early days it was really something of an art form,' Delia
admits. 'We used to try to imitate steam but it never quite
looked like steam and people could tell you had cheated. They
used to use mashed potato for ice-cream. You can imagine what
happened otherwise under hot lights. But the standard in

commercial photography today is so incredibly high that they insist on reality.'

One of the photographers she worked with was Max Logan, who had a studio just off Cambridge Circus. He met Delia at the time she was contemplating becoming a food writer and describes what she was like in those early days. 'Delia was a nice, unassuming, pleasant person who knew what she was doing and just got on with it,' he says.

'She seemed to be someone with a vision. She told me she had a job looking after a person in Harley Street, but was free to do other things in the day. She was doing some casual home economics and would come to the little studio I had in the basement in Earlham Street.'

The two became friends and when Delia told Max about her plans for the eighteenth century cookery book, he offered to help her. Describing how they put a presentation together to help sell the idea, he says, 'We were dreaming up a book which she was going to be involved in and we did a cover and a couple of spread pages inside.' But despite Max's help, Delia still had no idea how to go about getting the book published.

Then came a turning point in her career. In 1969 Delia met a young American woman called Deborah Owen. Keith Cheng, an actor and designer who worked with Max Logan, introduced them. It was a portentous meeting. Owen, who had just arrived from America and was starting her career as a literary agent, would prove to be one of the most influential people in Delia's life. In time the women would forge a powerful partnership that would make them both immensely rich and successful. In the meantime, however, the two became friends and Delia was able to offer the newly wed Debbie some useful culinary tips to keep her husband happy.

Debbie had recently married a handsome young doctor called David Owen, who later became the politician and statesman Lord Owen. As a new bride, she had no idea how to cook David's favourite food, and rather shame-facedly confided her lack of culinary expertise to Delia. Delia's calm and clear explanation of exactly what she should do not only inspired Debbie to don a pinny and get cooking; it also made her realize that here was someone with a rare gift for inspiring confidence. 'I thought if she can dispel all my hang-ups and fears, she can help anyone,' says Debbie.

'Delia got me on track when I was newly married and taught me how to poach an egg and make good soups,' she recalls. 'I had been existing on a diet of yoghurts and salads and now I had a husband to feed. David is passionate about poached eggs and I simply could not work out how to break the egg in the water and not have it spread out to all sides of the pan. I started talking to Delia about this and she told me that the whole thing entirely depends on the freshness of the egg. Then she told me how to tell if an egg is fresh by making sure that it floats in water.'

Delia mentioned the planned eighteenth-century cookbook, explaining that she wanted to remind people that English food hadn't always been so lousy. The book never materialized because they couldn't find a publisher, but Debbie Owen still decided to sign Delia up as one of her first clients. Later that year, she heard of an opening for a cookery writer on a magazine that the *Daily Mirror* was launching and suggested Delia for the job. Despite the fact that she had no writing experience, it was the 1960s and, as Ken Toye says, if you were young and bright you got the job. One might add that having a well-connected agent helped too.

Delia joined the staff of the *Mirror* during the golden era of national newspapers when all the papers were still situated in or around the corner from Fleet Street and circulation had yet to be affected by television. In 1969, the *Daily Mirror* was the biggest-selling newspaper in Europe with a daily sale of 4,250,000 and had an enormous staff. The *Mirror* offices were housed in an imposing if ugly red and blue 1950s monolith at Holborn Circus, within easy striking distance of the journalists' favourite watering holes in Fleet Street.

At the time Delia arrived everyone was talking about an exciting new tabloid that had just been launched. The *Sun* hit the streets on 17 November 1969 and immediately set itself up as an arch rival of the *Daily Mirror*. The *Sun* had previously existed as a rather dull broadsheet for five years in the 1960s as part of the Mirror Group, but had been sold off after losing more than £12 million. It was bought by an enthusiastic young Australian called Rupert Murdoch who took it over with one aim in mind: to challenge the *Daily Mirror*. Murdoch saw a great opportunity to steal readers away from the *Mirror*, which he felt had lost touch with the younger generation, and by Day 3 the new *Sun* claimed sales of 1,650,000 – twice its daily sales as a broadsheet.

Mirrorscope, the *Daily Mirror*'s colour magazine, was launched in a bid to ensure the *Mirror* kept its lead over its rivals. The editor was Mike Molloy and he recalls how easily mini-skirted Delia got the job, admitting that her employment had more to do with the way she looked than her ability. It was also a case of 'it's not what you know but who you know', as Molloy knew Debbie Owen and respected her judgement. 'We were looking for someone to do the cookery column and Debbie told me she had met a girl who wanted to do a book about medieval cooking but had no writing experience,' he says. 'She said there was definitely something about her. Delia came along to see me. She was very warm and enthusiastic. Very attractive. She said she wanted to write about food, so we gave her a go.'

It was an enormously lucky break for Delia and one that would be perhaps less likely to happen in today's cut-and-

Delia Smith

thrust newspaper market. But Delia discovered that writing for a national newspaper was a lot more difficult than she had thought. Without any journalistic training whatsoever, unable to type and scarcely able to spell, her work failed to make the grade. 'The first piece she wrote was terrible,' admits Molloy. 'I told her to do it again, as if she was writing to her mum.'

Michael Wynn Jones, the magazine's deputy editor, remembers Delia's interview with Molloy. 'Mike asked her if she had any experience writing for a newspaper and she admitted she hadn't, but, to his eternal credit, he told her to go off and try her hand at writing a few columns,' he says. 'She went off and agonized like mad over a few sheets of paper but eventually, in long hand, wrote something that Mike and I thought was just right.'

Her first menu for the *Mirror* magazine was a three-course meal of kipper pâté, followed by beef in beer and cheesecake. The kipper pâté was a simple, no-nonsense recipe using frozen kipper fillets, and the beef in beer was made with good old-fashioned beef dripping. The menu showed a remarkable empathy for *Mirror* readers' tastes and budgets, which impressed her boss. She had taken her inspiration from what restaurants were serving at that time and carbonnade de boeuf à la flamande, as beef in beer was rather grandly called on bistro menus, remains one of her staple recipes.

She has served it up to her readers many times: it features in her *Complete Cookery Course*, in *Delia Smith's Christmas* – albeit with Guinness instead of beer – and, more recently, in the *Winter Collection*. In her latest version she cleverly updated it for the 1990s by calling it 'beef in designer beer', thereby successfully appealing to today's generation of image-conscious young cooks.

Perhaps in a bid to pre-empt any criticism that she was recycling old recipes, she defended her decision to include the

Flemish dish. 'Like other once hackneyed sixties recipes, I think it's been neglected and there's a whole new generation now who probably haven't yet tasted it,' she wrote. 'For them, here is the nineties version, the only difference being that we now have a vast range of beers with smart labels to choose from. Not sure which one to use? Do what I do and go for the prettiest label!'

When she handed in her first columns for the *Daily Mirror*, Delia's precise style was evident right from the start. Mike Molloy was impressed by the way she nursemaided her readers, telling them not to panic: 'Just trust me.' This particular style of guiding her readers every step of the way would later become her trademark. During her time on the magazine she suffered only one catastrophe, when she gave a recipe for a Christmas cake with nuts and raisins but forgot to say when to mix them in. It was a valuable lesson, and one that she has kept in the forefront of her mind ever since. 'It taught her you can't be too careful,' says Molloy. 'From then on she made sure to tell readers exactly what to do at every stage.'

Delia would have further call to be grateful to Mike Molloy. For, as well as giving Delia her first job as a cookery writer, he unwittingly played cupid when, realizing that her writing could benefit from a little fine tuning, he introduced her to Michael Wynn Jones, his deputy, and told her, 'This is the chap who'll be handling your copy.' Like Molloy, Wynn Jones was favourably impressed by the pretty mini-skirted brunette who shyly shook his hand, little realizing that she was in fact being introduced to her future husband. Delia reported directly to Michael, who tried to knock her copy into shape while still retaining its 'no-nonsense' quality. They became friends and soon friendship turned to love.

In many ways it was an attraction of opposites. Michael Wynn Jones was an extremely bright, Oxford graduate and a talented journalist; Delia was still shy and lacking in confidence and embarrassed about her obvious lack of academic qualifications. Like Louis Alexander, Wynn Jones was a man of the world and was possessed of the confidence and self-assurance that Delia so lacked. But, unlike Louis, he had his feet firmly on the ground. He had the healthy cynicism that is characteristic of many newspapermen and, despite being the son of an Anglican vicar, was an agnostic.

This last difference between him and Delia posed a potential problem. As a committed Catholic, it must have been hard for Delia to contemplate falling in love with someone who not only wasn't a Catholic, but also didn't even believe in God. Michael Wynn Jones's lack of religious belief could have served to put Delia off him, and the fact that it didn't probably owes a lot to Louis Alexander's treatment of her. No doubt having been jilted by her first love, not for another woman but for God, a relationship with a non-believer must have seemed an attractive proposition to Delia. Here at last was a man who would put her first and love her above all else.

And, in any case, Michael Wynn Jones was quite a catch. At twenty-eight, he was three months younger than Delia, young, single, talented and considered by everyone who knew him to be extremely good company. 'Wynn Jones was a rather dapper sort of fellow, a sophisticated sort of chap,' recalls journalist John Knight, who worked with him on the *Mirror*. 'He was part of the good life; the £300 lunches in Fleet Street when the going was good. Lots of champagne in El Vino, the favourite Fleet Street watering hole, and then on to a really swanky restaurant in Soho.'

He was also good at his job. 'The *Mirror* magazine was a really good magazine,' explains Knight, the paper's former diary editor. 'He's a lay-out man really; he was an extremely able design journalist.' And, crucially for Delia, he could type whereas she couldn't. As well as fulfilling all her romantic requirements for a partner, Michael would also prove to be an enormous asset in her career. Together with Debbie Owen, Michael would be instrumental in shaping Delia's rise to fame and has watched over and guided her career for more than thirty years.

'She could not have done it without Michael,' one friend was reported as saying. 'He has tasted every meal she has ever prepared, checked every word she has ever written, even typed all her stuff out for her because she can't use a typewriter. They are very different. Michael is a typical English middle-class lad. He went to public school and read Greats at Oxford. Delia is a non-smoker. Michael chain-smokes. He has a mandarin mind. She is intuitive and enthusiastic, full of ideas and inventive. She is deeply religious. As far as I know he is an agnostic.'

Photographer Norman Hollands, who has known the couple since they were first together, agrees that they are like chalk and cheese. 'They are very different really, although they are very close. Michael doesn't believe in God; I think he is too educated actually! He is the type of person who does the *Times* crossword before breakfast. He's smashing. When I first met him he was the archetypal academic: shaggy – he had quite long hair in those days – and interested in everything. He has this ability to impart information and he knows so much about so many things. Delia, on the other hand, has always said she is undereducated but I don't think she misses it; it certainly hasn't done her any harm.'

Food writer Tom Jaine was at Oxford with Michael and remembers him as being 'a tremendous high-flyer at the time, and now a very cute cookie indeed'. He says: 'After we came down he roomed with Terry Jones, the guy from *Monty Python*; a friend of mine called Nigel Walmsley who is now Carlton Television's Director for Broadcasting; and the opera singer

John Godber. My first wife lived in Lambeth and they took the house over from her. That's when I ran into him again; it would have been about 1964/65. I remember him being very personable, as he still remains, and I was quite impressed because he and Nigel Walmsley owned their own magazine.

'It was a little magazine called the *20th Century* which was an intellectual review that they bought for a pittance. They produced it periodically in the 1960s and Michael was the publisher and editor of that. It was a very clever idea. Michael was obviously full of energy and it was very professionally done.'

When he began to realize that his relationship with Delia might be the Real Thing, Michael took her home to Norfolk to meet his mother Dilys and clergyman father Edward. During the visit they went to see a Norwich City football match and Delia was hooked. She hastily abandoned Leeds United, the team she had supported up until then, in favour of the Canaries. It was the start of a life-long love affair with the club that would later turn from a hobby into a high-profile business interest. Michael also took her to her first international match at Wembley, where England was at home against Ireland and they watched George Best and Bobby Moore.

Within a few months, Delia had moved in with Michael at his flat in London's Primrose Hill. She was 'living in sin' which despite the Swinging Sixties, was still frowned upon, certainly by her parents' generation. It also went against everything that Catholicism stood for and, bearing in mind her commitment to her faith, was a daring step for her to have made. One explanation may be that during this time in her life religion was not as important to her as it had been when she first converted to Catholicism. She has admitted to having had 'early wobbles' in her faith and her experiences with losing her fiancé to God can't have exactly endeared religion to her.

She and Michael set up home together at 8 Elsworthy Court, where a newlywed couple called John and Norma Major were close neighbours. As well as her recipe column on the *Mirror* magazine, Delia was still doing the odd shift at The Singing Chef, as well as working as a food stylist on photographic shoots. Now she was on the staff of a national newspaper she was also able to push some work in Max Logan's direction. 'I did a lot of pictures of her when she wrote in the *Mirror* colour supplement,' he says.

'Sometimes we would do PR shoots but most of the stuff was for the *Mirror* magazine. We also did an Aga cookbook and in fact I've still got the peppermill that she used for it. It's a socking great big thing that was in my studio for ages. Now I've got it at home on my Aga. It's always a good topic of conversation when people come to dinner to tell them they are using Delia Smith's peppermill.'

The job at the magazine was short-lived and in 1971 Michael and Delia were made redundant. John Knight recalls how the magazine, launched amid a fanfare of publicity, came to a disastrous and embarrassing end. 'We used to get early copies of the magazine as it came off the press, three or four days before it was put in the paper, and when they delivered my early copy to me I couldn't believe my eyes,' he says. 'The main feature was all about contraception and there were very explicit drawings of people's genitalia showing how to put these things on. It was something that really shouldn't have been going into a family newspaper, bearing in mind it was only the early 1970s. It wasn't pornographic, it was quite clinical, but it was medically explicit and it was completely wrong.'

John Knight wasn't the only person to be shocked by the article. 'When the editor of the paper saw it there was a huge kerfuffle and it went all the way up to Cecil King, the chairman of Mirror Group, who had to make the decision,' he says. 'He closed the magazine down and trashed all 5 million copies of it. It never appeared again. Things have changed a lot in the past thirty years but even today I would be very wary about putting that in an all-purpose newspaper. It was very poor judgement. The people who buy Delia Smith's books would have been very shocked if that magazine had ever gone on to the kitchen table. But then again Delia and Michael got good redundancy money so explicit diagrams of prophylactics pays off, doesn't it!'

In fact the couple got a sufficient pay-off to be able to buy themselves a house. Delia had always dreamed of living in the country and Michael was happy to live wherever she wanted to live. They spent £4000 of their redundancy money on an eighteenth century cottage in Combs, a village near Stowmarket in Suffolk. It was small but to Delia, none the less idyllic – painted pink and with a chocolate-box style thatched roof. They named the house 'Little London Cottage' and it was everything that Delia had always dreamed living in the country would be. The cottage had welcoming open fires and was surrounded by wheatfields. They still had Michael's flat in London in which they stayed during the week, but their weekends in the country were the times Delia treasured the most.

Later that year, on 11 September 1971, they were married in a low-key wedding at the Catholic Church of Our Lady in Stowmarket. There were only a handful of guests – most of them close family. 'We wanted it that way,' says Michael. 'There were only thirteen guests because we both come from small families.' Delia had turned thirty-three months before, while Michael was just six days away from his thirtieth birthday. Under 'profession' on her marriage certificate, Delia, interestingly, did not write 'cook' but described herself as a journalist like her husband. Their best man was fellow journalist Dennis Hackett who, along with Michael's father, also acted as a witness.

Early on in their married life, the couple continued to spend weekdays at the London flat as they both pursued their separate careers, dashing back to Suffolk on a Friday night for their precious weekends in the country. Despite their very obvious differences, they made a solid couple who complemented each other very well. Friends describe how, after almost thirty years of marriage, they instinctively seem to know what the other is thinking and are able to make important decisions by simply glancing at the other's face.

Their friend, the cook Prue Leith, tells how she once met up with Michael and Delia to ask for their help in setting up a National Centre for the Culinary Arts, and witnessed their natural telepathy at first hand. She says: 'The centre will represent the whole spectrum of British cooking and is an enormous, £25 million project. At the beginning I needed £80,000 to do a feasibility study, to make sure the public would come to it and that we weren't barking up the wrong tree. I took Mike and Delia to lunch one day and explained it all to them.

'Delia said, "I think it's absolutely wonderful, it's so important and we really need to be proud of what we do, you're absolutely on the right lines. What can I do for you?" So I looked at Mike and I said, "Well, Mike, needless to say, what I'd like is money because we need to get the feasibility study done." Delia and Mike just looked across the table at each other and then Mike said, "How would £25,000 do?"

'Most people would have wanted a proposal and to know how much they were going to get out of it, but worst of all, making sure they got the right publicity or something. But there was not a bit of it with Delia and Michael.' Prue could be forgiven for feeling pleasantly surprised at the readiness with which Michael and Delia made their decision, for, at the very least, most couples would want to discuss it between themselves before deciding to hand over such a large amount of money. But, according to her, one look at the other's face seemed to be all that was needed for Delia and Michael to make a unanimous decision.

Delia describes how the two, while unalike in many ways, have proved to be a successful partnership. 'My husband is very patient,' she explains. 'We are total opposites but we balance each other. He is laidback, thoughtful and considered, whereas I want everything yesterday. He needs a shove sometimes and I need reining in.'

Their friend Ken Toye, Delia's old boss at The Singing Chef, is a big fan of Michael's. 'He is a very gentle man,' he says. 'Gentle and kind. I've never seen any other side to him. I only argue with him because he smokes a lot. Sometimes opposites are suited but he and Delia have the same gentleness and patience.'

While working with Max Logan at his studio, Delia met a photographer who was just starting out in the business. Norman Hollands was working as a photographic assistant to Max and he and Delia became good friends. In time they would work together on many of Delia's lucrative projects, but, says Norman, the friendship came first. 'We met through Max when Delia was just starting to get into food,' he explains. 'Max did some experimental stuff for her and pointed her in the right direction. She was in her twenties when I met her, just beginning her career. She looked much like she does now, but younger. She's not changed an awful lot.'

Norman introduced Delia to his then girlfriend, a young home economist called Caroline Liddell. She too would later work with Delia, becoming her right-hand woman and helping to devise many of the recipes, but back in the late 1960s their relationship was purely social. The two couples saw a lot of each other and Norman remembers he and Caroline being invited to dinner at Delia's and Michael's flat and being amazed to find that the famous chef Ken Lo was cooking dinner.

He recalls: 'Delia and Michael said, "Come round because Ken Lo is cooking dinner." It was quite something because Ken Lo was very well known – I suppose he was the Ken Hom of his day – and to think that he was going to be preparing dinner for us was really exciting. The Primrose Hill flat wasn't very big. It had a living room/dining room and two bedrooms and a hall-way, and quite a small kitchen. But Ken came round and cooked and then sat down and ate with us.'

Delia and Michael were regular customers at Ken Lo's Chelsea restaurant, Memories of China, and Delia was particu-larly fond of the Singapore noodles they served there. Searching in vain for a recipe for the dish, she rang Ken himself and asked him how to make it. Not only was he happy to give her the recipe, which she later included in her cookery book *One is Fun*, he offered to come round and show her how to make it.

As well-paid writers on the *Daily Mirror*, Delia and Michael could afford to eat out when they felt like it and of course, in Delia's case, it was all in the line of duty anyway. She was always keen to try out new produce and sought out interesting delicatessens which in the late 1960s were still hard to find, even in London. One of her favourite shops was an Italian deli in Soho and Delia became friendly with the Camisa family who ran it. Alberto Camisa recalls how he first met her, almost thirty years ago. 'We used to have a delicatessen in Berwick Street, and Delia and Michael would come to shop there.

'In those days foreign delicatessens were still few and far between and she used to come in and see what new things we had in stock. Sliced charcuterie and pastas, and general Italian foodstuffs; she and Michael used to buy a load of stuff. Being an old-fashioned delicatessen we used to have a nice long chat and Delia would swap recipes with my mother. Delia and I are both interested in food and our friendship started from there.

'Nowadays I phone her up to tell her when I've found something new and ask her to give it a go and tell me what she thinks, and she calls me to ask if I've got any ideas, or if I know where she can source a particular product. Delia is not at all full of herself; she's almost shy really. Both Michael and Delia are really nice people, down to earth with no airs or graces, just straightforward. If Delia wants to say something to you she just says it straight, and if I have to say anything to her I say it straight.'

Alberto says that going to dinner at Delia's house is a surprisingly down-to-earth affair, but she says she still occasionally gets nervous when cooking for other people. This is surprising given who she is, but Delia says that is exactly why she gets worried. 'There is sometimes an additional stress because of who I am,' she admits. 'Obviously with close friends and family it really doesn't matter but with new folk I can be a bit nervous because of their expectations. When a woman who organizes very sophisticated parties came to dinner I gave her bangers and mash!'

But Alberto doesn't think she has much to worry about on the food front. 'Some people are born with a gift and she's one of them,' he says. 'Give her four items and she'll come up with a nice meal. But she doesn't stand on ceremony. We've been to restaurants where they've obviously made an effort for Delia, but she disarms them straight away because she's not full of herself. She puts everybody at their ease so it's just a nice evening. If she came round to eat at my place I'd probably just do a very simple pasta dish and she'd be quite happy about it. She wouldn't be expecting something fantastic just because she's Delia Smith. She doesn't expect a work of art; she just expects to be fed like anybody else.'

After the *Mirror* magazine folded, Debbie Owen got Delia a job writing a cookery column for the London daily paper the

Evening Standard. It was an association that would last for more than twelve years, during which time her fame would grow enormously. Landing the position at the *Standard* was also a springboard to greater things. It raised her profile and brought her to the attention of the right people. Although the paper's sales were confined to the capital, London was where the majority of media and television people lived and worked. Delia's daily column in the paper brought her into contact with influential people from the world of publishing and TV and it was only a matter of time before her career really took off.

Her first book and a television show of her own were just around the corner. Delia had begun her life-long work of teaching the British public how to cook.

6

Fame

Delia's very first book, *How to Cheat at Cooking*, was published by Ebury Press in 1971. It was a collection of 400 recipes and general culinary advice, and aimed to show people how to convince their friends that they were far better cooks than they actually were. Unable to type, Delia painstakingly wrote it all out in longhand before handing it to Michael, who devotedly typed it up for her, correcting her mistakes as he went.

'Have you always wanted to be a good cook but never had the time?' the book jacket asked. 'Do modern convenience foods set you free from the kitchen or do you find them dull and taste-less? Delia believes that you can easily have the best of both worlds. She shows you how to escape long hours of kitchen drudgery by a little clever cheating. Basing her recipes on quick convenience foods – canned, frozen, dehydrated and pre-cooked – she shows you how to add your own special touches to delight family and friends. Mealtimes come round all too often. If you have better things to do than slave over a hot stove, this is the book for you.'

The premise seemed solid enough: Delia, herself a busy working wife, had realized that as more women were pursuing careers they had less time to spend in the kitchen. Dinner parties were gaining in popularity, especially among the middle classes, and people were keen to impress their friends by serving up elaborate meals. But they soon discovered that laying on a lavish feast took considerable time and effort – time that they either hadn't got or couldn't be bothered to spend cooking. Delia would cleverly tap into this by assuring her readers that they could have it all. Aiming specifically at people who naturally viewed anything to do with cooking as being a bit of a chore, she bluntly told serious cooks that her book wasn't for them.

The reality, though, was far from convincing. Viewed today, *How to Cheat at Cooking* is notable mainly for its cringe factor. Even in 1971 Britain, the book seemed like a collection of ill-conceived and often dreadful-sounding recipes devised by someone trying just a bit too hard to sound sophisticated. Would the socially conscious, middle-class housewife seriously consider this particular dish for the delectation of her high-rolling dinner-party guests: baked fish fingers topped with a tin of tomatoes and tinned mushrooms? Other supposed culinary treats included a shop-bought sponge flan topped with a can of cherry-pie filling.

Delia set out her stall immediately. 'If you are one of those dedicated cooks who is a keen early-morning mushroom-gatherer and wouldn't dream of concocting a salad without using the just-picked variety then this book is not for you,' she wrote. 'The following pages are for those who like to eat and entertain, who want to cook but simply don't have the will or the time to spend hours shopping, preparing or cooking. The recipes are aimed at helping you to use fresh and convenience food to prepare meals reasonably quickly, and at the same time convince everyone that they are strictly home-made.'

Quite how it was not possible to give the game away when

serving up deep-frozen four-inch-by-one-inch blocks of reconstituted cod in a industrial yellow crumb is not fully explained. But, warming to her theme, Delia warned that, before they could start, her readers would first have to learn the rules of the game. She went on to list her 'Cheat's Charter'. Rule number one was that there are more important things in life than cooking. Cheats were people who enjoyed eating but liked to spend the best part of their lives in places other than the kitchen. They were not defeatists who hate to cook, she insisted, perhaps in a bid to avoid making her readers feel guilty.

Cheats were willing to have a go because they had to but they liked to make a good job of it without lots of unnecessary bother. 'Cheats have given up reading cookery books – instructions to "continue in the usual way" send them reaching for the tin opener,' she wrote. 'For all they know, brown roux is a species of butterfly and demi-glace a half-portion of ice-cream.'

Her next rule concerned time, and how to spend as little of it as possible in the kitchen. 'If it only took twenty minutes to make, so what?' The flood of cookery manuals, part works and television virtuosi seems to have convinced us all that we need to be frightfully painstaking cooks,' she complained. However, she warned, cooking for the sake of speed alone, regardless of the end product, was not part of the cheats' code of ethics.

Rule three could have been written only by an *arriviste*, Primrose Hill housewife. Displaying a singular lack of understanding of her constituency, Delia advised her readers of the delights of Fortnums, Selfridges, Justin de Blanc Provisions of W1 and The House of Floris. Quite what this meant to readers in Wigan who knew Delia from her *Daily Mirror* column is anyone's guess. Her skill for not talking down to her readers, later to become her biggest weapon, was far from honed here. Keen to show that she was no longer the shy, working-class girl from Bexleyheath, Delia displayed all the missionary zeal of the convert in showing off her obvious knowledge of the finer things.

'If you're not a good cook then you've simply got to be an extremely good shopper,' she said bossily. 'Experienced cheats know where the best bakers are; they always serve delicious crusty bread and fresh creamy butter. They know where to get cakes that pass for home-made. They have delicious tempting fruit bowls; they get to know about unusual cheeses. They know where to buy good coffee and which tea bags are best. All these things don't cost a minute's extra cooking time. Ice-cream should always be available (a couple of Bertorelli's specialities stored away and you need never be short of a dessert).'

Apparently oblivious to the fact that most people would have had no idea what Bertorelli's was, she added, 'If you live a long way from town, or the shops aren't particularly enterprising in your area, remember that several London food stores do a mail-order service for any item that will keep in the post.' She then went on to list the most expensive shops in the land.

Seemingly unaware of her own pretension, she advised: 'Fill your kitchen with serious-looking accoutrements and have lots of intriguing jars for your herbs and spices. They'll look very phoney if they're chockfull by the way, so never quite fill them up. Bunches of dried herbs hanging around create a good impression. Of course you must have plenty of top-drawer cookbooks placed in full view (needless to say keep this one well hidden).'

She then got down to the nitty-gritty of socializing. 'Going mad with presentation can be utterly vulgar,' she admonished. 'Boats and nests and baskets of any description are right out. So are tomato water lilies, radish roses or any other horticultural effect. Nothing flatters food more than a tasteful table, which means taking trouble with details like glasses (classical-shaped rather than off-licence tumblers) and colour schemes.'

Her advice about what to serve for pre-dinner drinks revealed Delia at her most gauche and affected. 'Vermouth is a pretty safe bet,' she said. 'I'd be surprised if at least one guest didn't ask what is it so choose an example that will give you the chance to drop the name of your wine merchant (don't say off-licence). Chambery, for instance, is very popular with gourmets.'

The concept for her first book had sounded encouraging enough: great results with minimal effort. But in reality it is hard to believe that, even in the culinary desert that was post-1960s Britain, anybody would have been fooled by Delia's 'tricks', the majority of which appeared to rely on lashings of cream and chopped parsley to disguise packet food. And the best china in the world could never make the tasteless ready-made soups of the early 1970s taste home-made.

But Delia was gung-ho. 'Never underestimate the touch of authenticity that an appropriate serving dish can give,' she wrote. 'Canned and packet soups will almost certainly taste better if you ladle them out of an attractive soup tureen.' Home-made flavours could be imitated by adding copious amounts of wine, sherry, brandy cream or soured cream to mass produced soups, she advised, while most tinned foods could be jazzed up by garnishing with parsley, mint, chives, croûtons or cream.

The book would have dismayed fans of Elizabeth David and Robert Carrier and if Delia's own fans were to read it today they would no doubt be aghast to see Delia Smith cheerfully advo-cating the use of packet sauce mixes and instant mashed potato. It is perhaps just as well that the book is now safely out of print. It was also strangely at odds with itself: one minute talking about Fortnum and Mason and tradesmen delivering shopping to your door and the next minute coming up with recipes for fish fingers or instant mash.

Whatever its merits as a cookery book, Delia was overjoyed

at having her first book published. Her dream of being a writer, that she had written about so prophetically when she was eleven years old, had finally come true. Seeing her name on the front cover of a book was a much bigger thrill than seeing it every day in the *Standard*. Somehow a book was more permanent, more solid, and Delia hoped that hers would be read time and again, becoming well used and well thumbed.

After the excitement of seeing her first book in print, fame of a different kind presented itself to Delia when she was recommended for a job in television. She had no idea if she would be able to do it, but decided to give it a go. 'I had no idea how to go about it, or whether I could even do it at all,' she admits. 'There aren't any schools to teach you that sort of thing, so I simply had to decide if I *wanted* to do it and then learn as I went along.'

Signing Delia up for her own series, *Family Fare*, was virtually the last thing that Paul Fox did as Controller of BBC1. In his final day in the job, a time when the majority of people would be more occupied thinking about the future than the past, he none the less found time to OK Delia's appointment. It was something that took him only a few minutes but his actions set Delia on the road to TV stardom.

Sir Paul, who was knighted in 1991, explains: 'I had gone in to see Huw Wheldon, the Managing Director of BBC Television, to say that I was leaving to go to Yorkshire Television. As was the custom with the BBC in those days I was told, "Off you go then, clear your desk and never darken our door again." I went back into my office and cleared my in-tray and saw a note from Betty White, who was a producer in the Presentation Department. It was a proposal for a cookery series with Delia Smith.

'It truly was my last half-hour there and I wrote, "Yes, agreed", and put it in the out-tray. That's how it happened. Delia has always been kind enough to acknowledge that and whenever she has a party to celebrate selling yet another five million books she is kind enough to invite me. She says, "Paul was the chap who made it possible." I like her very much indeed – I think she's a terrific woman.'

Sir Paul made the decision, not because he thought Delia was the best person for the job, but because he trusted his producer Betty White's opinion. 'I knew of Delia in the *Evening Standard* but I had no idea what she looked like or whether she'd be able to do it or not,' he admits. 'But I'd known Betty for a long time and I relied on her judgement. And, after all, it was only twenty minutes in the afternoon; it was not a time when cookery programmes went out at peak time.'

Delia made her television début at a time when TV cooks were few and far between. In contrast to the plethora of recipe programmes and celebrity chefs that dominate our television screens today, in the early 1970s there were still very few people preparing meals for the entertainment of people watching at home.

The first ever television cook was Phillip Harben who appeared on the BBC in the early 1950s. His 'studio' was a world away from the sophisticated sets of today's TV shows. He cooked on the same basic, cream-enamelled four-ringed stove that his viewers had at home, and used the same kind of ordinary Prestige saucepans that they used.

His show was first aired in 1952, two years after Elizabeth David published her first book, and a time when many basic ingredients were still rationed. There weren't enough supplies for any of the 'here's-one-I-made-earlier' demonstrations that so typify the high-tech programmes of the 1990s. Harben, working without today's advantage of plentiful ingredients, was able to make each dish only once and brought in his own family's butter and meat to do so. He was preaching to a generation that had all but lost the ability to cook proper English food. As Delia remarked, the post-war generation simply forgot how to prepare traditional English meals and relied on turgid Ministry of Food recipes rather than old family cookery books.

In many ways Phillip Harben was the Delia Smith of his day. Like Delia, he preached common sense and his style was exact: take a pound of this, add half a pound of that and cook for twenty minutes. And like Delia he was cooking primarily for the family. Viewers were urged to do everything just they way he did – much like Delia does today – and flexibility extended no further than allowing you to leave out the clove of garlic if you weren't sure that you'd like it.

'I think Phillip Harben is the one person Delia could be compared with,' says food writer Egon Ronay. 'He was a very widely known popular writer and television performer in the 1950s. He was so famous in his day but he wasn't a very appealing personality.' Harben, reveals Ronay, has interesting parallels with Delia. Flying in the face of his bosses at the BBC, who strictly forbade their stars from doing paid advertising, Harben agreed to sponsor a frying pan. Delia very publicly sang the praises of an omelette pan in her *How to Cook* series.

Delia called the ordinary-looking £7 aluminium pan 'a little gem' on her BBC2 show and instantly sent sales soaring from 200 a year to an incredible 90,000. But, unlike Delia, Harben made the mistake of getting involved in the business side of the frying-pan promotion. It was to prove to be his downfall.

'There were big advertisements with Harben's name on and everyone was appalled,' recalls Egon Ronay. 'Those were different times; now people sponsor things all the time; but in those days it was absolutely taboo for people like him to be involved in advertising. It was frowned upon and it was well known that it was the cause of his fall from grace. He lost his purity and I think that's why he didn't pursue his television programmes any more.'

But despite certain similarities, there were areas of Harben's presentation that were nothing whatsoever like Delia's. He introduced a certain element of theatre into his shows out of necessity: in a bid to prevent his audience from falling asleep. Without the benefit of being able to produce four or five of the same dishes, each at a different stage of completion, it was impossible to cook a full meal within the thirty-minute slot. Essential-but-boring acts of whisking and sifting and watching things boil were simply not enough to keep the attention of the viewer watching at home.

He would bound around the kitchen, teacher turned entertainer, talking to the saucepans and making little asides to the camera. He turned the mundane craft of roasting a joint into show business. It is nigh on impossible to imagine Delia cavorting around the studio like him or, still less, to picture her carrying on the way Fanny Craddock did on screen.

If Phillip Harben was the first television cook, Fanny Craddock was the first celebrity cook. Dressed outrageously in a full-length evening dress and wearing thick make-up, she first glided on to the nation's television screens in 1954. She was surely the most eccentric television cook we have ever seen, even compared to the extrovert antics of chefs such as Keith Floyd and, more recently, Ainsley Harriott.

Craddock was the undisputed *grande dame* of the kitchen, and it didn't matter if her recipes were thought to be lacking by some. The important thing was she entertained people. 'Fanny Craddock was really an act because she was not a good cook,' says Egon Ronay. While Phillip Harben had been cooking for the family table, Fanny Craddock appeared to be catering for small ambassadorial dinners. Assuming, like many television cooks, that people had far more time and were prepared to put in far more effort than was really the case, she offered up pretentious and time-consuming recipes to the ordinary British housewife.

She even boasted that her mother, who by all accounts had been just as eccentric as her daughter, had once cooked a dinner party consisting entirely of pink food: pink mousse on pink glass plates chilled in pink ice into which pink moss rosebuds had been frozen.

People took Fanny Craddock to their hearts and for many years she reigned as the nation's favourite cook. She and her downtrodden 'husband' Johnnie, who it later transpired was not her husband at all – she married him only in 1977 – became the most famous double act of their day. Viewers watched transfixed as a bizarrely made-up Fanny ordered her amiable partner around, mercilessly chastising him if he failed to follow her barrage of instructions. It was pure theatre and for two decades the Craddocks dominated the television cookery scene.

As well as being an infinitely more colourful character than Phillip Harben, Fanny Craddock also added an extra ingredient to her cooking. She awoke a gentle snobbery in her viewers. People were starting to give dinner parties and looked almost reverentially to Fanny to see how they should be doing things. During the 1960s people began to be more aware of food trends and realized that what they cooked – and how they served it – said things about them. The socially conscious wanted to get it right and turned to the confidence-inspiring Fanny to find out how they should go about it.

To her viewers she epitomized glamour and sophistication, an image she encouraged with remarks such as, 'Johnnie lines his coats with sable and I line mine with mink. We drink champagne before we go on stage and we drive a Rolls-Royce.'

But the reality was far less glamorous. Her fans would have been amazed to know that the cupboards in her own kitchen were packed, not with delicious and elegant ingredients, but with endless packets of cornflakes and cases of sardines. She claimed her 'houseboy' ate the cornflakes and that she ate the

sardines herself in her speciality dish the 'dog's dinner' –
mashed sardines and boiled egg, squashed on to brown bread.
During rationing she and Johnnie caught sparrows in the
garden and cooked them and often ate hedgehogs.

She went to great lengths in the service of television, even
undergoing plastic surgery on her nose when technicians told
her it was too big and cast shadows over the food. She was still
regularly appearing on television when Delia began her TV
career and for a few years they presented cookery shows that
could not have been further apart.

Her reign lasted until the late 1970s, when a reliance on drink
and drugs finally took its toll on the star. Her behaviour, always
erratic, became increasingly bizarre. She had always revelled in
being rude to people but in 1976, on the BBC programme *The
Big Time*, she went too far. Ferociously lambasting a Devon
housewife, Fanny shocked BBC executives into sacking her.
Realizing they had to act, they took the decision not to renew
her contract.

Later, in the 1970s when Delia was starting out, Graham Kerr,
better known as 'The Galloping Gourmet', dominated television
cookery. While Fanny Craddock had specified ingredients in the
finest detail, Kerr just bunged it all in. Every dish, it seemed,
was cooked in wine, and wine was measured in vague sloshes
– one for the pot and one for the cook. Every episode ended
with him sitting down to eat what he had just prepared, almost
always in the company of an attractive woman from the audience with whom he then proceeded to flirt shamelessly. Food,
he implied, was all about sex.

And then there was Delia: quiet, unassuming Delia. She first
appeared on our television screens on 12 September 1973,
dispensing easy-to-follow recipes in short, ten-minute bites.
Her début, working for the world-famous BBC, was far from
glamorous and her viewers would have been horrified if they

had seen the conditions she was expected to work in. The 'kitchen' was in an old weather studio at the BBC Television Centre and Delia couldn't believe her eyes when she saw it. 'The first series was filmed in a totally ill-equipped studio with no cooking facilities,' explains her friend Norman Hollands, who went along to offer some moral support. 'There were no washing-up facilities either, just a sink with a bucket underneath. It really was bad.'

Delia Smith, reported the *Daily Telegraph* the day after her first appearance, made 'an agreeable impression'. She was, the review continued, 'a friendly, unaffected young housewife, at ease in the kitchen'. Her first programme lasted twenty-five minutes and thirty seconds precisely, and was recorded straight through without editing or break. If she had not quite finished making her liver paprika in that time it was just hard luck.

Delia must have drawn on some hitherto undiscovered acting skills to make the *Telegraph* reviewer think she was at her ease. For, in reality, Delia felt anything but. Anxious and quaking with nerves, she found the first few programmes nothing short of an ordeal. 'She was very nervous, and I'm not even sure that that's changed a great deal now,' says Norman. 'She has a lot more self-confidence these days but I think she still finds it quite difficult at times.'

In fact Delia found it so stressful that for a while her new job made her quite ill. 'Working on television was rather nerve-racking at first,' she admits. 'I came out in huge red bumps all over my legs, which was due to stress, and I used to get eczema patches on my scalp. It got quite bad. My hair became thin and stopped growing. I had to rub cortisone cream into my scalp.' The fact that the signs of her stress were showing on her face made her extra nervous as she worried about television viewers being able to spot the blotches. It was a vicious circle.

Understandably for someone whose career involves being

filmed at close range, Delia has always been acutely aware of her appearance. Her hair is always meticulously neat and tidy and her make-up is carefully done: not too little but not too much. She even had lessons from top make-up artist Barbara Daly, who did Princess Diana's make-up on her wedding day and is now a friend of Delia's. Delia likes cosmetics and prefers the made-up look, but Barbara showed her how to make the finished look appear more subtle.

'I do like made-up faces and I use a lot of make-up,' Delia says. 'I never knew where to go next with make-up and got really confused so to have Barbara telling me what to use and how to apply it properly was the best thing that ever happened to me. The products I use are the ones she suggested.'

Delia's mother had brought her up to be smartly turned out and to be aware at all times that people are judged by their appearance. Knowing that she was well dressed made Delia feel better about what she perceived as her shortcomings. 'I've learned over the years that if you do care for yourself then it contributes to a whole sense of well-being,' she explains. 'Like people taking a bit of extra care with their clothes, it makes them feel better.' Now that millions of people were scrutinizing her in close-up on their TV screens, Delia became more self-conscious than ever.

Finding herself on national television was a strange experience for Delia. She was proud and excited about having achieved her 'big break', but she also found that watching herself on TV – always a strange experience for people – magnified her lack of self-confidence. While viewers saw a pretty, glossy-haired, rather shy young woman, Delia saw someone with crooked teeth and too many freckles.

'Oh God, it's horrible,' she once said. 'Seeing yourself on television is just awful. You think, "God, why didn't I lose weight?" It never gets any better. I don't like the way I look and I absolutely hate having my photograph taken. I never smile because my teeth aren't straight and I'm very conscious of them. Generally I have a very poor self-image.'

Seen as wholesome and nice right from the outset, someone for the middle-class housewife to aspire to, the BBC did none the less try to change the way she looked, particularly the way she dressed. Delia always favoured plain, no-nonsense clothes but the wardrobe mistresses, perhaps with Fanny Craddock in mind, endeavoured to persuade her to jazz herself up a bit. 'In the beginning they did try to change my image a bit,' she admits. 'They used to take me to the Wardrobe Department and show me the kind of clothes you would see people wearing at a Buckingham Palace garden party. They tried to get me into those, but they didn't have much success.'

Her words reveal a surprisingly steely side to Delia. It is clear that even back in those early days, when she was the new girl at the BBC – almost an apprentice really – she wasn't afraid to stick up for herself. While other presenters might have been willing to compromise their own ideas of how they should look rather than risk upsetting those in charge, Delia was always her own woman. An incident involving a pair of dungarees provides a further insight into how carefully Delia watches over her image.

'I remember when it was fashionable to wear dungarees, they took me to a designer who had made some out of quilted material,' she recalls. 'For somebody like me, who has always tried to keep slim, the thought of wearing another inch all over didn't appeal. Fortunately, the gods were on my side the day this designer turned up with the dungarees in the carrier bag. She left the bag in the canteen and couldn't find it before it was time to go on air. I wouldn't have worn them anyway, but it saved me from having a row.'

It is an interesting story, and one that says a lot about Delia's determination to do things her way. The Wardrobe Department had no doubt gone to a lot of trouble in searching out interesting and fashionable clothes for Delia, even taking her to meet the designer. But after all that, Delia was still willing to risk a confrontation with them if necessary, so keen was she to preserve her own identity. If the story had not involved the ever-so-proper Delia, one might be forgiven for wondering just how the carrier bag containing the dungarees came to be lost in the first place.

Her weight has been an obsession throughout her adult life. Ironically for a person who gave us such delicious-sounding treats as sticky toffee puddings with pecan toffee sauce, and chocolate soured-cream cake, Delia is on a permanent diet. While her readers are free to sample her deliciously fattening creations, Delia assiduously denies herself such luxuries.

'I'm normally very careful about watching my weight,' she admits. 'If I'm dreaming, my perfect weight would be about nine stone four, but I'm actually about ten stone two. When I start creeping up to about ten-and-a-half stone I know it's time to do something. I always put on a good seven pounds on holiday because I'll eat breakfast, lunch and dinner. When I'm working I taste everything I cook, but I don't eat anything. I have some cereal in the morning, fresh fruit at lunchtime and then an ordinary meal in the evening, but no dessert.'

Even her cookery books feature negative references to her weight, her remarks strangely at odds with the books' often fattening contents. Bizarrely, she even urges her readers *not* to make some of her recipes. Not content with telling them how to bake the perfect fruitcake she appears to want to tell them how to live their lives. Writing about a recipe for home-made doughnuts in her *Book of Cakes*, she says bossily, 'If you're very thin and have no weight problems, you can make some of these. If, like me, you feel fat just thinking about them, perhaps you'd better not.'

One can't help but wonder how many plump people, itching to try out the doughnuts, hastily abandoned the recipe – and possibly the book – having been reminded in such a school ma'am way about their weight problems. Settling down to read one of Delia's beautifully photographed, mouth-watering recipe books is hardly the time that most people want to think about their weight. But perhaps by admitting her own weaknesses Delia shows an empathy with her mostly female readers for whom dieting is a necessary evil.

'I'm sorry if you have to diet,' she wrote sympathetically in her *Book of Cakes*. 'I do too, most of the time, but every now and then we all need cheering up with something gooey and squidgy and very chocolatey. I'm afraid I have a terrible weakness for anything chocolatey: although I rarely buy boxes or bars, chocolate puddings and cakes are totally irresistible.'

In her Christmas book she gives her readers the go-ahead to indulge themselves. Preaching from the pulpit of abstention, she says, 'If like me you are constantly torn for the rest of the year between a passion for good food and an urgency to try and stay reasonably slim, you really have to regard Christmas as a holiday and a respite from the struggle!'

Delia allows herself to lapse from her strict eating regime only once a week. 'Sunday in our household is the feast day, and on that day I have no compunction at all in indulging in a cake or pudding or bar of chocolate (or all three),' she says. But her friend, television producer Frances Whitaker, expresses doubts that Delia ever truly over-indulges. 'She wants to make sure that she looks as good on television as she can and certainly when she's got television to think about she chooses to be careful,' says Whitaker. 'Treats on Sunday probably amount to a potato.'

It was in the early 1970s, when she had just landed her first television series, that Delia began working with Caroline

Liddell, Norman Hollands' girlfriend. Caroline, an enthusiastic home economist, started out as Delia's assistant, helping her prepare for her TV show and taste and test the recipes. She was to prove to be an important part of Delia's career, helping her to devise many of the recipes that appeared under Delia's sole name in her books.

'Delia and Caroline would develop recipes between them,' Norman explains. 'Caroline would write them up and give them to Delia and then Delia would put them into her own words and produce them. They thought along the same lines as each other and Caroline was a very important part of it all.'

Norman also recalls the unusual way in which Delia and Caroline transported equipment from Delia's flat in Primrose Hill to the BBC's West London Studios. Needing an enormous amount of cooking implements and pans and with no car of her own, Delia came up with a novel way to solve the problem. 'She got a supermarket trolley to put all her gear in because a supermarket trolley would go in the back of a black taxicab,' says Norman. But, typical Delia, instead of 'acquiring one' like some people might rather dishonestly do, Delia made sure hers was above board. 'We actually bought a supermarket trolley from Sainsbury's and she and Caroline used to trundle off to the studio with it,' he says.

Caroline Liddell was involved in several of Delia's early books and throughout the 1970s she and Delia and Norman and Michael were firm friends. 'We spent a lot of time together, more socially than workwise because at that time I wasn't a food photographer,' explains Norman.

'The four of us used to go to France for weekends. We'd stay in hotels and go bumbling around Normandy. Delia can be fun; she's got a good sense of humour. Her image on TV is quite dour but I think much of that is born out of the fact that she's not totally at home with the medium. I think you're always on your guard when you're on telly; she's very different in real life.

'When Caroline was doing a lot of work with Delia she and I used to be quite regular visitors to Delia's and Michael's house in Suffolk. We'd go up for weekends and it would be part work, part social. She and Caroline used to cook for Michael and me, and on other occasions we would go out for meals because Delia was quite in favour of supporting local restaurants.'

But with her new-found friends Delia displayed the same secretiveness that she had shown back home in Bexleyheath. Then she had kept things very much to herself, refusing even to unburden herself to her friends when her parents' marriage was disintegrating. Once she began mixing with a whole new circle of friends in London she was equally reticent about her early life. 'She has never spoken to me about her brother or her father,' says Norman. 'I know very little about her youth.'

Right from the outset of her career Delia cleverly played down her prowess in the kitchen. 'One thing I discovered about myself is that I'm not a great cook, not like Elizabeth David or Jane Grigson or Robert Carrier,' she insisted. 'What I can cook, anybody can cook.' It is an admission that has served her well. Her words make her readers feel confident enough to get cooking, while at the same time deflecting criticism from other chefs that she isn't a great cook.

Throughout the 1970s Delia was working extremely hard establishing her reputation as Britain's favourite cook. As well as having her own television series, she also had her daily recipe column in the *Evening Standard*. The first one appeared in March 1972 and by the time she left the paper twelve years later she had chalked up more than three thousand recipes. Hardly surprisingly, she frequently found it hard to think up enough new recipes to satisfy demand. 'The first six years were the worst,' she says. 'I used to say to Michael, "I have done lamb's liver in fourteen different ways and there is no fifteenth." '

It was a dilemma that other cookery writers would no doubt sympathize with, but for one as prolific as Delia it was especially hard to avoid repetition. Over the years the same recipes have cropped up over and over, albeit with minor changes or 'updates'. Her old standby, beef in beer, has appeared time and again, as have lamb in coriander and bread-and-butter pudding. More recently a recipe for a warm roquefort cheesecake in *The Winter Collection* was almost identical to a savoury feta cheesecake in the *Summer Collection*. Twice-baked roquefort soufflés in *How to Cook* appear strikingly similar to the goat's cheese soufflés in the *Summer Collection*.

'They say there is a certain recycling,' remarks food writer Tom Jaine. 'I think it's inevitable; it's just like pop songs – once you've heard one Elton John record you've heard them all. Once you've read one cookery writer's recipe, to a degree you've touched on the style and so it will be variations on a theme.'

'Delia always said it was jolly hard work getting those recipes into shape,' admits Ken Toye. 'I think it was hard to start with because she wasn't very used to writing.'

But once her first book had been published there was no stopping her. *How to Cheat at Cooking* was followed in November 1973 by *Recipes from Country Inns and Restaurants*. 'It puts her on a par with the greats like Elizabeth David and Robert Carrier,' wrote the *Daily Mirror*. Asked about her recipe for success, Delia said, 'Be different. I think people have got tired of the purists who use only the very best and most expensive of ingredients. My ideas are for the ordinary housewife who likes cooking.'

Other books followed: *Country Fare*, and *Family Fare*, which featured recipes from her television show, and in 1974, *Family Fare, Book Two* and *The Evening Standard Cook Book*, a collection of recipes from her newspaper column. She was moved to write the *Evening Standard* book by readers' SOS calls. 'So many kind readers have written asking for it – some of them with hard-luck stories to touch the coldest heart,' she wrote. 'I recall one lady whose clipping of poor man's stroganoff had become so yoghurt-splattered she couldn't read it any more. And the gentleman who had finally tracked down some juniper berries for his oxtail casserole, but alas he had lost the recipe! To them, to all those tales of woe about tatty, yellowing cut-outs or papers that were thrown out "in error" have moved me deeply, and to all faithful recipe-followers, this book is dedicated.'

Among the 250 recipes were such Delia favourites as kipper pâté, crêpes Suzette, coq au vin, roast duck with cherries and, her perennial favourite, beef in beer. During the 1970s Delia was a prolific writer and had no fewer than fourteen books published. All of them were laboriously written out in long-hand and then typed up either by Michael or Delia's secretary Gwyneth Phillips.

Delia found that her days soon settled into a pleasant routine. Naturally a morning person, she would wake up between half past six and seven – 'I never need an alarm clock because one of my cats jumps on me,' she laughs – and then spend an hour praying while Michael slept on. 'I'm not holy and I don't want to give the impression that I am,' she insists. 'But I find that this is a very wonderful way to start the day; just to be still, to be tranquil if you like. I'm not any good at prayer, but I find that it's very important to me.'

She would then jump in her car and make the twenty-five-minute journey to Mass in Bury St Edmunds. In between the hour spent praying and attending Mass in church, Delia would – somewhat bizarrely – dispense with the peace and quiet that she so valued and play her car radio at full volume. 'My great love is pop music and I record the rundown of the Top Forty on Radio One just to play in the car,' she says. 'My favourites are Phil Collins and Dire Straits. I regularly make up my own tapes for playing on a journey and play them rather loudly. Michael says he can hear the "flying disco" coming as soon as I turn into our road!'

She would be back at her desk by ten where she would stay for the next few hours before going for a half-hour walk in the fields by her home. 'I think violent exercise is unnatural,' she once said. 'I've never been sporty at all. I love walking more than anything, and it's a good reflective time. I love nature and it's very beautiful here.' After a snack lunch with Michael, of soup or bread and cheese, she would work for a few more hours, take another walk, work a bit more and then finally break for the day to make supper.

She enjoyed the often demanding work of trying to come up with new recipes and endeavouring to meet publishing dead-lines. Delia and Caroline Liddell meticulously tested each recipe at least three times until they were 100 per cent sure that they were fault-free. 'Delia spends an enormous amount of time testing her recipes,' says her agent Debbie Owen proudly. 'She knows we need to be guided. I use her books all the time – they are my bibles.'

Work was something that Delia took great pleasure in. 'I think I've got something in me that compels me to work,' she explains. 'I couldn't see myself not working at something. If I wasn't working to earn a living I'm sure I'd be doing something – learning a language or taking an A level.' But working so hard meant that she was often exhausted by the end of the day. 'I tend to go down with the sun. I can get rather grumbly and grumpy at the end of the day,' she admits. 'The later on it gets in the evening the worse I get. I find I really do get very tired and I don't like late nights. In fact I hate them. I seem to need that eight hours. If I don't get it I'll have an hour's nap some time in the afternoon. I have to catch up otherwise I'm just no good.'

Her hard work was paying off and the people who bought

her books realized they could trust Delia's recipes to work. On television her calm, measured behaviour also inspired confidence and she enjoyed a reputation for being well organized and professional.

During the period that *Family Fare* was being transmitted on BBC1, Delia was asked to do a cookery slot on *Look East*, the BBC's regional early-evening magazine programme for East Anglia. In 1975 she started appearing in weekly five-minute clips and was an immediate success with the viewers. As people came in from work and sat down to eat, they got used to watching Delia's regular appearances on the show and, as a result, East Anglians began to look on her almost possessively as 'our Delia'.

'She was enormously popular with the viewers,' explains *Look East*'s former news editor Dick Robinson, the man who hired her. 'The number of people who took the trouble to write in with a stamped addressed envelope for copies of her recipes was enormous.'

Delia's slots were filmed in a small BBC studio at All Saints' Green in Norwich. It was a world away from the sophisticated conditions she enjoys working in today. 'Regional television studios in the early 1970s were fairly basic and it was all a little bit rustic,' recalls cameraman Paul Cort-Wright. 'We had a cooker and a sink that didn't actually have a drain to it, just a bucket underneath. Delia worked at a trestle table with a plywood front around it. It was a very small operation. She didn't have her own assistant – the receptionist used to help her carry the food in from the car. The programmes were actually recorded in Birmingham and were fed down the line from Norwich so you really only had one go at it. That wasn't a problem with Delia because she was very good.'

Director Betty Bealy, who at that time was the floor manager, put a protective arm around Delia. 'I became involved simply because I happened to be the woman on the production team and was seen as someone to ease Delia's path,' she explains. 'I was her assistant; that's what it amounted to. She would come in mid-morning, having worked out what she was going to do according to the time slot. She was a well-organized lady, which was something I always admired about her. She'd do quite complicated things like hot cross buns, which are quite long-winded and not easy. But she got them sorted into a five-minute slot.

'We provided cookery equipment and china but she bought most of her own stuff with her. It would pretty much take all day. She would prepare the food in the morning and then at two we'd do a dummy run to get the timing right. She'd rehearse it so the cameraman could get the shots right and do the close-ups properly, and so on. Then we would just go ahead with it. It wasn't easy and she was nervous to start with – in our case justifiably so, because although we could record the items we had no editing facility so it was like doing a live performance. We didn't have all the electronic wizardry that they have today. But it was good training and I think Delia always felt that once she'd done that she could do anything.'

The crew eagerly looked forward to trying out what she'd made, particularly if it was a cake. 'Cakes were always the most popular,' laughs Betty. The cameramen even took their own forks to work with them. 'We'd have our forks ready in our top pockets and when the recording was cleared we would dig into whatever she'd made that week,' recalls Paul Cort-Wright. 'I used to award her marks out of ten and she'd get a bit sniffy if I didn't score very high. She'd get a little bit prim – how can I put it – her professionalism sometimes shrouded her sense of humour!'

Delia would occasionally cause consternation among the crew by keeping food aside to take home to Michael. 'She would let us eat what she'd made but only if we got the recording on the first time round,' reveals Paul. 'It was something that used to annoy us a little bit. She got an allowance to buy the food and she always used to get two of everything. We were told the second lot was in case somebody made a mistake during the recording and we had to do it again. But when I said on one occasion, "Let's do it again" because the camera shots weren't too good and the vision-mixer had made a couple of mistakes, she said, "Oh, no. I'm taking that home for my husband's tea".'

Delia and Michael always appeared to be a close and happy couple. 'I think she relied upon Michael and was more dependent upon him than it might have seemed,' says Betty Bealy. 'I don't know if he was the power behind the throne – I'm not sure I'd go that far – but it's possible of course. We used to say he could perhaps have done more – he could have been Johnnie to her Fanny – but that wasn't his thing really.'

In the mid-1970s Delia's career could be said to be going very well indeed. But, as is so often the case, just when things are going well everything changes. A new appointment at the BBC spelled trouble for Delia and her television career was about to hit the skids.

7

The Graveyard Shift

In 1976, when she had completed three series of *Family Fare* for BBC1, Delia's television career was dealt a crushing blow. Aubrey Singer became the new controller and decided that she lacked screen presence. Explaining to Debbie Owen that he was thinking of scrapping Delia's show, Singer searched for the right words. 'She's just not sexy enough,' he said finally.

While spared the humiliation of being sacked, Delia was forced to suffer the ignominy of being shunted to a late-night education slot on BBC2 – the television equivalent of Siberia. It was a particularly cruel way to demote someone. To question her ability to do the job or express doubts about the popularity of the show would have been acceptable, but to accuse a self-conscious young woman of not being attractive enough was guaranteed to cause pain. Aubrey Singer's damning verdict of her subsequently became legendary within television and media circles and as a result remains with Delia to this very day.

'Aubrey Singer became Controller, and he thought I wasn't sexy enough and needed jazzing up,' explains Delia ruefully. 'My agent took Aubrey out to lunch and told him off for wasting a talent, and he said, "Delia belongs in the Further Education Department." So there I went.'

But Delia is nothing if not ambitious and she determined to make the best of this latest setback. Deciding that as she was now in the education slot she might as well educate, she took cooking back to basics. It was a recipe that worked. Resolved to make a go of her new show, regardless of the fact that very few people would be watching so late in the evening, Delia worked harder than ever.

'I am very ambitious,' she admits. 'I always believe that if you are doing something, whatever it is, you should want it to be the best it could possibly be. I thought, if I'm in the Education Department I ought to try and teach people something. Why should they go out on a dark night to evening classes when they can watch television and learn at home?'

At this time Delia and Michael were still living in London during the week, dashing up to Suffolk for their precious weekends. When the *Mirror* magazine folded Michael had got a job working for *Lloyd's Log*, the in-house magazine for Lloyd's of London. They each pursued their independent careers in town, often getting together only on Saturday and Sunday. 'On Friday nights we would leave London, put the portable telly in the back of the car and drive to Suffolk,' says Michael. 'We would stop off at Mr Bond's fish-and-chip shop in Needham Market and get home just in time to watch Delia's programme on TV while we were eating our supper.'

Delia often found herself reluctant to return to the hustle and bustle of London on Monday mornings and, as a writer, was lucky enough to be able to work from home most of the time. After much humming and hahing, she and Michael eventually decided to give up the flat in Primrose Hill and reside at Little London Cottage full time. They became members of the prestigious RAC Club in Pall Mall which had rooms they could stay in when they needed to be in London. The exclusive and expensive club provided them with a home from home and proved the perfect alternative to keeping on two properties.

Having at last achieved something that she had dreamed about ever since she was a little girl growing up in Bexleyheath, Delia threw herself wholeheartedly into country life. 'There was the inevitable period when I spurned London, wrote my first book, posted off my newspaper column once a week and played at being a country person,' she says. 'You know the kind of thing: going on long country walks, making cakes for the cricket fête, baking quiches for church dos. I even sewed a patchwork bedspread – not really me at all.'

After the hustle and bustle of London, Delia found the peace and quiet of East Anglia refreshing. Although she had lived there for only a few years, she realized that she had found home. Bexleyheath had never really been home for Delia, it was just somewhere she happened to live during her childhood and adolescence. From the moment that she moved into Little London Cottage, however, living in Suffolk felt 'right'. Today Delia describes herself unhesitatingly as an East Anglian.

'Living in Suffolk has fulfilled all that I wanted it to,' she says passionately. 'I really appreciate living here. I feel very strongly rooted and I have no desire ever to live anywhere else. I always feel the thrill of coming home and am totally wedded to East Anglia. It's delightfully empty and underpopulated, for a start; people don't pass through on the way to somewhere else – it doesn't go anywhere. It's blissfully un-chic, but at the same time appeals to people of taste in an understated way. Although the landscape lacks the contrasts of peaks and valleys to be found in other parts of the country, the Suffolk skies provide an unparalleled blaze of colour and drama.'

Her love for the area in which she lives is obvious and, in turn, her fan base there is stronger than anywhere else in the country. 'My sister lives in East Anglia and she tells me that up there Delia is Queen Bee,' says Denise Hatfield, Delia's old schoolfriend.

Delia was working extremely hard, as she has continued to do ever since. She had her column for the *Standard* to write – which appeared five, sometimes six days a week – as well as her cookery slots to prepare for on *Look East*. She appeared inexhaustible at this time and her appearances on *Look East* led to the inevitable spin-off books: *Country Recipes from Look East* and *More Country Recipes from Look East* in 1976.

Despite the set-back of her TV show being moved, her career was going well. She had a lovely home, plenty of money and the lifestyle she had always dreamed about. And in Michael she had a husband who both loved and supported her in every way that he could. The only thing that was lacking in her life was children. Delia had always taken it as read that in due course she and Michael would start a family. It was something that both of them wanted, and to which they attached a great deal of importance. As a Catholic and a Christian, she had been taught that children were the most important part of the union between a man and woman, and that marriage existed primarily as a backdrop for raising a family.

Delia dearly wanted to have a baby and looked forward excitedly to the day when she would become a mum. The type of work she did could easily be fitted around family life but although she was ambitious she was more than willing to give up her career for the sake of having children. It would be a sacrifice she would happily make for, as far as she was concerned, having a baby was the most important thing in the world.

But after several years of marriage no children had materialized. Like many women who are desperate for a baby, at times Delia felt desolate. When friends told her they were pregnant there was a little voice inside her that said, 'Why not me?' and at times she could think about nothing else. Seeing newborn babies would make her feel full of longing and she also worried about how Michael felt about not yet being a father.

Her faith helped her to keep her hopes up but at other times she allowed herself to contemplate the dreadful thought that it might never happen. As time went by and there was still no sign of parenthood, Delia and Michael had to face the possibility that there might be an underlying problem. Eventually, after much soul-searching they consulted doctors, hoping as much as anything that they would be able to put their minds at rest and tell them it was only a question of being patient. The devastating realization that they would never be parents hit them like a bombshell. All their worst fears had been realized and it remains the biggest sadness in their lives. It is something that as a woman Delia found particularly difficult to come to terms with and, understandably, it is a subject that she has chosen to keep private. Friends were given the deliberate impression that it is a subject that should be avoided and to this day even her own brother Glyn has no idea why she and Michael were unable to become parents. 'I don't know why Delia never had children,' he says. 'I wouldn't ask.'

During interviews Delia shies away from discussing her personal life but – perhaps in a bid to counter rumours that she was a hard-headed career woman who didn't want children – she has admitted she would have liked them. 'We were told it wasn't possible, so we just got on with life,' she says. 'We didn't dwell on it, although I do love children.' Her husband is similarly reticent about discussing something so personal. 'I'm pretty sanguine about the fact that we couldn't have children,' he says. 'It just didn't happen. It wasn't to be.'

As time has passed, Delia became resigned to the fact that she was unable to have a child. 'Maybe one of the reasons I have been so successful in my career and keep going on with it and taking on new challenges is because I haven't had children,' she admits. 'I think if I'd had a family I would have gone into being a mother wholeheartedly and given 100 per cent to it. So perhaps the fact that I haven't is what has given me the energy to put everything into my career.

'I'm sure the joys of family life are something I have missed out on, but it just wasn't possible to have them so I don't waste time thinking about it. If I had a family I would be happy with that. As I don't, I don't mind. The trick with life is to make the most of the situation; to learn to be happy with yourself. It was a misfortune but life just went on in a different way. Half of me thinks it would have been good to have children, but the other half says well, I wouldn't have been able to do what I've done. So you just make the best of it really. I've got my career, so I am a fulfilled person.'

None the less, it is something that is obviously still on her mind because in 1998 she surprised an interviewer by suddenly asking her whether she thought she would have made a good mother.

But one of Delia's closest friends believes she is in fact a mother to many youngsters. Paul McAuley, a Catholic missionary who has known Delia since 1978, cares for underprivileged children in Peru. His work is funded almost entirely by Delia and Michael. 'If they haven't had biological babies they have certainly got lots of spiritual ones,' he says. 'There are many people in the world who are good at producing physical bodies but don't produce much life or energy, whereas these two – by exploiting their energy and ideas and creativity – have done an immense amount of re-procreation. Delia has got thousands and thousands of babies out here in Peru. She's got lots of adopted sons and daughters – there's a whole tribe who would be ready to go and live with her tomorrow. She has learned to exploit the energy that she would have perhaps focused on a family of her own and apply it to her writing and her way of communicating with people. I don't know whether she would say it, because it might be unpopular, but I think that, for Delia, family is exaggerated in its importance. She believes in community but I am not sure that she would give all the importance to the nuclear family – mum, dad and two children – that we are led to believe is the ideal. Like many people, she has discovered that you make family, relationships, and community, at all sorts of moments in your life. It is very restricting to think of children as being the only sign of success in forming a community. Someone who hasn't been able to have a baby can actually be an extremely successful person in terms of forming a human community.'

Delia's ninth book was a special one and showed a serious side to Delia that hadn't been glimpsed before. *Delia Smith's Frugal Food* was published in 1976 and she pledged to donate all royalties from the book to Christian Aid and the Catholic Fund for Overseas Development. In doing so she revealed a more solemn side to her nature: one that was clearly troubled by the irony of writing about food for a living when so many people were starving. 'There simply isn't enough food on this planet to feed all the people who live on it,' she wrote gloomily. 'Rich nations like our own are just beginning to feel the pinch, while two-thirds of the world's population continues to suffer from the grave effects of living below subsistence level. It is a paradox which concerns me personally a great deal.'

Delia the Catholic was much in evidence. 'As individuals, are there really any of us who, if we found ourselves living next door to a family whose children were starving, would not give all the help we could?' she asked, almost in the style of a vicar giving a sermon. 'But the truth is we *are* living next door, on the next continent, on the same planet.'

Predicting that 'our days of unrestricted choice in eating are strictly numbered', she said, 'We shall still be well off compared with the greater part of the world, which is not to say that we should feel guilty about cooking good food but rather that we should have some sort of responsibility to make the most of it and not squander it.'

It was all very worthy and very Catholic. She had written the book, she said, 'For people like myself, those who have lived and cooked during the affluent years and now find themselves caught up in the spiral of inflation, rising prices and impending world food shortages.'

But her scaremongering predictions of world food shortages turned out to be as accurate as 1920s claims that by the year 2000 people would pop a pill instead of eating. Far from our choice of food being restricted, supermarkets would go on to import every kind of food imaginable from all corners of the world.

Her next words will have driven fear into the hearts of super-markets such as Sainsbury's, for which she would later work. Years on, Sainsbury's would pay Delia to encourage people to buy expensive food items, but back in 1976 she was busy urging shoppers to be parsimonious and keep their money in their purse. 'The seductive cunning of commercials will now meet its match – in you,' she promised conspiratorially. 'Nothing will be tossed lightly into your basket: you'll know how much it weighs, what it costs, and how much it cost last week.'

She included her own thrifty tips: home-made food costs less than ready-made so make your own; buy things in season as they will be at their most plentiful and therefore cheapest; keep the kettle regularly descaled as it will boil faster; make olive oil go further by cutting it fifty–fifty with groundnut oil; and use cider to cook with instead of wine. Cream could be replaced by the top of the milk.

Delia was inspired to write the book partly to counter allegations that her recipes were too extravagant, and partly because her Catholic conscience had been pricked by the obvious gap between the starving of the Third World and the over-indulgence of the West. As a churchgoer who attended Mass every day, Delia was troubled by the suffering and starvation that she saw and read about in the news. She found it hard to reconcile the fact that she wrote about food for a living but the recipes she concocted were out of reach for so many poor people.

Unlike the majority of people, who exclaim in horror when they see pictures of starving children on the television news but then forget about them as they go and make their supper, Delia wanted to do something positive to help. Donating the proceeds from her book to charity was the one thing she could do that would help to make a difference. Written by a well-known writer with many fans, *Delia Smith's Frugal Food* sold well and is still in print today. It has earned many thousands of pounds for the two charities that she nominated.

A sensitive person prone to worrying, she gave a rare insight into her often troubled soul in her book *A Journey into God*. 'I do suffer from not being able to heal sick friends or prevent famine; from failed relationships or insecurity; from the threat of nuclear warheads and the catastrophes flashed nightly on to the television screen,' she wrote. 'There in a literal sense, I could switch off the pain by turning a knob, but in blotting out the reality might I not be switching off also the hope of redemption from it?'

As well as raising money for worthy causes, *Frugal Food* was also an opportunity for Delia to put paid to the accusations that the ingredients she used were somehow too lavish. She says, 'One lady, I recall, was outraged by my making a bread-and-butter pudding on television with cream; I ought to have been teaching people to economize in this day and age. Well, perhaps in the context of this book the appearance of a little cream here and there does call for an explanation. For me, quite simply, cream is the one ingredient that makes frugality tolerable!'

The front cover of *Frugal Food* featured a photograph of a demure-looking Delia wearing a frilly-necked lace blouse and smiling warmly – although of course with her mouth clamped shut to avoid showing her teeth. Her make-up was subtle and kept to a minimum and the only jewellery she wore was her plain gold wedding ring. It was a pleasant image and one that appealed – as it was intended to do – to men and women alike.

As the man who first employed Delia, Ken Toye has kept a watchful eye on her career and he believes he has pinpointed the secret of her success. 'My theory is based on something somebody said to me,' he explains. 'I asked a friend's wife why she liked Delia and she said, "Because she's like my sister." I asked around the dinner table and the men in the party said it was the same for them; they saw Delia as being like their sister. She can please everybody.'

It is exactly this blend of approachability and ordinariness that makes Delia's fans feel that they know her. Throughout her career she has had a weighty postbag of letters from her readers, not all of which are complimentary. People wrote to ask her why their meringues crack, or whether she could send them recipes that they had mislaid. One woman wrote and said that she had carefully cut out Delia's recipe for spinach tart from the *Evening Standard* and put it behind the clock on the mantelpiece, but her husband had lit his cigar with it.

But others felt that she needed putting straight on one or two things. In *A Journey into God* she recalls how she was criticized by one of her television viewers for using alcohol. The woman wrote to tell Delia that she had been horrified to note that, as a Christian, she had given such a bad example to others by using wine in a recipe. 'Of course she knew the Scriptures, she added, and had read that famous line where Paul tells Timothy to "take a little wine for his stomach",' relays Delia. 'But she assured me that what Paul had actually meant was (wait for it) to rub it on!'

Delia also learned very early on that there were some people who only watched her cook in the hope that she would slip up and make a mistake. They weren't actually interested in what she was doing at all. Delia found recording in front of a television crew nerve-racking enough but her ultimate horror was having to do a live cookery demonstration. During her very first one she was horrified to spot just such a person sitting in the audience. 'I will always recall seeing a fierce lady in the front row, arms folded,' she says. 'Sure enough she was there for no other reason than to point out my mistakes. In the end her very presence was enough to cause me to make mistakes! It was such a relief later on to be able to do all my demonstrating in front of uncritical television cameras.'

It is perhaps no coincidence that Delia decided almost then and there that she would not do any more live demonstrations. It is something she has stuck to and even today she refuses to cook in front of an audience. Fellow cook Prue Leith, whom she met while she was writing *Frugal Food*, has often tried to persuade her to change her mind but with no success. She says, 'Delia has fans all over the place but she's quite retiring, you know. She won't ever do a live demonstration. We used to try to get her to come to Leith's Cookery School and demonstrate to the students. She would come and talk to them but she wouldn't cook. She is very nervous. She said, "I can do it with a camera, that's easy." It's funny, isn't it?'

Prue, who subsequently became a friend of Delia and Michael, recalls being impressed by the effort Delia put into *Frugal Food*. 'Delia's full of good works,' she says. 'The first time I got to know her was more than twenty years ago when she was doing a charitable book. She spent six months of her life producing this book and I think she asked me to write a chapter for it or something.'

Delia's follow-on book from *Frugal Food* had an infinitely more appealing title: *Delia Smith's Book of Cakes*. It came out in 1977 and featured the same wholesome photograph of Delia on the cover, together with a recipe book and a traditional Easter simnel cake. Every kind of cake you could think of was recorded within the book's 188 pages, including such delicious-sounding delights as amaretti chocolate cake, fresh lemon-curd cake, and strawberry and orange gâteau.

Her friend Norman Hollands, encouraged by Delia to become involved in food photography, photographed the cakes. 'I had taken photographs of Delia when she had her television series on *Look East* and I did the cover shots for the *Family Fare* books and an *Evening Standard* one,' he explains. 'But the *Book of Cakes* was the first job I ever did for her where I actually photographed the food.'

Delia took a keen interest in her friends' careers and would often encourage them to branch out if she saw an opportunity for them. Whenever possible she also liked to involve her friends in her work. One of her early programmes featured Alberto Camisa, the friend she made while shopping in his family's delicatessen in Soho. 'We made pasta above our shop in Berwick Street in those days and Delia came in and did a programme on pasta and pancakes,' he explains. 'We spent the whole day there with ten or twelve people all crammed into one room trying to make pasta for the TV cameras.

'While they were setting up the lights, Delia and I sat on the stairs and started swapping recipes. I was telling Delia how my mother cooked and she told me, "You should write these down and write a book." ' Fired up by Delia's enthusiasm for his family's Italian recipes, Alberto did as he had been told. 'I did go home and write a book but you don't realize just how difficult it is,' he says. 'You have to measure everything exactly for a recipe book but we had never measured anything in our lives – we just throw it all in.'

Watching his friend in professional work mode when they filmed the pasta programme, Alberto saw a different side to Delia. Browsing in his shop she always had time to stop for a chat, but once the crew had finished setting up and the cameras were rolling her mind was solely on the task in hand. 'She's very straightforward and professional when she's working,' he says. 'Delia likes things to be done correctly and the people she has around her are the same. There is no mucking about, everybody knows what has to be done and it gets done without any fuss. If an outsider came in and had a look they would probably say, "That was quick." She likes to get it right first time because that's how it should be anyway. But I've never seen her ruffled as such. She's very calm – quiet and reserved.'

In December 1977 Delia's younger brother Glyn was married and eighteen months later his daughter Hannah was born, making Delia an aunt. It was a joyous moment and one that made Delia extremely happy. Her brother's child was the next best thing to having a family of her own and she immediately poured all the love and affection she would have lavished on her own children into her niece. In March 1981 Glyn's wife gave birth to a second child, Thomas, and Delia became an aunt for a second time.

Delia and Michael doted on Hannah and Thomas, whom they looked on almost as surrogate children. Delia enjoyed spending time with them and buying them toys and games and as they grew older the youngsters would often travel from their home in Lewisham, South London, to stay with their aunt in Suffolk. Having Hannah and Thomas to love was a great comfort to Delia and they became instrumental in helping her come to terms with her own childlessness.

'I've been lucky because I've been very close to my niece and nephew,' she says. 'They are very important in my life. The thing I like most when I'm not working is to be with them, and they spend a lot of time with us.'

Delia's appearances on *Look East* inspired two more spin-off books in the 1970s: *Recipes from Look East*, in 1977, and *Food for Our Times*, in 1978. After that she gave up the programme to dedicate her time to an important new project: devising her *Cookery Course* TV series and books. 'A lot of the recipes Delia did with us eventually appeared in the *Cookery Course*,' explains Betty Bealy. 'She always wanted to do something like that. Her agent was not keen on her doing things for *Look East*. She was ambitious for her and felt Delia should go on to bigger and better things.'

And Paul Cort-Wright says the fact that Delia used to appear on *Look East* is left out of the BBC's Internet information service. 'If you look at BBC On-line the references to *Look East* and her early cooking days are discreetly missed out,' he says. 'I suppose it's because they weren't particularly glamorous. It was only a small regional station but it gave her a damn good training in television.'

When Aubrey Singer banished Delia to the late-night education slot known as the graveyard shift, he did her – and her fans – a huge favour. For it was there that she decided to take things back to basics and developed her famous *Cookery Course* series. The books that accompanied the television programme were eventually amalgamated into what is considered to be her definitive work: the *Complete Cookery Course*. It is still in print more than twenty years on and remains the best example of her particular style.

'There was a basic need for a book that told you not only *how* but *why*,' Delia explains. 'Why mustn't you add the egg quickly so it doesn't curdle? Why should you seal meat? Why mustn't

Delia (second row from front, fourth from right) aged nine, when she was a pupil at Upland Infant School in Bexleyheath. Her childhood friend Denise Hatfield is pictured in the same row, third from the left.

90 Belvedere Road (right), Bexleyheath, Kent, the house in which Delia grew up. Her grandparents Marshall and Ellen Smith lived next door at number 92 (left).

Delia Smith with actor David Meredith.

(UNIVERSAL PICTORAL PRESS)

By 1973 she was already the author of four cookery books.

(UNIVERSAL PICTORAL PRESS)

Delia – the young television cook – photographed at her home in Suffolk.
(MIRROR SYNDICATION INTERNATIONAL)

Girl about town.

(Mirror Syndication International)

An early photograph of the aspiring cook.

Delia in October 1976.

With husband Michael Wynn Jones in 1985.

With her revised *Complete Cookery Course*. Delia updated her bestseller because she was concerned about criticism that some of her recipes were 'unhealthy' for the 1990s.

Delia examining the seafood at Billingsgate Market.

Delia proudly displaying her highly successful *Winter* and *Summer Collections*.

(CAPITAL PICTURES)

Signing copies of her *Winter Collection* – the book that made publishing history.

(CAPITAL PICTURES)

Delia Smith, after collecting her OBE, with her mother
Etty Smith and husband Michael.

(UNIVERSAL PICTORAL PRESS)

The passion that means more to her than cooking: football.
(REX FEATURES)

Delia Smith with Bruce Oldfield, Sarah Thomas and Norwich
City FC players, for the launch of their new kit in May 1997.
(UNIVERSAL PICTORAL PRESS)

Delia and comedienne Dawn
French sporting red noses in
aid of Comic Relief.

(UNIVERSAL PICTORIAL PRESS)

With husband Michael Wynn
Jones, editor of *Sainsbury's The
Magazine*, which the couple
co-own.

(REX FEATURES)

you over-beat egg whites?' If Delia herself couldn't provide all the answers then she made sure she found someone who could. 'I worked with a food scientist and I asked her, "Why is it that choux pastry puffs up like that?" ' she says. 'And she said, "Give me the weekend."' Then she rang back and said it was the water. One of the main ingredients is water; the water turns to steam and pushes the pastry up. So I was able to explain that.'

Nothing was left to chance. 'I do go to a lot of trouble to give people information,' she says. 'I take them by the hand and lead them through – I don't leave them in any doubt. I would never say, "Cook the sauce until it thickens", I would say, "Cook the sauce for about six minutes until it thickens." ' She also told her readers exactly what happens when they bake a cake: 'The egg white conveniently forms a layer around each air bubble and, as the temperature of the cake rises in the heat of the oven, this layer coagulates and forms a rigid wall around each bubble. I enjoyed discovering things that had never been put in cookery books and making it simple and accessible for people. I wanted somebody to pick up the *Cookery Course* book and say, "Right, I've never cooked anything in my life and now I can with this book." '

Part One of the *Cookery Course* was printed in 1978, followed by Part Two in 1979 and Part Three in 1981. Each section sold half a million copies in paperback and Part Three even toppled a sexy American novel to become a bestseller. 'It's a bit of a laugh that food has overtaken sex in the book charts,' Delia said. 'It's good to know the British have their priorities right!'

In 1982 the three were combined and the *Complete Cookery Course* was published. Not everybody was a fan of the book, which actually contained a recipe for 'eggs: boiled'. 'She writes as she cooks: with one hand in the flour jar,' the food writer Paul Levy wrote, implying that Delia's style was stodgy. 'The dull soul of Middle England,' groaned another critic. But by the following year the *Complete Cookery Course* had sold 250,000 copies in hardback. It has never been out of print and has sold more than a million copies.

The book made unwelcome headlines when a Cambridgeshire woman discovered that warming treacle tins in the oven could make them explode. She had been following Delia's advice that pre-heating the treacle made it easier to pour, but ended up needing four stitches in her head after being hit by a flying metal lid from a stored tin. Delia had neglected to mention that the lid of the tin should be removed before placing it in the oven. Several other people were also reported to have had narrow escapes from exploding tins.

And, once again, she came under criticism for her liberal use of fat. 'During the *Cookery Course* television series I had a letter from the coronary unit at the Middlesex Hospital, saying, "We are trying to save lives here, and you're plastering your chickens with butter," ' Delia says. 'So I tried to find out all I could but I always come back to the fact that a balanced diet is what it's all about. It is excess, imbalance and lack of exercise which make problems arise. And, frankly, the excesses of animal fats are usually through junk foods.'

The *Complete Cookery Course* was a weighty tome that endeavoured to cover everything the domestic cook needs to know. With lengthy instructions about equipment, in which she compared the advantages of aluminium and cast-iron pans and metal and wooden spatulas, Delia left nothing to chance. She even stipulated what kind of rolling pin her readers should use (a long straight one, not one with handles!)

The first section of the book was devoted to eggs, Delia's favourite ingredient. She was pictured on the front cover holding a single brown speckly one and she dedicated eight pages to educating her readers in all things oval. She included a chart showing the exact weight of a size 1 egg, compared to a size 3 or 4 and detailed how exactly to tell a fresh egg from a stale one. She also said that the only difference between brown and white eggs is the colour of the shell.

'The contents are identical,' she said. 'In this country we tend to find brown eggs aesthetically pleasing and happily pay extra for them. And I admit if I had a pretty breakfast tray all set with a fine china egg-cup, I would personally choose a brown egg, preferably with speckles.' Ironically, years later Delia would change allegiance and create a rush of demand for white eggs by putting them on the front cover of her *How to Cook* book.

When the MP Edwina Currie caused chaos in 1988 by declaring that the majority of British eggs were infected with salmonella, the government tried to get Delia to reassure people. Faced with widespread panic and plummeting sales in the egg industry, they knew one word from the nation's favourite cook would go a long way to undoing the damage caused by Currie's remarks. They invited Delia to be involved in a pamphlet of reassurance about eggs and chicken. 'But I wouldn't,' she says. 'There was so much confusion. Anyway, I have said often enough that chicken should be cooked right through.'

The *Complete Cookery Course* included comprehensive sections on bread and yeast cookery, stocks and soups, pâtés, fish and baking. Meat and the various ways of cooking it featured on seventy-seven pages. Delia likes meat and has often said that she could never be a vegetarian. 'Vegetarians themselves have been known to make rash claims, such as that vegetarians are slimmer, healthier, and less aggressive than carnivores,' she wrote. 'Rubbish. I know a number of rather plump vegetarians who are subject to the same bouts of flu or rheumatism as the rest of us – for that matter I also know slim meat-eaters who seemingly never have a day's illness!'

And she was triumphant in the next stage of her argument. 'The facile connection between eating meat and aggression (a theory derived, I believe, from a comparison between the fierce, meat-killing lions and tigers and the peace-loving, plant-eating elephants) does seem to crumble when you consider that the most aggressively minded man of recent history, Hitler, was – guess what – a vegetarian.'

Her obvious lack of interest in vegetarianism showed in the lacklustre veggie options that she dished up. The meat-free meals that Delia offered her readers in the early days were typical of the uninspired food that vegetarians had to endure in the 1970s: brown rice salad, ratatouille, cabbage leaves stuffed with rice, brown rice and vegetable gratin. To be fair to Delia, she wasn't the only cook who struggled to get her head around the concept of vegetarianism. Brown rice was a favoured meat substitute for many chefs, but for a self-confessed carnivore like Delia it must have been especially hard to imagine meat-free meals.

In *Frugal Food* she appeared to take the view that vegetarianism was something that people needed to be cured of. She included a chapter called 'Who Needs Meat?!' in which she wrote: 'I do, for one. I could never be an out-and-out vegetarian, although I must admit the thought does cross my mind from time to time. But then all I have to do is conjure up a picture of a steaming steak and kidney pud bursting at the seams with fragrant juices or imagine the sound and smell of bacon and eggs sizzling, and I'm instantly cured.'

Her veggie recipes for that book stretched to three different quiches, pizza with two different toppings, a soufflé and four other vegetable dishes. It appeared to be a token effort and was hardly likely to encourage people to give vegetarianism a go. It wasn't until the dawn of the 1990s that Delia bucked up her ideas about vegetarian cooking. In the twenty years that she had been writing recipes a lot had changed. A growing army of veggies was no longer prepared to accept second best when it came to food. Coming up with exciting and unusual vegetarian recipes was a challenge that could no longer be ignored. But, typical Delia, it was one to which she rose magnificently. The meat-free dishes that she dreamt up for *Delia Smith's Christmas* and her *Summer* and *Winter Collection* books were some of her best recipes ever and were guaranteed to please even the most fussy vegetarian gourmet.

But that was all another ten years off. As the 1980s began, Delia's mind was not really on food at all. Nouvelle cuisine was waiting in the wings but it would all but pass her by. For Delia had another calling that she felt she must attend to. Having written thousands of recipes in fifteen books and spent more than twelve years teaching the British public how to cook, she felt she had done her bit. She wanted to educate people about something else; something that to her mind was far more important.

That something was God. Delia wanted to spread His Word and attempt to do for religion what she had done for cooking.

8

Spreading the Word

As she grew older, religion became an increasingly important part of Delia's life. It was something that brought her comfort and security and, most importantly of all, a sense of self-worth. One positive aspect of not having a family to bring up was that she was able to devote plenty of time to prayer and religious contemplation, time that as a mother of young children she would have found almost impossible to find.

Despite her discouraging academic start in life at Bexleyheath Secondary School, Delia had always been keen to learn. Wanting to find out as much about religion as she could, she decided to seek instruction in the Scriptures. Within their words she found the answers to numerous questions and Delia promptly fell in love with the ancient teachings. 'One of the most joyful aspects of discovering Scripture at a deeper level is to find that it contains all the teaching we will ever need,' she said. 'It is a deep well of information and inspiration that never runs dry.' She also went on religious retreats, where she could immerse herself in reading and praying for weeks at a time.

Through religion Delia had found the self-confidence that had been lacking all her life. Her low self-esteem was still evident at times but over the years her faith had helped bolster her confidence. 'When it comes to ourselves, we can often be our own cameras creating our own self-images,' she wrote in her book *A Journey into God*. 'I may feel much more like St Paul's "cracked earthen vessel" than a rare and exquisite Ming vase, but my feelings are not the true lens. I exist because God created me and wanted me absolutely as I am. When I come to perceive in prayer, however gradually, God's love for me then I can begin to accept and love myself.'

Realizing that she was loved by God, and that in his eyes she was something truly special, had been an important revelation for Delia – perhaps *the* most important of her life. Full of the happiness that religion had brought her she wanted to share her experience with others. Early in 1981 she was given the chance to do so. She received a telephone call from BBC producer Sue McGregor, asking her if she would take part in a television series she was making called *Home on Sunday*. The theme of the interview would be nothing to do with cookery, she was told; they wanted her to talk about religion.

It was just the opportunity Delia needed and, on a sunny day that summer, a TV crew arrived at her house in Suffolk and filmed a forty-minute programme about her faith. Delia Smith the Catholic was not nearly so well known as Delia Smith the best-selling cookery writer and those who saw the programme were no doubt surprised to see this other side to the nation's favourite cook. It brought her to the attention of a whole new audience and her appearance on the show was to set in motion a chain of events that, at one stage, threatened to stop her from ever publishing another recipe book.

After a decade of writing nothing but cookery books, Delia was ripe for a change. The pressure of having to come up with enough recipes to satisfy both her readers in the *Evening Standard* and the book-buying public had taken its toll and she was fast running out of both ideas and enthusiasm. It was a dilemma. Writing about cookery was what she *did*, and it was hard to know what she would do if she wasn't coming up with ideas for recipe books. But then fate stepped in. The simple yet eloquent way in which Delia had talked about her love of God on television was impressive, and she was offered the chance to become more involved in spreading His Word. After the programme had been transmitted she received a letter from the Bible Reading Fellowship asking her to share some of her personal reflections on Scripture in a book for Lent.

Discovering that people were actually interested in hearing her thoughts and opinions on religion came as a pleasant, and not altogether unwelcome, surprise to Delia. It was a subject close to her heart and one that meant infinitely more to her than cookery ever had, so why shouldn't she write about it? Putting her piles of recipes to one side, for the time being at least, she put pen to paper and began work on her first religious book.

A Feast for Lent was published in 1983. Little more than a hundred pages long, it was made up of psalms and prayer readings for each day of the holy period. Delia dedicated the book to Frances Hogan, who she said had 'taught me how to see, hear and understand God in Scripture'. As she had done with *Frugal Food*, Delia decided that all royalties would go to charity, this time choosing The Sick Children's Trust at Great Ormond Street Hospital.

She paid 'grateful thanks' to Michael, who had once again edited and typed the manuscript for her and, she said, 'guided me throughout'. The fact that her husband, an agnostic, was willing to involve himself so wholeheartedly in Delia's religious writing was a measure of his devotion to her. Where many non-believers might not have wanted to be involved in a tribute to God, Michael did all he could to help his wife, knowing how important the project was to her. The priest and congregation of her church in Stowmarket also received warm thanks. 'It is in this community that I have been formed as a Christian, and I thank them for their encouragement, support and prayers,' she wrote gratefully.

The foreword to the book was penned by Victor Guazzelli, Auxiliary Bishop of Westminster, who said that he hoped Delia 'may be able to do for the Scriptures what she has done for the kitchen'. As the Bishop pointed out, Delia was writing about her own voyage of discovery and what she wrote did indeed give a rare insight into her emotions. It revealed a sensitive person who was often troubled by the suffering and anguish in the world but who none the less had an unwavering faith. Whatever life threw at you, she said, God would help you to cope, provided that you opened your heart to him.

'In every human being there's a deep-down ache that only God can satisfy,' she wrote confidently. 'For some the ache can be dulled by extreme activity or ambition; for others the ache is recognized but not understood, kept carefully hidden behind an appearance of contentment. Every serious sin has its roots in need: the sexual pervert, the drug addict, the alcoholic, the person who commits adultery, all are crying out with a desperate need that none of these things can satisfy. A bottle of whisky may dull the ache, but when the whisky wears off the ache returns.'

The main tone of the book was peaceful and studiously concerned with the serious matter of prayer and worship. But occasionally Delia would raise topics about which she feels particularly strongly and then proceed to rail against them. Astrology and the occult are two such subjects. What she considers to be the 'evil' of astrology is something she finds deeply disconcerting. In *A Feast for Advent*, her Christmas follow-up to *A Feast for Lent*, she appeared almost despairing. 'It sometimes seems to me that the only spiritual nourishment many of our children get nowadays is from the fringes of the occult – not least, I have to say, on breakfast TV with its analysis of "the stars", fortune-telling of a kind that denies God,' she wrote disapprovingly.

'We see pornography openly displayed in high streets, children having access to macabre and sick videos. Bookshops even give shelf space to studies of the occult and Satanism, which (and this is one of the most alarming facets of our secularized society) itself gains momentum.' At times in her religious writing she displayed all the zeal of the convert. 'ANYONE WHO FAILS TO LOVE CAN NEVER HAVE KNOWN GOD – it is these words that should be flashed across our TV screens several times a day, because in them lies the real meaning of the word,' she wrote passionately. But, perhaps mindful of how such ardent declarations might be perceived, she tempered her remark. 'Sometimes we can become over-zealous – perhaps for reasons of pride,' she admitted later on. 'We can want to do great things for God – we have often read about born-again Christians wanting to give up everything and preach the Gospel.'

As she considered all the evil threats in the world her imagination occasionally slipped into overdrive: 'Today, with the build-up of nuclear weapons, falling social values, and a general atmosphere of insecurity, the ache of dissatisfaction grows more pronounced and people become more vulnerable to the influence of strange and powerful cults,' she warned. 'On the surface these seem to offer some kind of answer, but in reality they cause havoc: young people are brainwashed, families split, idols – pictures of ordinary human beings – venerated and worshipped.'

Another of her pet hates is noise. In *A Feast for Lent* she slammed what she called 'the evil of noise'. 'We live in a world of high speed and much noise, and we are vulnerable to every kind of medium of communication imposing its hidden pres-

sures on us,' she wrote crossly. 'The reason so many tranquillizers are prescribed is because people have forgotten how to be
tranquil. Stress is said to be a contributory factor in many
modern diseases, and it's my own belief that noise causes and
aggravates stress. We not only have radios and televisions in
our homes, we have car radios, personal walking stereo
systems, piped music in shopping centres and supermarkets,
restaurants and pubs. It is little wonder that people go to their
doctors in desperate need asking for tranquillizers, which in the
end can only patch up like sticking-plasters, but never heal the
problem.'

It was a favourite theme, and one that cropped up again in
her third religious book, *A Journey into God*. 'We are woken up
by clock radios (depriving us of those few precious reflective
moments between sleeping and waking), and noise then
follows us around for the rest of the day, piped into supermarkets, pubs, stations,' she wrote. 'We take it around with us in
personal stereos, except that they are anything but personal.
Television and radio programmes span the clock, not always
listened to but switched on just for the steady input of noise.'

As the readers of her religious books would by now be fully
aware, her faith was something that Delia took very seriously
indeed. It was also something she worked at. She spent an hour
a day 'talking to God' as well as attending Mass at least once a
day. 'I am very lucky in that I have the peace and quiet to think
about these things,' she said. But while she might not have had
children who required her attention, she did have a busy career
to attend to. As a writer and broadcaster who was much in
demand, it wasn't always possible to devote as much time to
God as she would have liked. At times it had proved far from
easy to juggle her spiritual life with her private and professional
life and this was something she found deeply frustrating.

Realizing that her readers might have similar problems, she

confided to them how hard it had initially been to devote time to God. Satan – 'the enemy' – always seemed to provide distractions, she said. 'When I was being taught how to read the Scriptures prayerfully for an hour a day, the first decision I had to make was that this was going to be a priority and some other activities would have to go,' she wrote. 'Then once the time has been allocated, the next step is to take pencil and paper and write down the enemy's suggestions for alternative uses of your time (because he'll be working overtime trying to get you to work overtime!)

'This is how it goes: first I must just phone my publisher … I must peel the potatoes … must just listen to the news … and so on. Then consider the list. Is there anything on it that (a) is more important than my relationship with God, and (b) can't wait one hour? Of course not, and I can also testify that once you're committed to this, the enemy's tactics cease and you can dispense with pencil and paper!'

She willingly confessed to her readers what she considered her own failings to be. 'Any growth in faith will only be possible if we can openly come to terms with our great enemy, the ego,' she said. 'And the stark truth is that we would much rather not, we would prefer to keep it hidden, especially from ourselves! I know when I prayed for a deeper faith and knowledge of God, the first thing he did was to let me take a little peep at myself; and what I saw was a mountain of self-centredness!'

Delia is a firm believer that people's spiritual growth is more important than endless moneymaking bazaars and fêtes. It is an opinion she formed when she visited a country parish where the vicar and his wife had decided to do away with coffee mornings and sponsored events. 'Instead they would have family prayer meetings and invite a speaker to give the people some spiritual help,' she explained. 'The net result, I'm happy to tell you, is that the parish's income has increased 50 per cent in the first year. I found it a wonderful witness to the truth of Jesus' words, "seek ye first the kingdom of God, and then all will be added".'

This view was also shared by the parish priest at Delia's own place of worship, the Church of Our Lady in Stowmarket, where she and Michael had been married. Delia was a stalwart member of the congregation and, accordingly, when it was announced that they were getting a new priest she was eager to make sure that he got the right welcome. Father James Walsh was a novice priest about to take on his first parish and he was naturally nervous about his new appointment. 'How you are received by the parish depends to a certain extent on how popular your predecessor was,' he explains. 'If he was well liked it can be hard to fill his shoes, and if he was unpopular you might be seen as an improvement. But either way you never really know how you will be received.'

Father Walsh was grateful to find himself welcomed warmly by Delia. 'She was very supportive and very helpful,' he recalls. 'She went out of her way to welcome me and invited me to her house for a meal and a chat. The church is medium sized with a lovely parish of about a thousand people. It is a large parish in the sense that it covers a very wide area because Suffolk is not a very Catholic part of the country. Delia was very involved in parish life. By then her time was already at a premium but she did what she could and took an active part in the prayer life of the parish, which is especially important in a scattered community.'

During his ten years in Stowmarket Father Walsh got to know Delia very well. The two became friends, a relationship that has now lasted for twenty years, and he saw a side of Delia that people rarely see. 'There is a contemplative, prayerful, reflective side to Delia,' he reveals. 'When she is in the middle of a television programme and all the publicity and caught up in this very active and demanding life, I think she finds it very difficult. Part of her enjoys it but another part needs the quiet and the reflection. This is why I think she makes a point of getting to Mass every day – because that assures her.

'A number of her friends, people like Sister Wendy Beckett, are contemplative people who spend a good deal of time praying and I think that also meets a need within Delia. It's also reflected in the religious books she's written. *A Feast for Lent* for example is her own thoughtful, prayerful thoughts of what she has read and heard in church.'

Realizing that Delia had a natural talent for communicating with people, Father Walsh encouraged her to become even more involved in the activities of the church. In 1980 she took the important step of becoming commissioned as a lay minister, meaning she could help distribute communion at Mass and take communion to people in their homes. Visiting the sick and elderly who were unable to get to church was an important part of parish life, and one that Delia enjoyed. Helping to spread God's word was a responsibility that she took very seriously and was something that she was also extremely good at.

If people, expecting to be visited by a lay minister, were somewhat taken aback to open their door and be confronted by the famous cook Delia Smith, they didn't remain awestruck for long. Delia would put them immediately at their ease by frankly volunteering her own shortcomings. 'When I go out and talk to people about prayer, I can see that they are visibly relieved and reassured when I tell them that I very rarely feel like praying (to be honest, I frequently don't feel like it),' she admitted in *A Journey into God*. 'Sometimes I don't feel like being married, or working, or running a home. But I carry on doing all these things, knowing that I am committed to them, that I am committed because I made a choice because deep down that was what I wanted.'

At church on Sunday Delia would assist Father Walsh with communion, helping to distribute bread and wine to the congregation. 'We needed at least four or five people to administer communion and as a lay minister of the Eucharist Delia would be part of the rota,' he explains. 'She was popular in the town. People liked her, very much so, but to most people she was just an ordinary member of the parish who happened to be rather well known. I don't think they were particularly in awe of her because that's not what she would have wanted anyway.'

As Delia started to become well known for her religious writing, she found herself much in demand to talk about her faith. She forced herself to overcome her natural shyness to speak in churches and parish halls across the country and even talked to a party of seventy MPs at the House of Commons. Delia made a good lay minister and Father Walsh was disappointed and saddened when she told him that she was too busy to continue. 'She had to give it up after a while because she just didn't have the time,' he says regretfully.

While she was a lay minister Delia was busy collating the three parts of her *Cookery Course* into one volume. She was still appearing on *Look East* and had her column in the *Standard* to write and she was also occupied researching and writing her religious books. But it wasn't just her career that she was referring to when she told Father Walsh she didn't have the time to spare. She reluctantly realized that her extra duties as a lay minister were preventing her from devoting enough time to God. She began to question her motives in carrying out 'good works' like visiting the old and sick and realized that she could reach a far wider audience – and spread God's word further – by making use of her skills as a writer.

She shared some of these quandaries with her readers, at

times appearing hard on herself. 'If we work backwards we'll often find that the reason for an overburdened life can be pride, and the cause of that pride simply a lack of self-acceptance, a fear of not being good enough,' she said. 'Therefore an enormous amount of energy is expended on the effort to be somebody loved, accepted and highly thought of. One of the most seductive monopolies of our time (and I speak from personal experience) is that of "helping others", to gain acceptance and esteem. If one is not careful, the self-appointed healer and comforter can find themselves far from raising up "those crawling on their bellies in the dust" but simply keeping them company. If they complain "but I can't hear God in my prayers", it is probably because they are utterly exhausted from everyone else's problems.'

The most important way to serve God, she was sure, was not necessarily by helping others, but through prayer. 'It has taken me quite a long time to discover how dispensable I am, and how well able the Lord is to care and provide for people without any help from me,' she said in *A Feast for Lent*.

In all three of her religious books Delia opened herself up to her readers, sharing her thoughts on everything from astrology to the January sales. And as a cookery writer she could not resist discussing the parable of the yeast and the dough. 'If you make an unleavened dough, what you will have is a mixture of flour and water: it will feel like a large heavy lump, quite dull and lifeless,' she wrote. 'If you add yeast (which is alive and active) and begin to work at the dough by pummelling it (that is, putting a bit of effort into it!) very quickly you will find it springing back. You feel that it comes to life and, soon, it will be so alive that if you try to make an impression in it with your thumb you won't be able to because that impression will spring back into a smooth surface. As the dough rises and increases in size it becomes something life-giving.

'The spiritual analogies of bread-making are endless. But suffice it to say that a bag of flour that stays on the shelf has nothing to offer; but if it is given water (grace), yeast (the word) and the fire of the oven (the Holy Spirit) it will be transformed into a substance that can feed and sustain life.'

The general decline in moral values was also something she felt obliged to comment on. 'We live today in an age of compromise, when anything seems to go and when Christian values have largely been shrugged aside as irrelevant to modern requirements,' she complained. 'Even within the churches the message gets a sugar coating, its challenge muted. Society has been "led astray" and we can observe violence and crime on the increase, family life disintegrating with so many marriages ending in divorce and thousands of children growing up insecure.'

She wrote with feeling on this last point. As the product of a broken home herself, Delia knew only too well the anguish that children face when their parents split up. It had taken her most of her adult life to shake off the lack of confidence and low self-esteem that had typified her childhood years.

Her foray into religious writing led, almost inevitably, to her being dubbed 'Saint Delia' by the press. It is a tag that she hates and when *A Journey into God* was published in 1988 she insisted she was not a Goody Two Shoes. 'Anne Elliot, the heroine of Jane Austen's *Persuasion*, admits she is quite eloquent when giving advice to others on a subject that in her own life "could ill bear examination",' Delia wrote. 'I can identify completely with her, and am anxious to point out that what is contained in these pages is offered by one who shares the struggle, who is still journeying and not one who has in any sense arrived anywhere.'

None the less, her passionate declarations about God did lay her open to ridicule. 'Ever since I first talked about my faith publicly, I've had to accept that some people will say, "Delia Smith's a religious maniac, she's a teapot," ' Delia acknowledged with a smile. 'But this book is something I had to write. Some people have said that it's very brave of me. But in the same way as I felt I ought to write clear, straightforward cookery books which would tell people what to do and why they were doing it, I felt that I could explain in a simple, accessible way why God is important to us all. I felt I could fill a spiritual gap in many people's lives and provide some answers for everybody who thinks, "There must be something more to life" but doesn't know what that something is.

'That something is God, but he's had a bad press lately. I'm just trying to put the record straight. I quite understand anybody who doesn't want to wear a badge saying JESUS LIVES on their lapel, or to go to some damp, miserable church full of old people who seem to relish the threat of hellfire and brimstone for all those who aren't as holy as them.'

She confessed she'd found it difficult to put her message across in a way that wouldn't put people off, and had even agonized over what to call the book. 'An American publisher told me he couldn't sell anything with the word "God" in the title. "Won't move, no way," he said. But everything else sounded like a Barbara Cartland novel – "The Restless Heart", "Journey of the Heart" – and made me hoot with laughter. In the end I decided I had to be honest.'

While some people chose gardening or golf as hobby, Delia's was religion. 'The thing I enjoy doing most of all is writing and reading something spiritual,' she admitted. 'For the last five years I suppose you could say my hobby has been studying the Scriptures. What I want to do is try and give people the whole spiritual journey from day one, from very simple beginnings. I think there are a lot of people who want a spiritual life; they want to develop the spirituality that's within them. I want to try and help them to do that on a one-to-one level in their own home, if they happen to be unable to find it within a church community or whatever.'

Now quite used to people asking her about her faith, Delia has a ready stock of witty replies. Prue Leith recalls: 'She talks to God for an hour each morning and I said to her, "Come on Delia you can't talk to God for an hour every morning, what on earth do you say?" and she said, "Well when I get really stuck I ask him to help me with my shopping list"! She is one of those people who are full of good works without being at all nauseating.'

But Father Walsh believes being called 'Saint Delia' often wounds Delia. 'She's a sensitive person and I think she's quite easily bruised,' he says. 'She'll laugh it off but I think sometimes she gets rather irritated, and hurt too, by some of the rather sharp, harsh and flippant remarks that are made about her. But if you're in the public eye that's the price you pay.'

The priest also got to know Michael well, although he was not a churchgoer, and witnessed at close hand the strong bond between him and Delia. 'Michael is one of the nicest men you could ever meet,' he says warmly. 'Sometimes we would have discussions about God. He is highly intelligent; you think twice before entering into a theological discussion with Michael. You have to be very sure of your ground. But he is very good with Delia in the sense that he is very supportive of everything she does, including her religious writings and religious activities. He never made any difficulties for her at all.

'Delia loves company. I have seen her entertaining people when I've been there for dinner and she's a very good hostess. You don't get a huge lavish banquet; the food tends to be simple, good, well cooked, and nicely presented. What you would expect from Delia really – nothing over the top or fussy. I don't think I have ever cooked for her – you think twice about inviting Delia Smith to lunch. She probably suffers from that and if you did invite her she would actually be very kind and very appreciative. She wouldn't fuss or turn up her nose at the state of the cabbage, she'd be quite happy with whatever you gave her. If it was good-quality food that you'd cooked yourself, however simple, and not something from the freezer or microwave, she would appreciate that.'

'She enjoys cooking for friends and she enjoys having a convivial evening with a few drinks and nice food. I think that's quite important to her; it's one of the ways she relaxes. Methodists frown on alcohol but Catholics don't have any hang-ups about alcohol; sex possibly but not alcohol!'

While she was writing her first religious book, Delia would often turn to Father Walsh for advice. She also spent a lot of time with the Sisters of Jesus and Mary, an enclosed order of Carmelite nuns who lived at a convent in Ipswich. She thanked Father Walsh and the nuns in the book's acknowledgements. 'I can't remember what she thanked me for, she might have asked me a few things,' he says modestly. 'Delia got to know the Sisters of Jesus and Mary well. She told me that around the time of her conversion to Catholicism she had cooked for a Carmelite convent in London.'

Father Walsh draws an analogy between Delia and her work as a cookery writer. 'Her cooking and her approach to life are very much of a piece,' he says. 'I think the great thing about Delia, that is reflected in her television series, is that she is very keen to use good-quality basic materials in her cooking. That seems to me in many ways to sum up the person. Basic good quality: quality of life and quality of values.

'I don't see her very often now because she is in another parish, but I see her on the occasional Sunday evening and we stop and have a chat and catch up on the news. She will come here to the church if she has had a busy week and can't get to

Mass. She will come in quietly and go into the back of the church, dressed in very ordinary clothes, and with no make-up because she doesn't want to be noticed. Generally speaking she doesn't like fuss.' Delia admits she deliberately dresses down so she can rely on peaceful anonymity. 'I'm hardly ever recognized if I've not got my hair and make-up done and I'm in jeans,' she says. 'On the occasions that I am it's usually only the voice. I'll be stood at the supermarket checkout and say something and the person behind me will say, "I know that voice." '

Reading her religious books, it is obvious that Delia is big on the concept of a merciful God. 'Fundamentalist Christianity can be pretty uncompromising and Old Testament and I think Delia has certainly found in Catholicism the kind of God that is far closer to us than this judging and avenging and angry God,' says Father Walsh. 'And that is the God she talks about when she writes; that comes over quite clearly. She may well have been brought up with an angry God.'

To Delia's delight, her mother had eventually decided to embrace Catholicism. Etty had left Bexleyheath in 1980 and moved to Suffolk to be near her daughter. She bought a house in the next village and visited Delia on a daily basis, bringing her recipe ideas and feeding Delia's and Michael's cats when they were away. Delia wanted nothing more than for her mother to become a Catholic, but it was something that Etty was far from sure about. Father Walsh well remembers her reservations. 'Delia used to bring her mother to Mass on Sundays, and sometimes during the week,' he recalls.

'She was a Welsh Methodist, although I don't think she was a practising one, but she wasn't very pro-Catholic at that time. She came and asked me various questions about the Catholic Church and I said, "Look, we've got a group for people who are enquiring about Catholicism. Why don't you come along once a week and have all your questions answered?" So she did and she decided to join the Church. I received her about a year later. Etty is lovely, I have always got on very well with her.'

Becoming a Catholic is not something that one can do overnight. It is a long process that involves in-depth discussions with a priest. By the time a person is confirmed there is very little about their life that their priest would not be aware of. It makes it all the stranger, therefore, that Father Walsh got the distinct impression that Etty was a widow. Even though he has known Delia for two decades, as a friend as well as her priest, he firmly believed that Delia's father was dead.

Harold, in fact, was alive and well and living in Bexleyheath, but he was never mentioned by Delia or her mother. Discovering the truth about Delia's father came as a big surprise to Father Walsh. 'I presumed that he was dead and Mrs Smith was a widow,' he says, astonished. 'Delia's never spoken to me about her father. I never met him and as far as I knew he never came to visit either her mother or Delia. I thought he had been dead for many years.'

When Etty and Harold were finally divorced in 1986 – almost thirty years after they separated – it was kept secret by Delia and her mother. In 1989 Harold married Barbara Fitzgerald, a widow with whom he had been living for several years. This too was kept quiet by Delia. Divorce is something that, as a Catholic, Delia is dead set against. 'Regrettably the concept of commitment is fading from modern life and its importance urgently needs to be re-established. A marriage that "didn't work out" was not a serious commitment,' she wrote disapprovingly in *A Journey into God*.

Even where divorce might be looked on sympathetically, remarriage was strictly taboo. 'Divorce is sometimes necessary for financial reasons or whatever,' explains Father Walsh. 'But remarrying afterwards is certainly not acceptable. We believe that people don't remarry unless their partner dies. Then they're free to marry. But that was a side of her life Delia never spoke about. We became friends as well as priest and parishioner and I used to go to her house from time to time. She would also invite me out for meals with Michael and, sometimes, with her mother, but she never mentioned her father. She never spoke about her brother to me either.'

Strangely, Father Walsh wasn't aware that Delia even had a brother. One explanation for this might be that Glyn too had caused Delia unhappiness. As well as having to contend with her parents' divorce and her father's remarriage – events that simply served to rake up all the hurt and resentment again – Delia was dismayed to discover that her brother had been having an affair. His marriage to Catherine was heading for divorce and all the memories of her own parents' marriage break-up came flooding back to Delia.

Her first concerns were for her beloved niece and nephew. Hannah was only eight and Thomas just six and the thought of them having to go through what she and her brother had suffered simply didn't bear thinking about. Glyn and his New Zealander lover had a baby daughter called Rosie, whom Delia visited when she was a young baby. But just before the youngster's first birthday a family crisis meant that they all had to go back to New Zealand. 'My girlfriend's brother had a really bad accident and we went back to New Zealand so she could be near him,' Glyn explains from his home in Nelson. 'It was supposed to be a holiday but I ended up staying. I came here for three months ten years ago.'

Delia and Michael threw a protective arm around Hannah and Thomas, whom they now became even closer to. It broke Delia's heart to think of them growing up without a father and she worried to think about how they would cope. But she didn't turn her back on her brother. 'Delia was supportive when my marriage broke up,' says Glyn. 'And she's helped my kids quite a bit.' Glyn subsequently split up with Rosie's mother and has had only intermittent contact with all three of his children. But Delia has kept in touch with Rosie, who is now twelve. 'Delia might still write to her,' says Glyn. 'And last year Hannah came out here to live for a while and stayed with Rosie at her home in Wellington. They're friends.'

But, in contrast, Delia wouldn't see her brother for more than ten years.

During the 1980s Delia wrote only one new cookery book. She had combined her *Complete Cookery Course* into a single manual at the beginning of the decade and edited a book of recipes for Comic Relief in 1986 called *The Food Aid Cookery Book*, but she no longer found cookery writing fulfilling. In an interview that year she appeared disillusioned. 'Cooking used to be something I was very interested in,' she said, deliberately using the past tense. 'Learning and discovering it used to be a hobby, but now the terrific turnover of work I've done in the cookery field has kind of played itself out. I enjoy good food but it never dominates me. I hate it when people get intense about food and it starts to become a cult and everything has got to be terribly pure. It's just a part of life.'

Part of her disenchantment stemmed from the fashion for nouvelle cuisine that flourished in the 1980s. It was a style of cooking that existed at the exact opposite end of the spectrum to the one favoured by Delia and she failed to see its appeal. Nouvelle cuisine, meaning 'new cooking', originated in France but by the time it had crossed the Channel it had lost something in the translation. From being primarily about the importance of flavour, it became stereotyped by incredibly small-but-fussy recipes, with ingredients elaborately decorated to within an inch of their lives. During the money-obsessed era of the yuppy, nouvelle cuisine was all the rage and well-heeled city traders and businessmen willingly forked out obscene amounts of money for a few pounds' worth of market vegetables and a tiny square of meat.

Chefs such as Raymond Blanc, the Roux brothers and Anton Mosimann were kings of the nouvelle-cuisine movement and their high-earning customers would think nothing of paying £200 for a meal at one of their exclusive upmarket restaurants. Delia found it quite off-putting, both as a professional cook and as a restaurant-goer. 'I enjoy going to restaurants, but then again I think that food in restaurants has become a bit precious nowadays,' she moaned. 'You've got three different coloured sauces and so on, and I don't like that kind of food.'

Delia wasn't the only one who viewed the trendy new food with dismay. Chef Gary Rhodes reckons it was responsible for putting the final nail in the coffin of British cuisine. 'It was when nouvelle hit these shores that I believe we finally lost the confidence in our own traditions and techniques, and dropped them in favour of the new ideas,' he said in his book *Rhodes Around Britain*. 'The most renowned of modern French chefs, Fernand Point, had led a whole brigade of famous chefs away from the heavy and tyrannical traditions of classical French cookery as characterized by Escoffier. Point believed – as we in Britain once did – that flavour was of prime importance, that chicken should taste of chicken and needn't be disguised.

'However, we first encountered nouvelle cuisine in the form of cuisine minceur, food for slimmers and for health introduced by Michel Guérard, the three-Michelin-starred chef of Eugénie les Bains. We made a mistake yet again. Instead of embracing the true principles of the new French cooking, we thought the Guérard alternative was what it was all about – light, pretty and not very much of it. We dropped everything that was British and combined all sorts of new flavours and ingredients to make small pictures on large plates, to make a riot of colour rather than big tastes.

'Fish would be served with two or three different sauces, and decorated with half-a-dozen sprigs of chervil or chives. Looking back at that nouvelle period, I can remember that, for most chefs, cooking consisted of pan-fried medallions of pork, veal or beef, or chicken breasts, served with kiwi fruit or raspberries. I certainly passed through this phase, believing I was a culinary artist, and that tiny crayfish garnishing each fish dish was the ultimate in modern cookery.'

Rhodes believes the British totally missed the point of the new cuisine. In France even the most chic modern restaurants continued to serve traditional favourites alongside the new dishes. 'They still cooked their boiled bacons and hams, and beef and lamb stews, whereas we had foolishly left all that behind. They still cherished their traditions,' he said.

Cookery-wise the 1980s passed Delia by. The writer and broadcaster Libby Purves has said that like *King Lear*'s Cordelia, she told truths too simple to be interesting. It is true that compared to the exotic creations being conjured up by Raymond Blanc and the Roux brothers Delia's offerings seemed to be somewhat bland. It was a feeling that cut both ways. Unlike Gary Rhodes, who was considerably younger and just beginning his culinary career, Delia couldn't get up any enthusiasm for the new trend. It was something she despised and was actually offended by.

'I'll never be a vegetarian, ever, but I really don't think animals and birds should give up their lives to be dissected and have their skin and fat taken away,' she says firmly. 'I'd rather have vegetarian food than rip the breast out of a duck, fan it out on a plate and serve something that bears no relation to what a duck should taste like.'

Writing about her favourite restaurant, Bibendum, in a newspaper column she admitted that eating out had been 'a frustrating, sometimes even painful experience'. 'What we have been

treated to of late is Art, not food; culinary cabarets on a plate …
I am thankful others share my disquiet. Have they, like me,
suffered a surfeit of things "raspberry" – vinegars, coulis,
purées? Just think of the man hours involved in hollowing out
a tiny broccoli stalk and stuffing it with a turned carrot, in tying
up Lilliputian vegetables into little bundles or puréeing and
moulding them into baby-food mounds.'

Delia felt out of synch with the food of the moment, and the
only cookery book she wrote in the 1980s was *One is Fun!* – a
collection of recipes for people living alone. She had been
inspired to write it after hearing how Simon Jenkins, then her
editor on the *Evening Standard*, had eaten when he was single.
'He described a typical meal in his bachelor days as sitting alone
in front of the television with an open jar of commercially made
tartare sauce into which he dunked his fish fingers before
consuming them,' she said. In a friendly dig at her old boss's
eating habits the book jacket promised 'to inspire even the most
confirmed devotee of the frozen fish finger'.

Explaining her absence from the cookery market she claimed
she had run out of things to say. The *Complete Cookery Course*
had been a three year project involving thirty programmes,
three books and a video. 'I ended up with a book of six hundred
recipes and I had nothing left to say,' she admitted. 'I didn't
want to do things for the sake of doing them. I needed a strong
motive.

'It's unusual to find a gap in the cookery market. Subjects
tend to get covered over and over again. But we are all forced to
eat by ourselves from time to time. In Britain 24 per cent of
households are single-person households. When I do a book-
signing I ask people what they want. One man told me he
enjoyed making my country pâté but the recipe was for twelve!'
Single people, Delia pointed out, actually outnumbered families
yet they were often the victims of culinary discrimination. This

was a situation that Delia was not prepared to allow to continue.

'A lot of people have a poor self-image and feel it's not worth bothering just for themselves. But I've learned over the years that if you do care for yourself then it contributes to a whole sense of well-being.' In *One is Fun!* she came up with a collection of delicious meals for one and the book became a number one bestseller, proving that you didn't have to produce a lavishly photographed £25 tome about nouvelle cuisine to sell books.

But after that Delia again turned her back on cookery to concentrate on writing *A Journey into God*. She did her last television cookery show of the 1980s in 1985 to accompany *One is Fun!* and then disappeared from our screens for the rest of the decade. She was replaced by the bow-tie wearing, booze-swigging Keith Floyd who cavorted around the television studio sloshing wine into pans and engaging in good-natured banter with his long-suffering cameraman. Floyd was hugely popular and became a big star, famed as much for his string of marriages and pretty girlfriends as his skills as a chef.

Unlike Delia, Floyd left the confines of the studio and went on location to add extra interest to his programmes. He was filmed cooking fish while standing in the sea in Australia, and making huge meaty stews in the middle of the Spanish countryside. It was all very amusing for the viewer sitting at home, even if they didn't actually learn much.

While Floyd dominated cooking on the BBC, Anton Mosimann had his own show on Channel 4 showing people how to prepare restaurant food in their own homes. But while being impressed by the cleverness of the dishes he created on TV, the majority of viewers would never have had the confidence and experience to attempt to re-create them at home. There was still a market for a cook who could teach people how to prepare simple, no-nonsense food, but Delia was not available.

Ken Toye, Delia's old boss from The Singing Chef, became reacquainted with Delia during this period and was amazed to see the change in her attitude. 'When I first got to know her again after I had been living in France she told me she was not going to cook any more,' he recalls. 'She'd had enough and said, "I don't think I'll make another recipe." Then she wrote those three books of prayer and said, "I'm not going to cook any more." I don't know what happened; something happened. She either refound her interest or felt she needed to make some more money, but I was quite surprised when there was this kind of rebirth and up she came again, stronger than ever.'

9

Resurrection

The first hint that we hadn't seen the last of Delia came in 1989 when she brought out a revised edition of her *Complete Cookery Course*. She had updated it in response to the new trend for healthier eating but remained adamant that there was nothing wrong in using fat. It was moderation that was needed, she insisted. 'I don't know how you cook a chicken without butter,' she admitted. 'The answer to all these health scares lies not in cutting out but in cutting down. I don't see why people shouldn't eat sticky toffee puddings on Sundays as long as they're careful most of the time. Italian mascarpone has the highest fat content of any cream cheese, but use it half and half with fromage frais and you get the beautiful flavour and half the fat.'

The book was designed to appeal to a completely new generation of cooks. Billed by its publishers as *the* modern classic cookery course, indispensable to every kitchen, it categorically promised that every one of Delia's recipes could be trusted to work. That people should be surprised when recipes work out is something that puzzles Delia. She tells how at one of her book signings a woman said to her, 'What I like about you, Delia is that all your recipes work – even for idiots like me!' 'This started me thinking,' says Delia. 'How incongruous it is that any published recipe shouldn't actually work.'

But her big comeback came in 1990, after she had been out of the culinary limelight for half a decade. Writing the three religious books was something that she had felt she needed to do, but having completed them she decided to return to what she did best. Nouvelle cuisine was on the wane and she felt emboldened to try her luck in the cookery market again. The truth was that Delia had missed having a large audience. *A Feast for Lent* and *A Feast for Advent* together sold a very respectable 125,000 copies, but compared to her enormous cookery book sales it was small fry and she couldn't help but feel disappointed.

On her return she felt the need to account for her absence from the cookery scene. Having been so prolific in the 1970s she was keen to reassure her readers that she hadn't abandoned them. She explained that she had decided she could serve God better by making the most of her biggest skill: helping people with their cooking. 'Religious books go into religious shops and are bought by people who have lots of religious books already,' she reasoned. 'Belief in God for me is not a mystery but common sense, but perhaps God as a subject is incommunicable. Religion seems to be moving away from the rest of life, whereas I think God is in the warp and woof of everyday living.

'He is just as interested in helping people with their cooking as with prayers, and I began to wonder if cookery were not more spiritual than the spiritual.' While no one would deny that Delia has a talent for teaching people how to cook, she appeared to see it as something far more important than that; almost as a mission from God. 'There is something about having a gift and giving it that is a spiritual thing,' she said, a touch immodestly. 'It's a service. You give what you have to give, and serving others is what life is about. I feel that the gift I have is not my gift. It's God's gift to other people through me.'

Delia seemed not to care that she might raise a few eyebrows with her assertion that the Supreme Being worries whether people can make a proper omelette, or that he put her on this earth to ensure that they can. 'To put it very simply, I think that in the whole of God's creation, part of his plan is to help people with their cooking and I'm just one little bit of that whole,' she said assuredly. This inevitably led to accusations of conceit. 'Has fame finally gone to her head?' asked the *Independent on Sunday*, going on to say that it was doubtful that God's plan included supermarket shelves being emptied of whatever ingredients his messenger proclaimed to be important.

Her 'gift' to the British public came out in November 1990. *Delia Smith's Christmas* was an instant success and was to propel her into a new league of television supercooks. The book contained all the ingredients for a perfect culinary Christmas, including 130 mouth-watering recipes and tips to ensure the festive period went swimmingly. By the middle of December the £12.95 book had sold 300,000 copies, breaking all previous BBC records. Within weeks of it hitting the shelves and her television series being aired 'Delia Power' was in full swing. Hanging on their heroine's every word, housewives stripped supermarket shelves bare of the ingredients and utensils that she praised so fulsomely.

Liquid glucose sold out all over the country when she included five tablespoons of it in a recipe for chocolate truffle torte, broadcast on 6 December 1990. The recipe was borrowed from the chef at London's Athenaeum Hotel and she told her 4.7 million viewers that it was, 'quite simply the best dessert I have tasted in years'. She helpfully pointed out that it was available from chemists. Within days Boots' West Country warehouse had cleared its stock and two weeks later there was none to be had in Europe.

Scottish chemists were caught 'with their breeks down', said a leading Aberdeen shop, Charles Michie and Sons. 'First we sold out, then the manufacturer sold out,' said a spokesman. 'We were caught on the hop and the run on the stuff was massive.' Alan Wiseman, a pharmacist in Ewell, Surrey, said: 'In two hours we sold our entire Christmas stock and it is impossible to get any more. People were pleading.'

The largest maker of the glucose, Evans Medical of Horsham, Sussex, said the shortage could have been avoided. 'If only Delia had given us the tip we could have produced extra,' they said. 'By the time we get production going again in the New Year people will have lost interest.' But Delia insisted she had tried to warn people. 'It has happened before and it will happen again,' she said. 'The power of television is very, very, very big. The thing that annoys me is that I try to alert kitchen shops and catering supplies to a possible rush before the programme goes out, but they don't seem to take any notice.'

It wasn't just liquid glucose that was in demand. Lattice-cutters for pretty pie toppings became unobtainable after Delia praised them, miniatures of cherry brandy – used in Delia's Creole pudding – also disappeared from the shelves. Pickled walnuts, a key ingredient in her venison cooked in port and Guinness, were impossible to find. The book became an immediate bestseller, earning more than £1 million in only a few weeks. Her fans were clearly glad to have her back and everyone wondered how they had managed without her for so long.

It was a brilliant comeback and one that dumbfounded her critics. Accusations that Delia was bland or boring appeared absurd in the face of such creative delights as little mincemeat soufflé puddings, cheese choux pastries filled with mushrooms in madeira, roast goose with spiced pickled pears, parmesan baked parsnips, and iced chocolate chestnut creams with white chocolate sauce. Delia was delighted with the response. 'It's been really phenomenal,' she said. 'We thought it would do well but it's really exceeded that. I'm so pleased about it. I've always known there was more interest in Christmas than any other time of the year.'

Having been away for so long she had worried whether there would still be a market for her particular kind of television programme. 'I hadn't done a television series for five years and a lot had been done in quite different ways,' she admitted. 'I wasn't sure whether a straightforward cookery programme would hold up but it had the most enormous impact on viewers.' The downside to being so successful was that lots of her readers were disappointed when they found themselves unable to buy the things that she had recommended. 'I know it's very frustrating for my viewers because I get lots of curt letters from them,' Delia sympathized. 'I'm often accused of not thinking of them, or even of advertising products. But I think it's a good thing to introduce new ingredients and pieces of equipment. If I'm putting on a new programme I've got to come up with new recipes after all.'

She was clearly glad to see the back of nouvelle cuisine. 'The foodie culture passed over my head,' she admitted. 'As for all the patterns and fiddles I agree with Elizabeth David who said that nouvelle cuisine was nothing but theatre on a plate. I hated nouvelle cuisine: they never let you use flour. Imagine! I think a bit of flour improves things.' She added, 'It has been a funny period but if you look at France now, after nouvelle cuisine and the rest, you find that they are going crazy about what they call cuisine grandmère: just like granny used to make. I suppose that's what I'm all about. I think that people have gone further on with food during the last decades. They are a lot more sophisticated. But the fads have come and gone and they still need practical advice, and easy ways to do things.'

BBC book director Chris Weller said that Delia had made at least £1 million for the BBC in just two months. 'The success of it has been incredible – unlike anything we have ever seen here before,' he said. 'It has made Delia the biggest selling cookery writer of our time. Obviously we are delighted with the success of Delia's books. She has a gift for communicating recipes and making people want to cook.' But although Delia had made a fortune for the BBC, she played down her own riches. 'Books haven't made me a millionaire yet,' she said. 'Obviously I have made a lot of money, but I have also brought in revenue for the publishers, the BBC and the retailers. One bookshop owner said to me, "You have paid for my Christmas dinner this year." '

Speaking about the phenomenal influence she exerted over her readers, and how it caused supermarkets to sell out of key ingredients, she explained: 'I have a philosophy that if things are clever and good they shouldn't be exclusive, but available to everybody. Problem items eventually become stock items. It needs this kind of exposure so that one day people will be able to pop into Sainsbury's and get all these things.'

This last remark of Delia's was a deliberate spot of advertising for Sainsbury's. Unbeknown to her readers and viewers, in 1989 she had become a highly paid consultant to the store, a high-profile connection that has at times proved controversial.

With her *Christmas* book Delia, it seemed, had thought of everything for a perfect yuletide. She included a countdown to the big day that began at the end of October with a recipe for the classic Christmas cake, and went right through to Christmas Day itself with a timed step-by-step guide to cooking the festive lunch. Her army of readers had long considered Delia to be a friend, a role she liked and sought to perpetuate and she insisted unbelievably, that her own festive arrangements were often disorganized and stressful. 'If there's one person in the world who probably needs this book more than anyone else, it's me,' she said. 'For years my own Christmas preparations have been, to say the least, fragmented and fraught: recipes here, notes there and fading memories of what I might have done last year if only I could be sure! What I needed, it seemed to me, was a sort of personal organizer, something I could reach for in October and keep by me as a guide all the way through to the point when the last of the Christmas leftovers have been dealt with.'

Delia, rather touchingly, dedicated the book to Etty 'for all the lovely Christmases'. Caroline Liddell had once again helped create the recipes and the two women, together with Delia's assistant Mary Cox, had diligently tested each one at least three times. But *Delia Smith's Christmas* was the last book that Caroline and Delia would work on together. They had been friends for twenty years but their close working relationship ended somewhat abruptly at the beginning of the 1990s.

Puzzlingly, Caroline declines to explain why they suddenly stopped working together after almost two decades. But it is interesting that after years of seeing her imput rewarded by only a brief mention in the acknowledgements of Delia's books, she has gone on to publish a book in her own right. After working in Delia's shadow for so long, she now has the glory of seeing her name on the front cover of a book: *The Book of Ice-Cream* which she wrote with her husband Robin Weir. She has also collaborated on a book about Elizabeth David.

'Delia and Caroline parted company on a professional basis some years ago,' says Norman Hollands, Caroline's ex-boyfriend. 'As far as I know they haven't worked with each other for quite a long time. I don't know the reason for it but I think it can be quite difficult when you have worked with someone a lot, and been close friends in the past, and then don't see much of them.'

The new television series was to mark a departure for Delia. Instead of a TV studio it was to be filmed in her own home. The plan was to bring a more relaxed and less intimidating feel to the shows and had the added advantage that Delia did not have to travel to work. Millions watched as Delia, standing in the middle of her enviably large and bright kitchen, her immaculate English country garden tantalizingly visible through the glass, effortlessly cooked up delicious-looking festive feasts. She appeared every inch the perfect housewife, even down to her pristine silk blouses, upon which she never seemed to get a spot of sauce or a smudge of butter, despite not wearing an apron.

But, like most things in the world of television, it was just a mirage – a façade. In reality the 'kitchen' was not Delia's own kitchen at all, but an elaborate TV set that was built from scratch at the beginning of each new series and dismantled at the end. And the majority of the food preparation was done by Delia's three assistants in a large industrial unit parked alongside the cottage.

'You need certain facilities in order to be able to film,' explains Caroline Hawkins, director of the *Summer Collection* television series. 'And if you've got a sink and an oven that are up against a wall, which most kitchens have, you can't get a camera in front of it. We had a kitchen specially built for the show. It was hand-made and took ten days to assemble. We had a set designer and a lot of planning went into it before the thing was even built. We do try and give the impression that Delia is being filmed in her own kitchen.'

Delia was prepared to go to great lengths to create the right impression, even allowing parts of her garden to be dug up. For the *Christmas* TV series, transmitted in November and December, was actually filmed in March when all Delia's spring-flowering bulbs were in full bloom. As the crew prepared to film Delia in the conservatory the daffodils and crocuses were clearly visible in the background and had to be removed. 'All my lovely daffs and tulips had to go for the garden scenes because it was supposed to look like winter,' she revealed. 'It was very sad. But I persuaded the BBC to replace the bulbs for next year.'

Much has been made of the fact that, despite their wealth, Delia and Michael still live in the same 'small' house that they bought almost thirty years ago. But Little London Cottage has grown apace with Delia's career and today bears little resemblance to the tiny house it had once been. 'Delia's house is small – if you are used to living in something the size of Buckingham Palace,' says TV producer Frances Whitaker. 'The small cottage was extended and then they bought the house next door, joined the two properties together and built a fabulous conservatory. It is actually now a good size.'

Impressed by the success of her *Christmas* book and TV programmes, the BBC signed Delia up for a lucrative four-year project. The idea was for her to write two seasonal books, each accompanied by the obligatory television series. 'I want to reintroduce people to the seasons,' she said. 'Supermarkets have gone and clouded the whole thing. I want people to say, "Oh, there's rhubarb", and go home and cook it.'

Delia spent two years researching the first part of the project, the now legendary *Summer Collection*. It was published in 1993 and if people had liked *Delia Smith's Christmas*, they loved her *Summer Collection*. Everything about it hit the right note, even down to the simple yellow sunflower on the front cover.

The *Summer Collection* showed a marked change of pace. The recipes were livelier, more cosmopolitan, and more exotic than those concocted by the Delia of old. She had realized that food had moved on and that her readers had grown up and now expected more from her. It also reflected Delia's own odyssey. 'She has travelled a lot in recent years,' revealed her husband Michael. 'She's been to cookery school in Thailand and across America and Japan, always looking at food markets.' Delia had been one of the pupils on a Thai cookery course at the Oriental

Hotel in Bangkok and visited Tokyo to learn about Japanese food. 'It's a very, very exciting time to be involved in food,' she enthused. 'I think we are moving into an age of global cooking. Some very talented people are pushing at the boundaries.'

She revealed that a lot of her inspiration had come from the people she had met on her travels. 'I met this wonderful chef who is cooking Italian, Chinese, Indonesian, French – all with a kick of Japanese in it,' she said. 'It was amazing!' She was also inspired by reading upmarket magazines such as *Gourmet*, *Bon Appetit*, *Wine and Food*, and an Australian food magazine called *Vogue*. 'I like reading what people eat in restaurants,' she says. 'I may read that in California they are eating a roasted tomato sauce and think, "How would I tackle that?" '

Her increased knowledge of foreign cuisine showed itself in the rich diversity of recipes that she included in her *Summer Collection*. Keen to share what she had discovered with her readers, she included several Eastern dishes among the book's 130 recipes. She put in such unfamiliar delights as angel-hair pasta with Thai spiced prawns, red curry chicken, chilled lemon grass and coriander vichyssoise and Sri Lankan curry. The Middle East was represented, as was American and Mexican food. The only cuisine that didn't get much of a look-in, in fact, was British food. Traditional English fare was relegated, somewhat predictably, to the puddings section, with dishes such as rhubarb pie and gooseberry and elderflower jellies.

Delia's mother was still providing her with recipes, which she would write out on lined sheets of Basildon Bond notepaper before taking them round to her daughter's house. The *Summer Collection* included Etty's own apricot preserve and her coconut cake, the latter of which Delia adapted by adding limes. But by and large the book had a definite Mediterranean feel to it and many of the dishes were reminiscent of Elizabeth David's sun-drenched recipes. Delia included a starter dish of Piedmont roast peppers, which she explained was first discovered by Elizabeth David and published in her 'splendid' book *Italian Food*. Delia explained the complicated route by which it came to be in her *Summer Collection*: 'The Italian chef Franco Taruschio at the Walnut Tree Inn near Abergavenny cooked it there. Simon Hopkinson, who ate it at the Walnut Tree, put it on the menu at his great London restaurant Bibendum, where I ate it – which is how it comes to be here now for you to make and enjoy.'

But it didn't stop there. The Piedmont roast peppers became something of a culinary phenomenon that year. The simple yet extraordinarily delicious dish – which consisted of red peppers cut in half, filled with tomato quarters, anchovy fillets, olive oil and garlic and then roasted in the oven – was one of the most popular recipes of the *Summer Collection*. Beautifully illustrated in a full-page photograph and presented on a yellow Mediterranean-style dish, the juices glistened attractively on the peppers' shiny red surface. That summer it was frequently served up by cooks all over Britain. And it wasn't only Delia's readers who raved about the dish. The chef Prue Leith tried it and was immediately hooked. 'I've made the stuffed peppers with tomatoes a million times,' she says. 'We put it on the menu in all our restaurants and we put it into our catering company. All our chefs are given Delia Smith books and, let me tell you, they use them.'

The *Summer Collection* sold so well that for a while it became something of an in-joke among the dinner-party set, even inspiring diary pieces in newspapers. People could hardly go out to dinner with friends without being served up Delia's mixed-leaf Caesar salad, her chicken basque or the fromage frais cheesecake with strawberry sauce. 'When her *Summer Collection* cookbook came out you'd go to dinner parties and get exactly the same food wherever you went,' recalls Prue. 'I was as guilty of that as anybody. I cook her things all the time because I think they work.

I'm sure that the things of hers that I've cooked over the years are exactly the same as everybody else has: particularly the peppers and her famous jelly fruit terrine.'

One of the most striking things about the *Summer Collection* book was the beautiful way in which it was illustrated. It was an extremely visual book with glossy, full-page photographs and, unlike her earlier cookery books, did not look out of place on a coffee table. The photos were taken by Delia's friend Peter Knab and the book was surely sold as much on the appeal of the mouth-watering photographs as for the recipes themselves. The pictures evoked an image of lazy days spent eating alfresco in an English country garden; tables attractively laid with colourful table linen and decorated with pretty jugs, brimful of flowers from the garden.

The bright Mediterranean food was displayed on eye-catching plates and dishes such as peaches in Italian Marsala wine shimmered appealingly. Overflowing baskets of summer fruits were photographed among the prettiness of a wild-flower meadow and fields of cows were shown grazing peaceably in the sunshine. Aromatic bottles of olive oil and vinegars, seductively lit by sunshine, featured heavily and ripe juicy plums were pictured hanging plumply from a tree. A summer breakfast tray, laid with crisp linen and fine bone china and a dish of Delia's fresh apricot preserve finished off the idyllic image.

It was heady stuff. With one look at the delicious-sounding recipes and beautiful photographs, people seemed to forget that this country is famed more for its dreary weather and reliance on fast food than for eating freshly made jam in the sun. Inspired that they too could live and eat like people in the Mediterranean, they eagerly forked out £14.99 to buy themselves a little piece of summer sunshine. The must-have items that year were limes, capers and fresh coriander, all of which featured heavily in the *Summer Collection*.

Delia was keen that the highly polished look that prevailed in the book should be reflected in the television series and she was anxious to get the right director for the show. The job was given to Caroline Hawkins, a young director with no experience in food programmes. Delia was instrumental in her being hired. 'I am not particularly a cookery aficionado,' Caroline admits. 'I'd worked on *The Clothes Show* and I'd done a lot of fashion and consumer-type programmes and I think Delia wanted something slightly more visual than she'd had in the *Christmas* series.

'Delia is very visual; she really has very clear ideas about what works visually and what doesn't and she wanted somebody to bring a fresh contemporary look to it. We worked together very closely on achieving a very classy look to the series.' The team didn't have far to look when they wanted to film close-ups of idyllic summer scenes. 'Her garden is a gift for that and so is the whole area where she lives,' says Caroline. 'She's got a beautiful garden and it was very easy to get fresh fruit and other products and put them in the garden in wicker baskets under the sunshine. It all looked fantastic.'

The executive producer of the series was Frances Whitaker, with whom Delia had been friends for many years. 'I first met Delia over twenty years ago,' she says. 'It was entirely social: Michael, who was then her boyfriend, knew my boyfriend. She came to dinner and we hit it off. I was in television but not in the food area at all; I was doing general features. We became friends and she would ring me up for advice about the television she was doing, but it wasn't until the *Summer Collection* that we started to work together.'

The *Summer Collection* series took the best part of a year to film and involved more than a dozen people working full time at Delia's house. 'It was quite intensive,' says Frances. 'We would get there early so we'd have a full working day. There would be the cameraman, the sound recordist, the close-up cameraman, the PA, lighting men, and then there would be Delia's own team of people looking after the food preparation. We'd work all day. The emphasis is always on work. It's work, not fun. Just because it's on location doesn't make it a holiday. We would go there all week because once you have got the lights in there is no point taking them all down and putting them all up again, so we would be there from Monday to Friday – it's just like an office job really.'

In the back-up kitchen situated in the industrial trailers at the side of the house, Delia's three assistants would be working flat out to ensure that she never ran out of whatever it was that she was making that day. 'We needed a huge amount of ingredients and shopping for them was one person's full-time job,' Frances explains. 'And then it all had to be weighed out and measured accurately. We'd do one recipe in about two hours, and you'd need several of the same thing. For example, if we were doing a shot of something being sliced into we'd need more than one because inevitably you're going to want to do it again. It might not be as perfect inside as you want it to be or perhaps another one is better. So you always have more than one of everything. Depending on what you wanted to do you would have four or five and you'd also have all the ingredients ready to go again in case it went wrong.'

Mistakes inevitably happened. Mary Cox, who had become Delia's right-hand woman after Caroline Liddell stopped working with her, slipped up when she was making up the recipe for Delia's coconut lime cake. 'The cakes kept coming out as flat as pancakes, over and over,' recalls Frances. 'We couldn't work out why and then suddenly Mary realized what had happened and there was this rather sorry-looking face saying, "I know why they're so flat." She had forgotten to check over the ingredients and hadn't put the bicarbonate of soda into the mixture. They made good Frisbees though!'

Caroline Hawkins remembers other culinary cock-ups that happened during filming. 'By lunchtime the food had all been cooked and what tended to happen was that we'd all have a mouthful of it to finish it off,' she says. 'Delia had made something topped with very deep meringue and we were just appalled how salty it was. She'd made the meringue with salt instead of sugar and we all fell about laughing.

'And I remember we did a barbecue scene outside and we shot it from so many different angles that by the time I'd finished getting all the shots I wanted it was completely burnt. I made Delia stand by it with all the burnt chicken legs and we got some quite funny shots. Another classic moment that we often laugh about was when we were filming her cooking a chicken casserole. She swore by these Spanish terracotta cooking dishes that you could use in the oven or on the hob. On the first take she placed it on the gas ring, put in some chicken and tarragon and said, "This is fantastic and you can use it on the hob." But then she poured in some sherry and it just went Bang! It cracked down the middle and flames shot up in front of us. It actually blew up. It transpired that we'd had the gas on the wrong setting.'

If the food escaped being blown up or used as Frisbees it didn't survive the crew, who would wolf down any leftovers. 'The food certainly got eaten,' says Frances Whitaker. 'And Delia was actually rather disappointed if you didn't have some because she wanted to know what you thought of it. She wanted to know what the crew liked and was interested in their opinion. They would take dishes home for supper and the next morning she would ask them what they thought of it. They might say, "Well we liked that one but we thought there was too much lemon in this", or whatever. She was always interested in feedback – it's a good testing ground. Other food was taken to Delia's mother, who might have promised someone a cake, or to a church sale, so the food always got used.'

Delia Smith

Occasionally though, food would be rendered inedible by the difficulties of filming during hot weather, conditions that would have horrified Delia's viewers. 'We'd be in there in the middle of summer and it would be just like an oven,' recalls Caroline Hawkins. 'The kitchen was actually her conservatory, which wasn't designed with great ventilation, and with all our lights in there as well it used to get incredibly hot. The worst thing was the flies. It would get full of flies and we'd have to stop occasionally for Delia to get the fly swat out and swat them. Or we'd be blasting fly spray around and then nobody could eat the food because it was all infested with fly spray. It was immensely hot and we really were desperate. At the end of every take we used to open the door and all rush out into the garden and collapse on the grass.'

It wasn't just the weather that proved demanding. It is well known that Delia doesn't like retakes and the pressure was on everyone to ensure that things went smoothly. 'Like anybody, she obviously would prefer to get it all done in one take if she could,' says Caroline. 'It's very hard work and to pick up something in mid-flow is quite difficult. Normally we would do everything in one take; it's not like we'd have to go back and do endless pick-ups. That only happened if we didn't manage to get the shot, or if she read out the wrong quantity of something. But she is very professional. Because of her years of television experience she knows that you have to tip a bowl towards the camera so that you can see the ingredients in it, for example, and she's very aware of not masking things with her hands. She is a television professional in that respect: she knows exactly how to do things.

'The other thing that is a challenge with Delia, but also a virtue in a way, is that she won't cheat. You hear about people who will light a cigarette behind something to make it look as if it's steaming, but there is absolutely no way that she'll do that. And if a dessert comes out of the oven and doesn't look fantas-

166

tic then it's all cooked again and you carry on cooking until it does look fantastic. She won't put glycerine on things to make them look luscious, or use smoke or steam or anything like that; it has to be exactly as it comes out. It has to be true to her word really. It means that it all takes quite a long time to get done. She's a perfectionist.'

Frances Whitaker explains the reason that Delia is hardly ever seen to smile on television is because she is too busy concentrating. 'I think she is thinking about what she is saying, what the food's looking like and trying to remember if she's said everything, and I'm afraid smiling comes a long way down the list of priorities for her,' she says. 'And it's quite difficult to talk and smile at the same time. With anybody – whether they are in food or music or any other areas – you always work to the presenter's strengths and try to disguise any weaknesses, should there be any.

'She's not someone who is one of nature's extroverts, certainly, but her strengths lie in the fact that she is very much the person next door. She takes people by the hand and gives them confidence with their cooking. Her great skill, and what makes her different from other people, is that she's very happy to talk about the basics and help people – to give them the confidence to try things for themselves. Her attitude was always that the food is the star, not her.'

Despite the fact that she was by now a veteran of television presenting, Delia said in 1993 that she still suffered from tension and stress. 'The tension gives me back problems,' she said. 'The best thing for me is to have a sauna and a massage, which helps to relax the muscles. There have been mornings when I've had to think how I'm going to get out of bed because my back's been completely out. My husband is very good at making me relax. He knows the signs. He'll just tell me to have a rest for the day while he cooks lunch.'

Michael was on hand during filming to provide a calm shoulder for Delia to lean on when she got tired. 'Michael was around and was very much a confidant,' Caroline Hawkins explains. 'He'd be there to support her and sometimes he'd be watching on the monitor and giving her little tips and advice, but he didn't get involved in a major way. Delia's mother was also around a lot of the time.'

The series was still in post-production when it started transmission in May and the production office found itself inundated with telephone calls and letters from viewers. 'People would get half way through a recipe that they'd seen the night before and forget what to do next, so they would ring up and we'd have to talk them through the rest of the recipe,' recalls Frances Whitaker. 'People assume that Delia is sitting at the other end of the phone and is available to help them through a recipe. I think it's partly because people think that if it's been on the BBC there must be somebody who can tell them about it.

'They'd telephone the BBC and be referred to our production offices. It would happen at least once a week. We made sure we had the recipes to hand. If somebody has watched the programme and is standing in their kitchen with a half-made bowl of whipped cream, trying to remember what went into the ice-cream next, the least we can do is to do them the courtesy of answering their questions.'

One of the more peculiar aspects of being a television personality is that certain sections of society feel they have the right to point out your mistakes and question what you do. Frances witnessed at first hand the huge amount of letters that Delia's shows provoke. 'Because Delia is such an obvious target there are always people who complain that she is not using x, or she's using too much y,' she explains. 'She gets unfair criticism in that people will sometimes look at old recipes and say, "Look at all the cream and butter in this", without realizing that in fact the current version of the *Complete Cookery Course*, for example, has been entirely revised and all those old levels of fat and sugar have been reduced or replaced by other things.

'She realized that the recipes she'd done first time around were not appropriate for today's standards and lifestyle, so she spent a lot of time revising them and all the recipes were slimmed down. When we did the *Summer Collection* series we would occasionally get letters from viewers saying, "How can you possibly eat all of that in one meal?" but we never said that all these recipes were to be eaten at one time! Delia has to point out that it's not compulsory to eat it all, or to eat this course followed by that course followed by the other.'

One can only guess what such busybody types would say if they knew what Delia had got up to during the filming of the *Summer Collection*. They would no doubt have choked on their home-made pesto sauce if they had seen her during a raucous night out with the production crew. For when Delia discovered that the show's production manager Melanie Grocott would be celebrating her birthday during the shoot, she planned a surprise for her that was astonishingly at odds with her saintly image.

The birthday coincided with the end of filming, which it is traditional to celebrate with an 'end-of-term' party and Delia told the unsuspecting Melanie to book a table for them all at the Bow Window in Bildeston, one of Delia's favourite local restaurants. Melanie did as she was asked, never guessing what Delia had in store for her. Caroline Hawkins had also had a birthday while they were making the series and Delia had provided a bottle of champagne and arranged for a neighbour to bake her a cake. Melanie no doubt wondered whether perhaps Delia might lay on a cake for her too, but in fact Delia had a far saucier 'gift' in mind. Delia, plain, sensible Delia, the nation's bastion of respectability, had hired a Stripogram.

The group had just finished their meal in the small Suffolk restaurant when Delia sprang her sexy surprise. 'We had just finished eating when a good-looking young policeman walked in and asked for Melanie,' giggles Caroline Hawkins. 'He said he had come about a parking offence or something, it was something that Melanie knew she had done wrong anyway, and he had been well briefed. Melanie looked quite worried but then he suddenly took off his jacket and proceeded to strip off in the restaurant.

'We were all really shocked – Melanie especially. It was so unexpected. He was obviously a good Stripogram because he was quite convincing and looked realistic. He didn't take all his clothes off because Melanie was a bit embarrassed and said, "Stop that, I don't want to know!" We'd all had quite a lot to drink by then so it was quite funny. We had a jolly good laugh.

'The Bow Window is a very good-quality restaurant but I don't think they minded because it is only small and I think we had pretty much monopolized the whole place. It turned out that Delia and Michael had arranged it between them. That's the thing about Delia you see; she has this whiter-than-white reputation but she'd be the first to admit that she's a lot more fun than the public perception of her. This whole motherly image that she has got isn't true at all – she's quite wild really.'

Delia admitted to letting herself go at the meal, but only in so far as she ate three puddings. 'After weeks of eating sensibly and not drinking, I'm afraid there was no restraining me,' she admitted. 'It must have been the champagne that did it, but I ended up eating not one but three iced crème brûlées!'

Melanie forgave Delia her mischief-making and in fact Delia's sexy 'present' was partly responsible for Melanie agreeing to work for Delia and be her personal assistant. 'Melanie was so brilliant as production manager that Delia asked her if she would work for her; she poached her really,' says Caroline. 'Melanie is very close to Delia.' In her book *How to Cook*, Delia paid tribute to Melanie who she said was part of her 'life-saving team'.

The meal at the Bow Window was a one-off, says Caroline. 'When we were filming we didn't go out to dinner much because we were all too tired, and we were all so full of food anyway, having eaten all the stuff on the set. But Delia and Michael have taken me to the best restaurants I have ever been to and I've had some of the best meals I've ever had while I've been out with them in London. They are very generous people.'

Caroline also reveals that she and Delia are huge Victoria Wood fans and often acted out scenes from her TV series to cheer themselves up during filming. They especially liked the part of the show called *Acorn Antiques*, which is a spoof of a badly-made television show co-starring Julie Walters as the tea lady Mrs Overall. Caroline and Delia would happily swap catch-phrases from the comedy for a bit of light relief. 'I think it was the *Acorn Antiques* series that we found particularly amusing because obviously from a television programme-maker's point of view they put in all the clichés in the book: the swinging sets, the awful camera moves, the bad acting and people being cued on set at the wrong moment,' Caroline laughs.

'Sometimes during filming we would go into a Julie Walters voice and say, "Do you remember the two soups sketch?" And then we would act out the sketches between us, especially the trolley sketch where she used to say, "Can you point at it, is it on the trolley?" We used to find it quite a tension-killer when we were all very tired and it was very hot in the conservatory. Everybody got tired occasionally and if I felt that Delia's tone, her delivery, was a little bit downbeat I'd do a Victoria Wood sketch just to get her to laugh. Then she'd have renewed energy.

It provided little light moments and after we finished the series she booked a box at the Albert Hall and took me to see Victoria Wood live.'

10

Delia Incorporated

Delia was flavour of the month again. After being noticeably absent from the cookery scene for so much of the 1980s she was now bigger than ever. No one could find a bad word to say about her *Summer Collection*. Even the Queen was a fan, awarding her the OBE in 1994. After collecting her medal at Buckingham Palace, Delia happily posed for photographers, allowing herself a rare smile for the cameras. Savouring her moment of glory, flanked by her husband on one side and her mother on the other, she must have wondered what her old teachers would have made of her achieving such an honour.

The *Summer Collection* book had sold more than 1 million copies by 1995, astounding booksellers and trend watchers alike. But her follow-up book, *Delia Smith's Winter Collection*, was to eclipse that figure within only a few days of its launch in October 1995. Selling faster than the proverbial hot cakes, the *Winter Collection* made publishing history – and led to one of the most famous food shortages of recent times.

It had started innocently enough. On her travels Delia had happened upon fresh cranberries and thought the bittersweet berries tasted rather nice. Keen as ever to share any interesting discoveries with her readers, and thinking that they would make a welcome change from the jars of cranberry sauce that most people were familiar with, she decided to include them in her *Winter Collection*. In fact, she liked them so much that she featured them in no fewer than seven recipes. There was rillettes of duck with confit of cranberries, a tasty supper guaranteed to liven up a cold winter's evening; cranberry and orange one-crust pies; venison steaks with cranberry Cumberland sauce; spiced sautéed red cabbage with cranberries; and spiced cranberry and orange jellies.

The berry even featured on the cover of the book, attractively wreathed in snow, and Delia talked seductively of its 'rich, luscious flavour' and 'jewel-like appearance'. Just a week after she praised its qualities in her *Winter Collection* television series, the Great Cranberry Crisis was in full swing. As a staggering 500,000 copies of the *Winter Collection* book were snapped up in one week alone, shoppers cleared the shelves of cranberries. In Sainsbury's sales increased by 200 per cent.

Despite being warned in advance by Delia's office to stock up on key items mentioned in the book – including dried porcini mushrooms, Italian pancetta, puy lentils, and cranberries – supermarkets couldn't keep up with demand. Importers increased their orders by 30 per cent but within days of the book hitting the shops stocks were already perilously low as cranberry frenzy took hold. One harassed importer spoke for the nation: 'It is murder,' said Mike Lloyd. 'We *must* have cranberries.'

There were two main reasons for the shortage: firstly, the cranberry growers had suffered a terrible harvest and secondly, despite Delia's acknowledged selling power, nobody could have foreseen just how popular the *Winter Collection* book would become. Its launch coincided with the abolition of the Net Book Agreement, which enabled booksellers to undercut the manufacturers' recommended price for the first time. Sales of the *Winter Collection* were helped by many of the large book-shops and supermarkets selling the £15.99 book for as little as £7.

BBC Books, who published the *Winter Collection*, had wanted the book to retail at £16.99 but Delia thought this was too expensive for her readers and demanded they knock a pound off. The BBC agreed to do so but is adamant that it didn't do any deals with booksellers. Any discounts, they said, were being met out of the bookshops' own profits. The price-cutting appeared worthwhile: one Manchester branch of Waterstone's sold 1,800 copies of the *Winter Collection* in one month.

Boosted by prominent displays and the hefty discounts, the book broke publishing records. In less than a month sales had topped the million mark and printers were running off 35,000 copies of the book a day in an attempt to meet demand. Sales were expected to reach 1.5 million by Christmas and it was announced that the price war in the high street had earned Delia a £2 million windfall. It also brought her an unexpected prize: The 'Cranberry Scoop Award' from America's Ocean Spray Cranberry Company, which was presented to her by the American Ambassador to London.

It seemed that the book was on everyone's Christmas list that year. While Delia's fans settled down to prepare such winter delights as her roasted pumpkin soup with melting cheese; warm poached egg salad with frizzled chorizo; and – everyone's favourite from the *Winter Collection* – her chocolate bread-and-butter pudding, the critics were preparing their verdicts.

'Many of her recipes are exotic, but they are passed through the filter of her Englishness, becoming in the process just like mother makes,' wrote one. 'She is doing more than anyone else to demystify foreign cuisines – which is fine if you don't relish the mystique ... There is no escapism here, no appeal to the senses, other than to a kind of atavistic love of hearth and home and England and St George.'

'Smith's cookery includes a signally unfashionable native hue: brown,' complained another. 'She cooks joints, refers to French onion soup as "comfort food" and pays homage to "that great British institution, bread and butter pudding".' Others thought she was dull. 'Where is the fun in foolproof cooking? The excitement is all in the danger – and failure a price worth paying. I can't help feeling I'd warm to Delia a little more if she got sloshed on the cooking sherry, or if her Linguini with mussels and walnut parsley pesto were just once in a while to go soggy.'

She also attracted derisory comments for daring to bring back dishes like black forest gâteaux and her old favourite beef in beer, part of what she called her 'Sixties Revival Menu'. 'The main body of the book confirms the terrible truth: there are dumplings, casseroles and – heaven forfend! – crêpe Suzette – and – spare us! – prawn cocktail,' wrote Delia's old paper the *Standard*.

But it was what some saw as Delia's tampering with tradition that caused annoyance among die-hard foodies. The recipe that caused the most consternation was her oven-baked risotto. 'I've always loved real Italian risotto, but oh, the bother of all that stirring to make it,' she said. 'Then one day I was making a good old-fashioned rice pudding and I thought, why not try a risotto in the oven.'

Traditionally, Italian risotto is made by ladling simmering stock on to heated rice, allowing it to be absorbed before adding a little more, and so on until the rice is cooked. This, said Delia, was a bore. 'People don't have the time to do this,' she explained. Instead she advocated baking rice with stock in the oven but still called it a risotto. Tampering so heavily with an authentic recipe was tantamount to sacrilege in some circles; many food-lovers believe authentic recipes should be protected.

Cookery writing is a surprisingly competitive world and it became apparent that the knives were out for Delia. When it was announced that she had won the prestigious Glenfiddich Award for food writing in 1993 she was hissed and booed by her peers. 'She is quite unpopular, is the foodie consensus for what it's worth,' a witness was reported as saying. 'Among the public she is far more popular than anyone else, which explains the antipathy, and worse still, she keeps herself to herself.' In 1996 she was not even shortlisted for a Glenfiddich Award. The absence of her *Winter Collection*, which had dominated the British book trade for months, was a snub on the grandest scale.

Instead the front runner was *The River Café Cook Book*, written by the two cooks at the trendy London riverside restaurant. The glossy £25 book had sold a mere 50,000 copies compared to Delia's 1.7 million. And in September 1995 at the Oxford symposium where foodies gather once a year to exchange information, one man stood up in public to pay, as he put it, 'tribute to gross mediocrity in the shape of Delia Smith'.

On the plus side, a survey on what men found attractive in women concluded that Delia came closer to the ideal woman than *Baywatch* beauty Pamela Anderson. The surprising verdict emboldened some men to come out of the closet and admit that they found Delia sexy. 'To those male viewers who are not the least bit interested in how to boil an egg, bossy Delia's slow-burning sex appeal is irresistible,' panted one lovestruck interviewer. Delia found it all highly amusing. 'I love all that,' she laughed with glee. 'I don't quite believe it, of course, although I do get wives coming up to me and asking me if I can sign my book for their husbands.'

Outside in the high street Delia was more popular than ever. Newspapers devoted many column inches to the cranberry saga and the phenomenon of Delia Power was discussed at length up and down the country. The phenomenal success of the *Winter Collection* served to underline the huge influence wielded by one woman and Delia found herself the focus of much interest from the media, not all of which she welcomed. Up until that point journalists had not been particularly interested in Delia, preferring to devote their attention to the more flamboyant TV chefs such as Keith Floyd and Gary Rhodes. Floyd's colourful love life and Rhodes's wacky hair-do were appealingly at odds with Delia's rather stuffy image and made good newspaper copy.

At the press launches for her new books, hacks were usually lured along more by the thought of the food that would be on offer than by the prospect of interviewing Delia herself. At one BBC press launch she was spotted sitting alone in the corner while reporters swarmed around the other celebrities present. It was a situation that suited Delia fine. Intensely secretive, as far as she was concerned the fewer questions that she was asked the better. She did interviews only when necessary to promote her new books and had become adept at deflecting any questions about her private life.

'She freezes up personal questions so badly that it's quite embarrassing,' remarks one journalist. 'She makes you feel very uncomfortable if you raise the subject of anything to do with her private life, even the most harmless question is met with iciness. It is definitely not encouraged.'

But with the success of the *Summer Collection* and *Winter Collection* her profile was raised and she was bewildered to find herself the subject of so much media interest. 'I'm only doing what I've done for twenty-five years – writing cookery books and cooking on TV – but suddenly I find I'm this sort of creature who has quite deliberately been made into an industry,' she lamented. 'It isn't very pleasant what they are saying about me and most of it isn't true, but I think it's par for the course, inevitable.'

It was at the time of the *Winter Collection* that rumours began circulating that Delia was not nice to work with. Stories of her berating her staff and reducing secretaries to tears started to be passed around within the food industry. Delia, it appeared, was not as saintly as her fans might think. Most of the whispers centred on the filming of the *Winter Collection* television series and it is true that the shoot was not a happy one.

Delia had not got on with the series' director Trevor Hampton and filming was marred by clashes between the two. Hampton had replaced Caroline Hawkins, who didn't want to do another cookery series, and he and Delia failed to see eye to eye. Her agent Debbie Owen revealed that Delia had had 'strong words' with him because she felt her image was being compromised. She was apparently annoyed when Hampton wanted to reshoot some dishes that came out looking less than perfect, and argued that she wanted her viewers to see that she was human and could make mistakes. 'She was sad that all the mistakes were edited out of this series,' explains Owen. 'She is certainly no Little Miss Perfect.'

Trevor Hampton remains guarded about the events surrounding their falling out. 'She is a very professional and very famous cook and to a certain extent television takes second place to the cooking,' he says carefully. 'She is known for the fact that everything she cooks works, so everything has to work on set or else she isn't happy with it. She accused me of making things look too neat and tidy. I don't really want to go into it to be honest.'

But he adds tellingly, 'None of the television team from the *Winter Collection* series went anywhere near the new series.' Asked whether he would consider working with Delia again, he wryly remarked, 'She hasn't asked me.'

The executive producer of the *Winter Collection* series was Delia's friend Frances Whitaker, who had produced the *Summer Collection* show. She admits that at times during filming things became difficult with Delia. 'Let's just say that it wasn't the happiest of circumstances for everybody,' she says diplomatically. 'The main problem was that Delia was extremely busy. For us the television series was a priority but for Delia it was just something that she wanted to get through as fast as she could.

'She had the book to write and her work for Sainsbury's and other things going on. She just was terribly, terribly busy. Reshooting, if that arose, was an inconvenience to her. I think lots of people enjoyed themselves but the fact that Delia was very busy was certainly a problem during the shoot.'

The twelve-part series took the best part of a year to film from the initial planning meeting in August 1994 to the final editing in autumn 1995. The actual shoot took two and a half days per programme, making six weeks in all. For most of that time the TV crew was packed into Delia's home, which at times proved stressful. 'It was pretty much all done at Delia's house,' Frances explains. 'There were some sequences that were shot in a studio and there were one or two little pieces that were shot at a mussel restaurant, but it was mostly filmed at Delia's.'

As tensions mounted between Delia and Trevor Hampton, Frances found herself in an awkward position. She had been Delia's friend for twenty years but, in her opinion, Hampton was not to blame. 'I would say that Trevor did everything that he was asked to do and more,' she says. 'He could certainly not be faulted in any way. He's an award-winning director who has worked with an amazing number of very big names who are temperamental and difficult and stupid, none of which are things that you could apply to Delia. I don't think he'd done a whole series of food programmes before we did Delia but I met him earlier and thought that he had the right credentials, certainly in terms of the way he could plan it and shoot it to make it look fantastic.'

Frances admits that the problems surrounding the filming of the *Winter Collection* series strained her friendship with Delia. They are no longer close. 'In those situations the professional hat takes over,' she explains. 'Things had changed anyway so even before we started the *Summer Collection* we weren't as close as we had been earlier. We'd grown apart; one does. I think most of us have changed in twenty years. She's reached that iconic status of only being referred to by one name and over the years we've gone in different directions. I got a Christmas card from her but I don't really feel I'm up to date on how she feels about things.'

Caroline Hawkins says she never encountered an unpleasant side to Delia when they were filming the *Summer Collection* series. 'She was never difficult with me,' she says. 'We had a very professional relationship and I think there was mutual respect. I was never on the receiving end of any unpleasantness; she never snapped or had any shouting incidents with me.' But she admits that less senior people might not have fared as well. 'Being the director, I suppose there was a professional level of respect that maybe people lower down the scale may not receive,' she says.

'I would say she is a perfectionist who would always strive for the top, which obviously makes the work quite hard, but I wouldn't say she was difficult. If ever I asked her to do anything she'd always do it. I was never aware of anybody being in tears but I never went out into the back-up kitchen where she was dealing with her people – I was very much on the set by the cameras – so I wouldn't know.'

But Caroline Hawkins recounts a story about the filming of the *Summer Collection* series that gives an interesting insight into Delia Smith the television star. 'Delia is quite a sport, we did quite a lot of wind-ups on each other, and on one occasion she was wearing a cream blouse and she decided to do a wind-up on me,' Caroline explains. 'She went upstairs into her room and sent Frances down to me. Frances said, "I think you'd better go and talk to Delia because she's spilt pesto on her blouse and she won't come down. She's in tears. You'll have to use your diplomacy and go and talk her round, she's saying she's not going to do any more work today." So of course I went upstairs and Delia was just standing there laughing and going, "Nah, nah, nah, nah." '

The story is meant as a humorous anecdote, but the fact that the director fell for it so readily speaks volumes about her perception of Delia. This is something Caroline acknowledges. 'I did believe it because obviously there are tensions in all filming and there are times when things don't go according to plan and you have to do retakes and things. It can be quite tiring. It's hard work for everyone really. The people in the kitchens outside worked very hard as well.'

People who know her well admit Delia can be difficult to work with. One colleague was reported as saying they thought it odd that she should attend Mass every morning and then come into the office and reduce her secretary to tears. Delia has alluded to this herself, recalling an incident in the office. 'I was getting cross, losing my temper, and I said to them, "Just think what I'd be like if I didn't go to Mass." '

'I think there's a certain amount of jealousy,' says her friend Norman Hollands. 'One hears horror stories about Delia, but I like Delia. I think she takes after her mother: they are both fairly go-ahead people. I don't think Etty would take any nonsense from anybody and Delia is the same. She doesn't like being thwarted or crossed. But she's big on loyalty and she's not afraid to muck in and get her hands dirty. People now think she's really posh and doesn't get involved in things, but I remember working in the studio with her four or five years ago and she was at the sink peeling spuds.'

Betty Bealy, who knew Delia on *Look East* in the mid-1970s, says she was always pleasant company during filming. 'She got on very well with everybody and was a very nice person to work with,' she recalls. 'What you see on the screen *is* Delia; she's a nice lady. People will always say that sort of thing – that she is not nice to work with – but I can only speak as I find and I can't believe Delia is any different now. She wasn't a young girl then so you don't change to that extent. People obviously do have pressures so maybe some people didn't get on. There's always going to be somebody who doesn't get on with some-body. It's a funny old business to be in – there's always a lot of carping.'

Antony Worrall Thompson takes the rumours with the proverbial pinch of sea salt. 'You hear about the Delia horror stories but I don't take them too seriously because as the story gets taken down the line everyone exaggerates a little bit more,' he reasons. 'It ends up a complete fabrication: whitebait becomes shark.'

But her husband admits that she can be demanding. 'She has very high expectations of herself and other people,' he says. 'She does feel depressed and very frustrated when those are not met. She has extraordinarily high standards and likes them to be reciprocated.'

Delia has never claimed to be a saint. 'Apparently, other people have this clean, sparkling image of me. They see me as the Mary Poppins of the kitchen,' she says. 'I suppose it's better than being called scruffy or unwholesome, but I don't really like it. I can be just as sharp and grumpy as anyone else. I get really het up when the pressure is on. I can explode and be really grumpy all day.' Debbie Owen agrees. 'Delia has got a huge personality – she gets very enthusiastic and very angry about things. Underneath there is steel.' Owen says Delia's religion provides her – and everyone else – with 'a vital safety valve'. 'Delia is not perfect,' she says. 'Her faith is important to her precisely because of that. She gets very annoyed about things sometimes and it helps soothe her, calm her down again and see things in perspective. I think she would admit herself that she would be unbearable to live and work with without her faith.'

'Delia is like a lot of people; she has very high standards and she expects other people to work to those same high standards,' says Frances Whitaker. 'Quite often when people are described as difficult it means that they actually expect quite a lot from the people they work with. Delia isn't the only person who has those high standards, indeed it is what makes people success- ful. She doesn't want to settle for anything less than perfection.' Delia willingly admits to this: 'I am a perfectionist and if they're going out to buy food for the photographs and the food they come back with is manky stuff, then yes, I do get cross. But I don't yell and I only snap occasionally.'

Delia's eyesight caused problems during filming of the *Winter Collection* and eventually Frances had to broach the subject with her. 'There came a point when we noticed that she needed to think about wearing either contact lenses or glasses,' she explains. 'There were certain things that she had difficulty with, just in terms of her focal length changing, and it meant that things had to be redone. She had problems putting the top back on the food processor because it wasn't always a model that she was familiar with. They are not easy to do if you have got perfect vision and are using your own at home that you've had for years. She was fine about it, I just think she hadn't thought about it until then.'

Delia is a careful guardian of her own image and works hard to ensure she strikes just the right chord with her fans. She once banned a newspaper from publishing an old photograph of herself with a Mary Quant hairstyle and short skirt because it presented the 'wrong' look. Two wardrobe assistants accompanied her on a two-day shopping spree to buy suitably inoffensive attire for the *Winter Collection* series. The look they were aiming for was 'warm and cosy, nothing too exotic or flamboyant' Frances explains. But it is interesting to note that in searching for her 'ordinary housewife' attire Delia chose Harrods in which to do her shopping.

The fact that she dresses conservatively and doesn't have any flamboyant mannerisms makes it hard for impressionists to imitate her. When Rory Bremner decided that he ought to have a go at 'doing Delia' he found it a challenge. The key to his brilliant take-off of her lies, he says, in her utter absence of overt personality. 'There's nothing in her delivery,' he explains. 'The voice is unremarkable, very measured and rather bland. There's a sense of control. It's there in her body language and it's there in her recipes.' Bremner is not the only person to have mimicked Delia. Julie Walters did a hilarious spoof of her in television adverts for Bisto. But whereas Bremner *was* Delia, Walters gave us a manic kind of Delia-on-speed.

Safe in her position as Britain's favourite cook and adored by her millions of fans, Delia seldom appears riled by the criticisms levelled at her. The rudest thing she has said about her critics is that they are snobs, but her husband and agent are always on hand to fight her corner for her. 'There seems to me a whole stratum of cookery, food writing and criticism that's so precious it's on a different level from the way most people exist,' Michael complains.

And while critics snipe at what they consider to be Delia's lack of originality, her books race up the bestseller list and stay there year after year. It is her populist touch that endears her to the masses. 'Basically she is a communicator, not an entertainer,' says Debbie Owen. 'She is one of us and she has never forgotten what it means to have to cook yet another meal. Delia has often said to me, "There are loads of people who are better cooks, but I seem to have a gift for communicating." Fame is a double-edged sword. I have seen a lot of people acquire it and, of all of them, she has dealt with it the best by ignoring it.'

Michael says, 'Delia's appeal lies in the fact that she's a housewife, not a chef or perhaps even a cook. She's just some-body who learned to cook like everybody else.'

But this assertion of Michael's was not strictly true. Delia was not a housewife. Housewives are women who stay at home and do not go out to work; Delia not only worked, she ran a multi-million-pound business empire. In the early 1990s she went from being a successful and comfortably off cookery writer to being a phenomenally rich and powerful businesswoman with swish London offices and a chauffeur-driven Jag. She had a full-time housekeeper to look after her home and a gardener ensured that her gardens were kept to National Trust standards. She and Michael had also splashed out on a two-bedroom river-side flat in London's exclusive Docklands with the proceeds from the *Summer Collection*. These were hardly the trappings of the average housewife.

Much of her new-found success was down to her association with Sainsbury's, which had by then turned into a very prof-itable liaison indeed. The supermarket had shown interest in the concept of producing a Sainsbury's magazine and discussed it at length with Delia, their food consultant. Michael had recently been made redundant when *Lloyd's Log*, the magazine he edited, had folded and Delia wanted him to be involved. She was confident he had the talent and vision to produce a fantas-tic magazine for the store.

But in the event the magazine would be launched without any money from Sainsbury's. In 1992 Delia and Michael formed their own publishing company, New Crane Publishing

Limited, on London's South Bank, and amid much secrecy began plans to produce a glossy, upmarket monthly food journal. Their friend Norman Hollands was involved in the project from an early stage. 'When Michael was made redundant he told me he and Delia had something in the pipeline,' Norman recalls. 'About six months later they started the magazine and asked me to do some stuff for the dummy. It was absolutely stunning. What the financial arrangements are I do not know, but the initial idea was not to carry any advertisements for Sainsbury's. It was not to be a direct puff for Sainsbury's at all.'

The company was started with £250,000, all of which was raised by Delia and Michael. They invested £156,250 of their own money and their good friends David and Debbie Owen put in £25,000. Peter Knab, the photographer whose pictures featured in the *Summer Collection* and *Winter Collection* books, invested £25,000 and other friends of the couple put up the remaining money.

It was to be a shrewd investment for all concerned. Launched the following year, in May 1993, with Michael as editor and one Delia Smith as consultant food editor, *Sainsbury's The Magazine* was an instant success. Although Michael was the editor, the magazine was built around Delia and her name featured on every front cover. Widely regarded to be one of the best food picture stylists in Europe, Delia personally oversaw the food photography and worked at the magazine four days a week. 'I don't like it when photographers want to play around with dappled lights and filters,' she says. 'I think food is, actually, very beautiful in itself.'

The publication was sold throughout Sainsbury's stores and by only its second year of trading the company was already generating a turnover of more than £6 million. Sainsbury's reportedly pays a percentage of the £1 cover price to New

Crane, which covers the production costs and keeps the advertising revenue.

In 1994 *Sainsbury's The Magazine* won four prizes, including the top foodie accolade, a Glenfiddich, for best food magazine of the year. By October 1995 it had a monthly circulation of 300,000 and within four years of its launch it boasted a circulation of 416,000 and a readership of 2.9 million. The benefit to Sainsbury's was equally impressive: when Delia illustrated a recipe in the magazine with a photograph of a saucepan of shallots, sales of the small onions soared by 2000 per cent.

Right from the start, Delia and Michael did things differently. Journalist Fiona Knight, who was commissioned to write the cover story for the all-important first issue, recalls the somewhat unusual manner in which her copy was delivered to the magazine. 'It was an interview with the actress Catherine Zeta Jones, who was to be featured on the front cover,' she says. 'Instead of me faxing the feature across when I'd finished writing it, Michael Wynn Jones said he would send someone to collect it. I was expecting a courier bike but was surprised to see his chauffeur-driven Jaguar turn up outside my office. The feature was ferried over to New Crane Wharf on leather seats.'

In 1997 turnover had reached £15 million and all the shareholders drew substantial dividends from the company. The highest-paid director, who was almost certainly Michael Wynn Jones, got £166,250 – probably his salary for editing the magazine. £550,000 was paid in dividends and Delia and her husband each pocketed £171,875. As well as being a director of New Crane Publishing, Delia is paid by the company for the work she does for *Sainsbury's The Magazine*. The last filed company accounts show that in 1997 she personally billed New Crane for £125,000 for her consultancy services. As a husband-and-wife team it would appear that in 1997 they earned in excess of £700,000 before tax, just from the magazine.

As directors with 10 per cent of the shares, David Owen and his wife received £55,000 after tax. Peter Knab also received £55,000, plus £76,595 for the photographic work he had done for the magazine. It was, as Del Boy would say, a 'nice little earner'. By anybody's standards the company had grown spectacularly quickly. 'It's a little bit unusual,' admits Bernie Hoffman, a partner in leading London accountancy firm Edelmans. 'For a company to start from scratch and go to £15 million in three years is a hell of a jump.'

But while Delia and her friends were feeling pleased with their little investment, not everyone was happy. Critics claimed that her tie-in with Sainsbury's was too cosy and the number of pages allocated to her in each issue led to it being dubbed 'The Official Delia Smith Fanzine'. She vehemently denies that there is any deal to advertise its produce but the relationship has become symbiotic and it is hard to disengage the two. It has also been pointed out that her best-selling *Winter Collection* was a BBC book, but included a list of Sainsbury's stores in the back.

The fact that Delia is able to enjoy such a close relationship with Sainsbury's when her books and television series are produced by the BBC is something that has astounded her peers. As a presenter on the BBC2 consumer show *Food and Drink*, Antony Worrall Thompson is forbidden from doing lucrative advertising work. But the BBC doesn't appear to mind the fact that Delia is closely affiliated to a major supermarket.

'Obviously there's a bit of incest there with the Sainsbury's magazine being run by her husband,' remarks Worrall Thompson. 'But if someone's not slapping her down, if the BBC are endorsing it when they are very strict with myself and others, then good luck to her. I'm not allowed to endorse any products because *Food and Drink* is a consumer programme. Gary [Rhodes] is allowed to do his frozen food because his isn't a consumer programme. Delia's isn't current affairs either: that's where the BBC clamps down.

'She's either brilliant or she's naïvely lucky, but I would have thought she's a brilliant businesswoman. And they treat her like an innocent – a total angel. To me she's a brilliant marketing lady, whether it's intentional or not it's fact. But I'm sure there's a huge amount of intention there.'

The BBC would not wish to risk losing Delia by interfering in her private business. It considers her to be one of its most treasured assets and during her twenty-seven-year television career she has stayed the course while other 'celebrity' chefs have been and gone. 'Delia is very important for us, and she's very important for BBC2,' says Suzanna Zsohar of BBC Books. 'The BBC, as a corporation, very much regards her as the jewel in its crown. We are all very seriously committed to her.'

Delia has tried to divert some of the flak by insisting that – shock horror – she actually shops at Marks and Spencer, but the disconcertion rumbles on. Delia has been accused of selling her soul to one supermarket and criticized for assisting the demise of small independent shops by promoting a chain of superstores. 'She regularly tells her viewers (more than 4 million for one episode) that an ingredient "is available at the supermarket" and we all know which one she means,' wrote the *Independent on Sunday*. 'Small specialist shops such as butchers, delis, organic veg suppliers and cheese shops need supermarkets like Delia needs cookery lessons … It is a shame that someone as influential as Delia, with her self-professed spiritual approach, seems so devoted to patronizing the multiples. A word from her about seeking out a superb butcher when choosing the Sunday roast would give a much needed lift to the struggling small shops.'

In both the *Summer Collection* and *Winter Collection* books, she applauds the variety of fresh fish available in supermarkets, whilst bemoaning the decline in high-street fishmongers. There is no advice to seek out a reputable fishmonger or to find a good butcher. But it was not always thus. In her 1974 *Evening Standard Cook Book*, Delia stressed the importance of finding a good butcher and chastised people who shopped in the supermarket. 'An absolute essential for any successful meat dish is a sympathetic butcher,' she wrote. 'So many people are fickle in their custom, just wandering into the nearest shop or buying meat pre-packed in a supermarket (a much more expensive method). I couldn't survive in my job without my butcher.' And she added, 'The best-flavoured chicken is undoubtedly the one bought from the family butcher.'

'It can certainly be said that by being tied in with Sainsbury's she is helping to stamp out the corner shop,' says David Benady, deputy editor of *Marketing Week* magazine. 'When Sainsbury's open superstores small shops close down. People have that criticism against the superstores but does it mean that anyone who works for those superstores is guilty of the same thing? I suppose that by association they are.'

One of Delia's former employees accused her of being too trusting. 'Sainsbury's obviously see her as an advertisement, but Delia sees it the other way round, which may be a bit naïve,' they were quoted as saying. 'She thinks she can introduce people to something and get it made available nationally at the same time.'

Sainsbury's does now appear to stock every ingredient under the sun and there can be no denying Delia's influence in this. Michael Wynn Jones says their relationship with the store is a 'two-way process' – sometimes he and Delia tell the store what to stock; sometimes the store tells them what to write about. 'Delia championed pancetta,' he explains. 'And although Sainsbury's stocked it, they did so in rather limited areas. But she uses it in quite a lot of recipes. Now Sainsbury's stocks pancetta in all forms – not just sliced – and has extended its distribution.'

Her husband counters criticism by saying that Delia has never endorsed products, or indeed the supermarket, and that she is very forthright with Sainsbury's about what it stocks. At times the flak appeared to be getting to Delia. In an interview with the *Daily Telegraph* in September 1995 she reacted fiercely to the suggestion that she had sold herself to the company. 'No way. You wouldn't believe the trouble I have with Sainsbury's getting them to stock things I want to put in my recipes,' she protested. 'They are incredibly stuffy and old-fashioned. Quite honestly I don't know how much longer I want to go on doing this.'

Sainsbury's, it must be assumed, managed to persuade her to carry on. 'From Sainsbury's point of view it is important to have someone like her on board because they're trying to point their customers in the direction of more high-margin products like fresh food, rather than tins of beans or frozen beefburgers,' explains David Benady. 'They make more money out of selling fresh fruit and veg and expensive ingredients like fancy olive oil. If you get someone who can speak to people on their level, in terms of cooking, it can act as a key to getting people to trade up to those more high-margin products. Having said that, it doesn't seem to have helped them that much as they have been doing fairly badly recently. Or maybe they're doing less badly than they would if they didn't have somebody like Delia on board.

'They have been lagging behind Tesco for a number of years now. About five years ago they had that campaign 'Everybody's Favourite Ingredient' and I think the problem with that was that it appealed to more upmarket people: people who had quite a knowledge of cooking and were confident enough to go out and buy those more expensive ingredients. Part of Sainsbury's problem is that it is seen as a place where rich people go. It is deemed to be more expensive than Tesco, which of course it is, so what they are now trying to do is reposition it as being better value.

'Sainsbury's has struggled with its own identity because it wants to attract higher-income customers but it also wants to attract lower-income customers. So how can you have a brand which is suitable for both rich people and poorer people? It's a bit of a marketing problem really. They are trying to have a foot in both camps. I think maybe having Delia Smith is part of that plan because she is not one of those upmarket cookery writers like Jane Asher, whom they used previously. That helps them to promote the idea that they are better value and not just there for upmarket people who maybe know a lot about cooking, but for general plebs like us.

'People are buying more olive oil, etc. I don't know if that is because of Delia, but I would imagine that it is. There are people who watch television and go out and do what they're told; people who see an ad for a new product on television and go out and buy it simply because it's new. In a culture like ours, where there isn't a strong traditional culinary base like there is in France, we are used to eating very simple stuff like egg and chips. I think we are probably quite responsive to being encouraged, told, and bossed, into trying out new things. Twenty years ago, who ate spaghetti?'

For Delia, one of the perks about owning her own magazine was that it gave her licence to travel – and get paid to do so. 'One of the best things about the magazine is that I can do something I've been wanting to for ages – ingredient stories,' she said when the first issue was launched. 'I've just come back from doing anchovies – a brilliant story – and this afternoon I'm going off to do crème fraîche.' Nice work if you can get it: one 'fact-finding' mission involved a trip to Mauritius to write about sugar, and there have been numerous pilgrimages to Italy with friends.

'I've been to Italy with Delia and Michael a couple of times,' says their pal Alberto Camisa, an importer of upmarket Italian foodstuffs. 'I go several times a year and because I know all the little outlets and producers, and where you can still get whole-some old-fashioned food. Delia picks my brain from time to time. We flew out for a couple of days last year to meet Martelli, who is the only importer of a particular kind of pasta. I've got to know Martelli pretty well over the years and Delia wanted to meet him so basically I put the two of them together.

'We also went to Parma for the *How to Cook* book and TV series. I took Delia to see the rice people and the olive people. It's fun, but it is hard work at the same time. It was a rush from one place to another, we could hardly keep up. The places we were visiting were scattered around Italy and sometimes the transport between them was a bit like being driven by a rally driver! We are basically two friends swapping information and pooling knowledge. She makes use of it one way and I make use of it another. It's all tied in. Delia and Michael obviously have the Sainsbury's magazine, Sainsbury's are always on the look out for nice things, and we supply Sainsbury's with about twenty lines for their Special Selection.'

Delia is generous to her friends, helping their careers when-ever she can. She was instrumental in launching the book-writ-ing and television career of her friend, the Carmelite nun and art critic Sister Wendy Beckett, and she has ensured that her friends benefit from her success wherever possible. *Sainsbury's The Magazine* is staffed almost solely by Delia's and Michael's friends. The editorial consultant is Mike Molloy, who gave Delia her first job on the *Mirror* magazine, and the publishing director is their friend Sue Phipps, who is also a director of the company. Delia's helpers Mary Cox and Celia Stone were also given jobs on the magazine and chefs Nigel Slater and Ruth Watson – two more of Delia's chums – are contributing editors. Norman Hollands is frequently commissioned to take photographs and her old friends, chefs John Tovey, Simon Hopkinson and Ken Toye, provide recipes.

As food editor, Delia has exhibited the same perfectionism that she applies to her books and television work. John Tovey, who used to own the famous Lake District restaurant Miller Howe, reports that she frequently sends back his copy for revision, and that she can be equally demanding as a friend. 'She wants nothing but perfection,' he says. 'But she also offers great support.' Michael Wynn Jones admits that all the recipes used in the magazine, even those from a leading chef like Simon Hopkinson, are tested three times by Delia's team before publication.

Some might consider this somewhat insulting. After all, these people are trained chefs who cook for a living, day in, day out. 'I gave Delia a recipe for bouillabaisse and Mike rang me up and said, "Can you just run through how you cook that," recounts Ken Toye. 'Then he apologized and said, "Of course we should be able to rely on you, shouldn't we, but we do check everything." So they checked on me. I felt fine about it. It's part of our job, we're professionals and you don't worry about people checking on you.'

Antony Worrall Thompson agrees: 'When I do recipes for magazines I get tested. It's quite interesting and a lot of chefs' recipes don't work when they are tested domestically. They probably do work but they're not being interpreted properly. I don't think it's insulting to check another chef's recipes, I think it's vital because a lot of them just convert them from bigger recipes. I would love to be able to afford a full-time tester like Delia can. It's good for the customer because they know the recipes are going to work.'

The success of *Sainsbury's The Magazine* marked a turning point in the way Delia was viewed by her peers. Those who had sneered at her in the past now realized an important new fact: *she could give them work*. Food writing is a small world and in her new role as food editor and owner of one of the best-selling food mags, Delia was not only the most popular cook in Britain, she was also the most powerful. Through the magazine she could give a platform to a host of respected writers – but only if she wanted to.

Simon Hopkinson and Nigel Slater, two of the chefs she uses the most in the journal, each declined to be interviewed for this book. But Slater, himself now a successful TV cook, is on record singing the praises of his sometime employer. 'She's an absolute sweetie and very generous,' he gushed. 'She's a great influence for good. She has got people attempting things they almost certainly wouldn't have done otherwise. They'll have a go for Delia because they trust her absolutely.'

When Sainsbury's expressed interest in Delia doing a series of cookery roadshows for them, she roped in John Tovey to accompany her. This solved her age-old dilemma of how to get out of doing live demonstrations, and had the added bonus of enabling her to spend time with one of her very best friends. Some thought it just as well. 'Delia is not much of an entertainer and even her most ardent admirers would hesitate to call her a wit,' said the *Daily Telegraph*. 'Three hours of unrelieved Delia might have been something of a strain.'

In November 1995 the pair took to the road on a two-week tour across England and Northern Ireland. Every show was a sell-out and by the end of the fortnight 6000 people had paid £12.50 for their tickets. The profits went to the Macmillan Cancer Fund. While the flamboyant Tovey whipped up treats such as twice-cooked vegetables and veal escalopes with caramelized apple wedges, Delia contented herself with a forty-minute question-and-answer session at the end of the evening. There was heavy product placement taking place on stage, with instructions not to 'forget to use Sainsbury's luxury mincemeat' and reminders that the canapés served during the interview were 'available in store now'.

During the question-and-answer session Delia apparently appeared awkward and ill at ease. And when a journalist asked her if she gets paid for promoting Sainsbury's products, her mood quickly changed. John Tovey was said to intervene by shouting 'Delia is a heroine to Sainsbury's!' but the question had clearly caught her off guard. 'Um. I work as a behind-the-scenes consultant to Sainsbury's, so I get paid for my behind-the-scenes consultancy,' she said. 'I have been working in this game for twenty-five years and I'm very pleased to say that I've never done any advertising for anyone in my career.'

Pressed, she added somewhat confusingly, 'All this talk about my multi-millions! Sometimes I sit on the train and think, well, what would I spend that money on if I really did have all that money, and I can promise you that if I did advertising then I certainly wouldn't be a multi-millionaire.' After the question-and-answer session the reporter asked her if she thought the public was confused about her role with Sainsbury's. 'There is no problem because the problem does not exist,' she reportedly replied, and then told the journalist, 'I think you should go away. I wish you goodnight.'

Delia is happier talking about her favourite charity, Zapallal: Sharing the Struggle. In recent years *Sainsbury's The Magazine* has donated more than £45,000 – and helped to raise £200,000 – to support a school for impoverished children in Peru. But what Delia has failed to mention is the fact that each year she secretly donates the whole of her salary as food editor of the magazine to the charity. In 1997 alone this amounted to £125,000.

She became involved in the project when she travelled to

Zapallal, a shanty town on the outskirts of Lima, in May 1996. She says it was a pilgrimage that changed her life and describes it as 'a journey that perhaps unknowingly I have been gravitating towards all my life'.

She and Michael were the guests of Paul McAuley, a Catholic lay brother and teacher whom she met more than twenty years ago. He set up the Zapallal School of Faith and Joy in 1992 and within six years the small community had become self-sufficient. In an area where rainfall is scarce, the people of Zapallal have, with Brother Paul's guidance, created a thriving 'Garden of Eden' where a variety of crops are grown. Housed in the school the townspeople built, the Zapallal programme has won two environmental awards. Delia says that progress is hampered only by lack of finance.

'The project is housed in a long enclosure – a remarkable patchwork of awnings, screens and straw partitions which from the outside gives no hint of the mini Garden of Eden inside,' wrote Delia in *Sainsbury's The Magazine*. 'It is a landscape of flowers, herbs, vegetables and shrubs that could be a million miles, not just a few miles, from the parched desert. It is based on the simple science of hydroponics – growing plants without soil, in this case in solutions of water and fertilizer. Considerable ingenuity has been spent on creating containers that allow the plants to dip their roots in the solution: crisp lettuces peek out of drainpipes, beets paddle in plastic trays and strawberries spread their leaves over troughs of bin liners, all cunningly balanced to recycle the water. All this is a triumph of determination. We have to keep reminding ourselves of the hardships of just surviving in the desert, never mind growing anything.'

Each month Delia and Michael devote a page of their magazine to give readers updates of progress in the town. 'Obviously what is needed first is, as always, resources, wrote Delia in one article. 'But we also hope the benefits will not just flow one way. By sharing the problems, by becoming involved, we can perhaps rediscover some of the values which inevitably get obscured by the material pressures of our life here.' The charity receives small donations from readers of the magazine, but Paul McAuley says it is the money that Delia herself donates that makes the real difference. 'The bulk of the help, the only real help we get on a permanent basis, is the help we get from Delia,' he says. 'If Delia didn't help us we would have to close up tomorrow.

'Thanks to her we now have a women's centre, a craft centre, a sewing workshop, and a wonderful ceramics workshop that makes pottery sold through Harrods. We are trying to do any kind of productive work that will bring in some income for local families. We have to combine an attack on poverty, youth unemployment, delinquency, and violence in the family, most of which is tied into income. If people have a dignified way of earning a living then we don't get many of the other problems.

'We've just had a postal service installed and it's housed in a little bookshop called Libreria Delia. Because people have got to know about us it means that we have got things like electricity quicker than we would have done. The next step is to get water connected, which is a priority. Zapallel is continually expanding. People can no longer afford to live in the centre of Lima so they come out to find any free land that's available and just invade. They put up their four little walls made out of straw and set up home. The whole of the outskirts of Lima is like an extended, growing refugee camp. There are now sixty thousand people living here; when Delia came out it was a little village with two thousand inhabitants.'

Brother Paul, who was awarded the MBE in 1998 for his charity work, tells how Delia personally intervened to help an ill Peruvian man who was struggling to look after his family. She wrote her friend a letter, telling him how the man was suffering from TB and his wife had left him with three children to support. 'Delia asked me to give him a job and he now works on the maintenance of the school,' he explains. And he promises that when Delia revisits Zapallel she will notice a huge improvement in the way people live. 'When she comes back she's going to get a lot of satisfaction seeing what she's done,' he says. 'She has made an enormous difference.'

11

Deals FC

If Delia Smith the business mogul is an unfamiliar concept to her fans, then Delia Smith the football club boss is an equally unlikely one. Both are intriguingly at odds with her mumsy image, but of the two, it is her position as director of Norwich City Football Club that is perhaps the most unusual.

Her love of football is something that many of her readers were not aware of until recently, yet it is a passion that means infinitely more to her than cookery. Fanatical fans of Norwich City, Delia and her husband have been season-ticket holders at the club's Carrow Road ground for more than a quarter of a century and have seldom missed a game. If the Canaries lose a match, Mr and Mrs Wynn Jones console themselves with fish and chips from their favourite chip shop on the way home. It matters not that the proprietor supports their arch rivals. 'Although he's an Ipswich supporter, he cooks the best fish in the world, fresh from the coast and always cooked to order,' Delia praises, perhaps mindful of the time when she herself supported Ipswich at the 1978 FA Cup Final.

Like many football fans, Delia and Michael haven't always approved of the way their club was being run, particularly when

Norwich City was relegated from the Premiership. But, unlike other fans, they had the financial muscle to be able to do something about it. When it became known that the club wanted new board members following the resignation of chairman Robert Chase, Delia and Michael became directors. They took their seats on the board in November 1996 and were reported to have paid off £1 million of the club's £7 million debts.

Becoming a director of a top football club was obviously going to make heavy demands on her already hectic work schedule, but it was something Delia really wanted to do. 'It won't be a major problem for me finding the time,' she insisted. 'It never is when you have a lot of passion and enthusiasm for something. But what it does mean is that one or two other things may have to go to make time for football. So I'm currently reviewing all the other things I do, and all this new work may replace some of them.'

Many saw Delia's appointment as no more than a sign that Norwich City was keen to improve its catering. Newcastle United's restaurant had just been included in the *Which? Good Food Guide*, highlighting the new trend for stadium food to move upmarket. At Manchester United's ground, Old Trafford, an international video theme restaurant had been opened, serving such exotic fare as paella, Cajun chicken, julienne of vegetables, and deep-fried pearls of mozzarella with a gooseberry and nectarine compote.

'Football clubs have rested on their laurels in the past, thinking they didn't need to make an effort because the fans would come anyway,' explains Lesley Williamson, food and beverage manager at Middlesbrough FC. 'But in no other leisure industry would you expect to put up with lukewarm Bovril and a cold pie.'

Norwich's 22,000-capacity stadium had a carvery to serve 300 and an executive restaurant to serve 200, but Delia admitted the state of catering at the ground was among the 'worst in Britain.'

The news that the nation's favourite cook was now on board was greeted with pleasure by many of the club's fans, who were no doubt anticipating feasting on some of the delights from her own recipe books.

Delia was indeed interested in improving the food at the stadium – one of the first things she did was sack the caterers – but to think that was her only agenda was to seriously misjudge her. For, as with everything else in her life, she was determined to make a go of her new appointment. 'I'm taking the work of a director very seriously,' she warned. 'I certainly won't be acting as some sort of cheerleader for the club. I'm very excited. It is every supporter's dream to have a say in the running of the team.'

She did her homework thoroughly. In true Delia style, she even visited former England manager Bobby Robson and ex-Blackburn Rovers manager Roy Hodgson to ask their advice, committing their every word to her tape recorder. 'I don't remember everything,' she explains. 'So I tape it and listen to it.' She spent an entire week at the club, looking at how it operated and making sure she had everything at her fingertips. For if she was going to be a director of the club it had better be a success. And not just successful within Britain: she has a 'burning desire' that the team should be the best in the world. But to do this, Delia and Michael first had to gain control of the club.

Joe Ferrari, assistant sports editor on the *Norwich Evening News*, explains how the odds were stacked in their favour right from the start. He says: 'Delia and Michael were received very well. They came in after Robert Chase, who was very unpopular indeed. We got relegated from the Premiership in 1995 under his splendid guidance. He left in May 1996 after protests and near riots calling for him to go, and having virtually bankrupted the club. So really Delia would have had to be pretty bad not to have been received well.

'But having said that, she is the sort of person who appeals to Norfolk people in that she's fairly homespun and straight-talking. She has a reputation for being a successful businesswoman and her husband is very successful too, albeit in a rather quieter, lower profile way. There is no doubt that they are fully committed to the club. They are both fans and I think that's one of many things that sets them apart from Mr Chase. You get the feeling that when Norwich lose it hurts them and when they win they're cracking open the bubbly.

'I have sat next to them in the Directors box, where the form is to clap politely no matter who scores. But Delia and Michael jump up and down, sing songs and generally behave like fans, which is very refreshing. There is definitely a feeling that, while they are quite unusual and not obvious football people, they do have good ideas about how to make money for the club and make a success of it. There was an interim period where there was a lot of speculation about who was going to take over, but they won the power struggle.'

At the end of 1997 Delia and Michael forked out a reported £700,000 to buy 42% of the club's shares, making them joint majority shareholders. By 2002 they had upped their stake in the club to 58%, making them more powerful than their predecessor. 'A lot of people used to say it was terrible with Robert Chase because he had too many shares and too much power for one man,' explains Joe Ferrari. 'Delia and Michael came in sympathising with those noises but they now have more shares and more power than he ever had.'

This was something that worried some of the club's supporters. 'We feel this could be a major problem,' admitted Roy Blower, chairman of Norwich Independent Supporters' Association. 'I have always thought it is dangerous for one person – or in this case two people – to have overall control. Any move they want to make, they could carry through.'

But Delia was ecstatic. 'It is extremely exciting and gives us an awful lot of pleasure,' she said after securing her shares. 'We are supporters and season ticket-holders and in the past year we have had a chance to see what happens behind the scenes. If you showed me a profit and balance sheet I wouldn't know which way up to hold it, but I have other gifts. I think everyone wants to give the talents they have. It is very nice when you reach middle-age and you can go in another direction.'

The club manager, Mike Walker, expressed delight at the news. 'It is a very pleasant surprise and stabilises the club,' he said. 'They have been successful in business and if they want to bring that success to the football club, it's got to be brilliant.' The Wynn Joneses said they had no interest in ousting the club's chairman Barry Lockwood. 'We are not going to go in with all guns blazing, and nothing like that is on the agenda,' Michael promised.

But within months both Walker and Lockwood were gone. Delia and Michael brought in their own man Bob Cooper, former head of trading at Sainsbury's, to be the new chairman. 'I think the official reason that Lockwood stood down was that he felt there was someone else who could add new impetus to the club, and that he wasn't leaving the club and there was no ill feeling,' says Joe Ferrari. 'But reading between the lines, Lockwood was very much behind the scenes, whereas I think they hope Bob Cooper will take a much more pro-active, dynamic role in the management of the club. They were obviously impressed with his business acumen at Sainsbury's and it is very much the case in football that people want their own people around them at every level.

'Mike Walker's contract was terminated by mutual consent, but I doubt very much that he walked in there and said, "I'd like to leave". He had two spells at the club and in the first spell the club did really well, and he'll never be forgotten for that. But in his second spell the club wasn't by any means as successful and he had more than his fair share of critics during the last few months of his reign.'

Delia admits that getting rid of Walker was not an easy decision. 'We went through terrible agonies,' she says. 'But in the end the consensus was that the team weren't playing for him. We had a lot of flak but I think it was the right thing to do. The newspapers are telling us that the fans are not in broad agreement but that's not our experience. On the way into Reading last weekend, a couple of fans shouted, "Well done Delia". At the end of the day you've got to take a chance on your instincts. And it's a tremendous responsibility. The hopes, the joy of so many people depend on it. And I want so much to serve them. It's frightening. All I can say is, we will do everything we can.'

She had set her sights on a return to the Premier League within three years and in securing former Arsenal manager Bruce Rioch as Walker's replacement, she was deemed to have done well for Norwich City. 'Rioch is a much more high profile character within the game nationally,' explains Joe Ferrari. 'He also managed Bolton and as a player he was a Scotland International. As a football figure he is probably one of the most high profile managers Norwich ever appointed. He was a very big catch.'

Having pleased the fans and the players by getting them Bruce Rioch, Delia set about winning over the players' wives. As the first female director in the club's history, she was only too aware that she had to operate in a traditionally male-dominated industry. She also realised that many people might assume that her talents were confined to cooking and baking and would fail to take her seriously as a football boss. But the way she handled this conundrum showed a touch of pure genuis.

Six weeks after she and Michael became directors, she hired a pub outside Norwich and threw an enormous party. 'We invited everybody – the senior staff, the players and their wives, the coaches, the directors and the directors' wives – and we had a knees-up,' she explains. 'The manager didn't think we had a cat-in-hell's chance of making it work, until we invited the wives. They were bowled over by that, because the wives never get invited to anything.'

It was good psychology. Once the players' wives and girl-friends had met Britain's favourite cook and been subjected to her full charm offensive, they all thought she was the bees knees – a Good Egg. And with the women singing Delia's praises to their menfolk, she had all but won the battle. 'The women tend to be perceived by the public, with some justification, as pretty young models; glamorous types who are happy to sit in their nice £200,000 houses on the outskirts of Norwich, cooking and raising kids while their bloke goes off and plays football every Saturday,' says Joe Ferrari. 'Delia dragged them out of their obscurity and thrust them into the limelight. That went down well with the women, and consequently with the players as well, and was pretty much a masterstroke.

'They've even got a nickname for her: they call her Deals. You know you've made it in football when you go from being Ms Smith to Deals. It means you're part of the in-crowd in the changing rooms. Certainly Mr Chase wouldn't have been Bob to the players, he'd have been Mr Chase.'

It is precisely this knack for putting people at their ease, says her friend Paul McAuley, that is Delia's greatest asset. 'In terms of human relationships with the players and their families – giving them a caring environment – Delia's got talent, the right touch,' he explains. 'She's very keen on motivating the club and her spiritual power has an excellent outlet in a football club. I think she realises that she's got to start working at that side of football. It's a long-term thing, but it's an exciting area. She is not for doing things by half. She's taken the club on and now she's going to put all her energies into making sure that it works.'

Delia is keen to make the game more female-friendly. 'I feel football lacks a bit of the feminine touch,' she says, rather absurdly stating the obvious. 'I read recently that one in six fans now are women, so hopefully I will encourage even more to come along to matches. I think a lot of women just tend to dismiss football without ever going along to a game and experiencing the atmosphere for themselves. I would love to see more women attending games. Supporting a team at a live match is completely different from watching it on television as a neutral. At the game you get very involved.'

She displays the same passionate commitment to the sport that she has shown for religion. 'Football has so much to offer,' she insists. 'It brings all that is best in the human spirit to the surface and creates a real sense of community among the supporters. It helps to bring back the old-fashioned feeling of belonging which is so often lacking in modern life.'

Within a month of taking over, Delia pronounced herself happy with the way things were shaping up at Norwich City. 'It has been wonderful the way things have changed at Carrow Road this season,' she said triumphantly. 'Before, I was just like all the other supporters, watching sadly as player after player was sold. Like everyone else I would get very distressed and upset. The standard of football also went down, but now no more players are being allowed to leave, and this season we are playing lovely football again. Just like it used to be.'

And in the summer of 1999, by and large the fans were happy too. 'The club has turned around,' admits Joe Ferrari. 'It was seven or eight million pounds in debt and that figure has been at least halved, although it's quite difficult to forecast with any accuracy because they are quite tight-lipped about the figures. But certainly the club is no longer losing money and is breaking even, if not making a small profit. They're not having to sell all their stars, which was Norwich's big problem for 10–15 years.

They've got two players on the books who are worth £5 million each and under previous regimes they would have been long gone.

'Delia and Michael have done a lot of work in that respect. They loaned the club half a million quid when they took over and they would have had to pay a substantial sum for their shares, probably just over a million pounds. Whether they have loaned any subsequently, I don't know; the only loan they went public on was when they first came in. They made quite a big noise about it at the time, saying, "Look, we're putting this money up front now". They have also attracted sponsors to the club and Delia was probably instrumental in that because she is a high profile, charismatic figure.'

But as Delia has discovered in her career as a cookery writer, she will always have her detractors. 'Delia is doing a lot of good but unfortunately for her – and she'll find this out if she hasn't already – the people who pay your wages, i.e. the fans, judge you purely on what you do on the pitch,' Ferrari explains. 'She has one or two harsh critics. When she was revealed as one of the richest women in the country, some people expected her to pay for players out of her own pocket. They said that if you are going to buy a football club and you need two players at a cost of a million pounds each, and you've got £14 million in the bank, can't you at least buy one of them yourself? But I have to say the critics are in the minority. People tend to focus on the manager and what he's doing right or wrong, rather than what people in Delia's position are doing.'

Delia's biggest – and most public mistake – at the club was to decide, off her own bat, to change the players' kit. For 26 years Norwich City had played in green shorts and canary yellow tops, hence their nickname, but Delia fancied a change. 'We decided it was time to smarten our players up,' she said bossily. 'All the other kits looked baggy, scruffy and out of date, so it was time for a change.' She commissioned the famous designer Bruce Oldfield to come up with a new-look kit, but ended up with egg on her face.

'Although Delia said she didn't want to change anything when she took over, she did change one or two things fairly drastically and pretty much unilaterally without consulting too many people,' says Joe Ferrari. 'She decided to launch a new kit, which is fairly standard in football every two years for merchandising purposes, but I'm not aware of any other club that has had a top fashion designer design their kit. It was launched amid great fanfare in London and got us some great publicity which the club had been starved of for years.'

But the replacement all-yellow kit was universally unpopular. Football supporters care deeply about such things and it caused a furore amongst the Canaries' fans. 'The colour has been described as mustard yellow and there was some rather unkind speculation that it was tied in with us being sponsored by Colman's, the mustard company,' explains Ferrari. 'It does seem a bit of a coincidence. Sponsorship by any high profile company is good for the club and Colman's is quite a high profile company to secure as sponsors. I don't think anyone was saying, "We don't want that mustard company sponsoring us", it was just that it seemed suspicious.

'We're a fairly traditional bunch in Norfolk at the best of times and when our newspaper, *The Pink'Un*, ran a campaign saying "Stand up if you want green shorts" we had 930 letters and e-mails from around the world. We got the club to agree to a vote and at the Bristol City game on December 19th 1998 everyone was given cards with green on one side and yellow on the other. Delia bravely stood up and brandished her yellow card in the middle of the noisiest section of the crowd, but she was swamped by green. It was 90 per cent in favour of green. She took it in good spirit, she's very sporting.'

Delia had failed to anticipate the fuss she would cause. 'Nobody understands me,' she complained. 'Men just don't get it, but if you are a woman you have an eye for these things. Football strips are unbelievably tacky and it's very satisfying for me to see we have this beautiful, well-cut strip. I didn't realise the colour was so important to so many fans. I'm happy to concede that green shorts should come back.'

Challenging Delia was not something that was taken lightly, even by the local newspaper. 'She doesn't like to be crossed and I was a bit wary when we decided to take her on about the green shorts,' admits Joe Ferrari. 'But if you go about things in the right way with her; if you make it clear what you're doing from day one and don't do anything that she perceives to be underhand or unsporting then you'll be OK. She's not a megalomaniac – she just happens to be very successful. And who amongst us wouldn't believe our own hype if we'd raised millions of pounds from scratch through our own good sense and hard work? She also hates it when newspapers use cookery puns when they're writing about the club: "Delia's cooking up a storm" – that sort of thing. It drives her mad.'

Other Delia alterations have also proved controversial. 'Some of the changes she has made are quite jazzy and we are certainly getting quite a lot of feedback in our paper,' says Ferrari. 'They now have what they call "Match Day Entertainment", with circus entertainers, dancing girls and various mascots tumbling around on the pitch and incredibly loud speakers playing pumping house music whenever there's a corner. It's all part of Delia trying to make it a more entertaining place to go with your families, but the traditionalists feel it detracts from the match.'

Delia admits she has come in for the odd insulting comment from fans. 'People do shout rude things to me sometimes, but on the whole I've had a lot of personal support,' she says. Being the nation's most popular and best-selling cook gives her a certain

211

amount of authority, and she adds: 'I mean, the fans are sitting there cheering on the team and they've all been brought up on my recipes.'

One City fan who has met Delia and Michael many times at the Carrow Road ground says they are like chalk and cheese. 'They are very different people and if you didn't know them you wouldn't put them together as a couple,' he reveals. 'Delia is very bubbly and everybody who walks into the Directors' lounge is greeted with a hug and a smile and a comment that is pertaining directly to them. She is very good at winning people over straight away. She comes across very much like she does on telly: like a down-to-earth, good-humoured, easy-going type but with a no-nonsense "make sure you melt your butter at exactly this point" streak.

'Michael Wynn Jones, on the other hand, is a very quiet man and when he talks he means business; he doesn't engage in frivolous conversation. He takes a back seat and is happy for Delia to swan around. While everyone comes over to mill around her and ask for her autograph he sits in the background. He's a bit like Denis Thatcher, but to be fair to Michael, he's a dynamic figure in his own right. He's not bothered with the limelight; he's a bit more sensible. But in terms of who has the influence in the club's affairs they are at least equal.'

True to her word, Delia doesn't appear to have any trouble combining her two careers. 'Football and cookery are the two most important subjects in the country,' she says. Within a year of taking over at Norwich she had introduced the players to high-carbohydrate, low-fat breakfasts and set about improving catering at the ground. But no doubt it came as a disappointment to her fans to discover that she wouldn't personally be donning a pinny.

'I am sure people will be expecting me to run the catering at Carrow Road,' she acknowledged. 'I will obviously be taking an interest, and it would be lovely to use my expertise to bring about some improvements in that area. We could perhaps have a new restaurant or wine bar. But I will have to find out a lot more about the club first before I can start thinking of any changes like that. We are going to do something new in catering. It will be at every level including kiosks. And we are going to have a restaurant as good as any in England. After all, if Newcastle can get in the *Good Food Guide*, so can Norwich City!'

But her credibility was dealt an embarrassing blow when the club failed to get a result in a national soccer-pie survey. Naturally enough, it was a humiliation newspapers were all too happy to capitalise on. 'Oh dear, Delia! Canary pies get the bird', was one headline. There were more red faces when *Total Football*, the magazine that had held the survey, launched an investigation into alleged vote-rigging after receiving dozens of votes for the Carrow Road pies – all in the same hand-writing.

For 12 years catering at the club had been franchised out to South Norfolk Caterers, run by Mervyn Philpott. But Delia sacked them and brought in Food East, the company run by her friends Ruth and David Watson. 'I was very unhappy with what was happening,' Delia says. 'It was British catering at its worst.' In November 1998 Mervyn Philpott issued a High Court writ against the club over £100,000 he claims his company was owed.

The new caterers also failed to impress. On their first day in July 1998, hungry supporters were reported to be furious about the quality of food and service when Norwich played Tottenham Hotspur in a pre-season friendly. Thousands went unfed as queues built up in executive dining areas and at food counters because staff were in short supply and could not work the tills. Diners paying a discounted £20-a-head for a ticket and a meal in the club's new carvery were left moaning about unpalatable meat, greasy roast potatoes and over-cooked vegetables.

John Farley, managing director of the Dunella waste management company who were sponsoring the match, wrote to complain, condemning the catering as 'an absolute disgrace'. He described the meal as 'chaotic, shambolic and disorganised, akin to food parcels being distributed in the Sudan'. 'The food was horrendous and a disaster,' he said. 'The caterers were behaving like a bunch of adolescents. I am sure Delia Smith would be mortified.'

Other diners found themselves at tables without salt and pepper, napkins and, in some cases, without chairs. Ordinary fans in the 16,000 crowd were annoyed that pies had gone up from £1.30 to £1.80. 'At best, the catering was a fiasco. At worst, it was a disaster,' said Roy Blower of the Norwich City Independent Supporters' Association. 'Most supporters did not think there was that much wrong with the old catering firm which was given the boot.'

Delia refused to comment but in May 1999 she fired Food East, despite the fact that the Watsons were personal friends. Announcing that their contract would end on July 1st, she said the catering would be dealt with in-house from then on. She was considering taking it over personally. 'I feel I would like to be more involved,' she said. I don't know at the moment how much time it would take because I have my other work, but in the long term it is something I would like to be involved with.'

But it is questionable how many football fans would be interested in being fed on such Delia delights as Piedmont roasted peppers with feta cheese and rosemary bread, or salmon steaks with avocado and crème fraiche. Catering for match goers is notoriously difficult. Rangers say it is doing a good trade in veggie burgers and has a selection of fine wines and champagnes at the Ibrox stadium in Glasgow. In London, Spurs offer Indian and Chinese takeaways and Arsenal is dishing out smoked salmon bagels. But Blackburn's attempts to introduce scampi hit the rocks when fans refused to ditch their pies – traditionally the soccer fan's favourite grub.

Vegetable samosas went down like a lead balloon among Newcastle's followers and pizzas got the thumbs down at Arsenal. There is a school of thought that says football fans don't want upmarket food. A spokesman for Newcastle FC summed up the mood in the Northeast: 'We provide basic food – hotdogs, burgers, pies – because there is no demand for anything more. As long as we stock plenty of brown ale everyone is happy.' Even Delia herself admits to opting for a pre-match meal at McDonald's. 'On the way to the game we pick up Big Macs and have a picnic in the car park before the match,' she says. 'I absolutely love Big Macs with fries and loads of ketchup.'

But while she may not be able to dictate what Norwich City's fans eat, Delia does have a say in what her players consume. Unsurprisingly for someone who has spent their career concerned with food, she is keen that the sportsmen follow a nutritionally balanced diet. In an interview with comedian and fellow football fanatic David Baddiel, she revealed she had been busy studying football diets. 'I've been finding out what their diet is – or should be – and persuading the players to do it,' she explained.

'They're supposed to have a high carbohydrate diet, and 24 hours before a match they're supposed to have what they call carbohydrate tracking. Apparently the continentals are very keen on this. It's all very experimental at the moment, but if it works we'd like to publish it so that everybody can do it.'

Already used to being the nation's nanny and telling people how and what they should eat, Delia has turned her attentions to implementing a strict meal plan for the Norwich City players. She personally oversees their diet and has put them on what she calls her High Performance Eating Programme. The players' specially designed carbohydrate-dominated breakfasts and lunches are prepared by her own chef, Mark Corbluth, at City's Colney training centre. And she even laid on a demonstration for the footballers' wives and girlfriends to show them what they should be cooking their men.

Delia's own recipes were obviously included; such as sun-dried tomato risotto and Italian bean and pasta soup, which are designed to provide maximum energy for football. But she didn't conduct the demonstration herself as she still refuses to cook in front of a live audience. Instead she brought in a team of helpers from Auxerre. 'The regime at Auxerre is incredibly strict,' she says, talking about the Auxerre team. 'Virtually no alcohol. Ten days a year they are allowed alcohol. I'm learning, I'm learning. It's water, water everywhere. The coaches, players, families all have dinner together on a Saturday night with loads of water, and with lovely food.'

How the different continental clubs operate is something that interests Delia enormously. On a trip to Italy with her friend Alberto Camisa she jumped at the opportunity to find out about the methods used by one of Italy's top teams. She was in the country to film sequences for her *How to Cook* television series and was delighted to discover that not only could Alberto intro-duce her to interesting food people, he also knew a leading Italian trainer. 'My niece's godfather is a scout trainer for Parma Football Club,' he explains. 'They're a top team – the equivalent of Liverpool – and about 14 of us went out to dinner with him one evening.

'We went to a nice old-fashioned restaurant where I know the owner. There was no menu – they just feed you. The meal went on for four or five hours and was great fun. The owner is a bit of a show-off and he and Delia were swapping recipes. But she spent just as much time talking about football. She discovered that in Italy the clubs are much stricter about what players do and eat. In Britain they play a game of football and then go to a bar. That wouldn't be allowed in Italy.'

'Delia's got a big bee in her bonnet about modelling us on

continental clubs, and in particular a French one called Auxerre,' explains Joe Ferrari. 'We now have a continental-style management team.'

Delia was impressed by what she saw at Auxerre and plans to run Norwich City in a similar way. 'Aspiring young footballers from the age of 5 want to be there,' she says. 'At 14, they select the best ones to go to the academy where they have a full-time education and football coaching side. We have a licence to have a Football Academy at Norwich and that is our vision. For us, it's not about making money.'

In October 1998 Delia said she and Michael had invested £3.5 million in Norwich City, but denied she was as well-off as people might think. 'There's no doubt about it, I've earned a lot of money,' she says matter-of-factly. 'I've been lucky, extremely lucky, but I don't have anywhere near what they say I have. And at the moment I have put it all into the football club. This year Michael and I have had to look carefully at how we paid our tax. We have pensions and things, we're secure, but to actually find the ready cash to pay the tax was a bit tricky.'

By 2002, the amount they'd invested had risen to £6 million and the couple held a 61% stake in the club. Delia admits they may never see a return on their investment in the club. 'We knew that when we put the money into Norwich City we would probably never see it again,' she says pragmatically. 'We are football fans, first and foremost. That's what we're interested in. We're not interested in villas in the south of France and swimming pools. We spend our money on hiring little planes to go to away matches.'

Football is the only thing that stops her thinking about recipes. She confesses, rather shockingly, that even going to church doesn't have that effect on her. 'I can make up a recipe in my head when I'm in church listening to a sermon but when I watch football there's nothing else,' she says. 'I find it really

217

good therapy. When I'm at the football, it's the one time I'm not thinking of anything else.'

Delia is keen to devote more time to football. 'I think there will come a point when people have all the recipes they need,' she says. 'I have been very tempted to give up my day job and go into football full-time. There is so much to do. I thought about it a lot, but we decided it wasn't the right thing to do at the moment. I would like to spend more or less full-time on football and I might consider working with the Football Association. I was asked to go on the Task Force but I didn't have time.'

At the beginning of 2002 the faith and hard work that Delia had put into her club appeared to be paying off. The team was playing well and Norwich was set to share in the multi-million pound bonanza television company ITV Digital had pledged for the rights to show Nationwide League matches. But when the company went under in April 2002 owing £178.5 million to the Football League, it threatened to throw the club into crisis. Norwich City was owed £2.5 million; money it desperately needed. Norwich chief executive Neil Doncaster spelt it out: 'To lose the ITV Digital money would mean that our position is not sustainable,' he said. 'We are talking about survival.'

'I am passionate about this club and I have put in lots of time and worked very hard to turn it around,' a clearly upset Delia told the *Mirror*. 'Now someone could take it all away and that's absolutely outrageous. They say 30 clubs could go out of business by the end of next season. Football clubs will go to the wall.'

There was a glimmer of hope on the horizon however. In May 2002, Norwich City stood on the brink of the Premiership – and a possible £25 million. If they could win the vital play-off match against Birmingham City, the club would enter the promised land of the Premiership and be entitled to a cut of the huge amount of money on offer to its teams in television revenue and sponsorship deals.

In what must have been the most stressful match she has ever watched, Delia was on tenterhooks as the two teams battled it out at Cardiff's Millennium Stadium on May 12th. At half time the score was 0–0, a stalemate that continued to full-time. Iwan Roberts pushed Norwich into the lead with a goal in the first minute of extra time and it seemed that Norwich had won the day. But 11 minutes later Birmingham city's Geoff Horsfield made it 1–1. In a finale that had supporters of both teams biting their nails to the quick, the match culminated in that most hated of endings – the penalty shoot-out.

Norwich's first attempt went in, courtesy of Iwan Roberts, but Phil Mulryne and Daryl Sutch both missed. Birmingham City, who had almost made it to the Premiership so many times before, finally had luck on their side and won the match 4–2 on penalties.

It was a horrible way to go and Delia was devastated. Speaking for thousands of fans she said: 'We have experienced seven years of pain and misery and being robbed when we were so close to the Premiership probably makes it eight years. Never mind, there will be a big party anyway.'

The lady who came out on top was Birmingham City's managing director Karren Brady. 'Delia and myself are great friends and we will stay that way,' she said. 'Don't expect me to be anything except overjoyed about the prospect of an extra £25 million or £30 million of revenue though.'

12

How to Boil an Egg

Delia had managed to keep her latest cookery project under wraps, but in June 1998 word got out. She would be taking on the mantle of Mrs Beeton with a 'How To' guide for modern cooks who had forgotten the basics. The BBC confirmed that the top-secret project was *Delia's How to Cook*, a two-volume book accompanied by a 22-part television series. 'A lot of people out there can chargrill a bit of monkfish but have never baked a loaf of bread,' explained a spokesman. 'We think it will help people who didn't get to domestic science and didn't learn from their mothers.'

As a concept it was unremarkable – boring even – but never has a recipe book caused so much fuss. Published in October 1998, it immediately opened up a heated debate amongst chefs, food writers and Delia's own fans. The nation was split into two camps: those who thought *How to Cook* was a good thing, and those who considered it to be condescending and banal.

Celebrity chef Gary Rhodes started the ball rolling by launching a blistering attack on Delia, accusing her of 'insulting viewers' intelligence.' Rhodes, one of her leading rivals for Britain's culinary crown, said: 'I do not need to be shown what boiling water looks like and I tend to think that the rest of the popula-tion doesn't need to be shown it either.'

While Delia kept a dignified silence, others waded in on her behalf. TV chef Hugh Fearnley-Whittingstall acknowledged that Gary Rhodes might be the more sophisticated cook, but said Delia's programmes had a staggering popularity. 'People do what Delia says to the letter and they get results,' he said. 'If you want to do a cookery show from the basics then its right to show people how to boil an egg.'

Former *Good Food Guide* editor Tom Jaine admits he has mixed feelings about the merits of *How to Cook*. 'Each year there are a million people entering the world of cookery for the first time and they need to be taught,' he reasons. 'But I did get slightly ventilated about this new series and was actually quite shocked that they could contemplate putting it out at prime time. That anyone with half a brain could sit and watch this old woman rubbing around a boring kitchen – well it just left me quite gobs-macked.

'It's so boring – deeply boring – and I can't believe that people were watching at 8.30pm. It seems to me that it's going out at the wrong time. The people who really need to be shown how to boil an egg are between the ages of 13 and 27 and will be watching at 6pm, at which point it would be really useful.'

Jaine also took exception to Delia's manner, which he declared to be 'exceptionally condescending'. 'When I first saw her on television I thought, "This is a woman of genius" because she was able to educate the unwashed exceptionally clearly,' he says. 'She seemed to have exactly what hopeless young marrieds need. But when I saw her recently I thought that she was educat-ing the unwashed in an exceptionally condescending fashion. That's my feeling.'

Delia's BBC colleague Antony Worrall Thompson is on her side. 'I am fully supportive of her latest series, and in fact any series she's done,' he says. 'The people who criticised it were purists and I say to them, "If you don't like it, don't buy it". If you can cook, you don't need the book. If you can't cook – which the majority of the country can't – then it's a bloody good book. If you look at Elizabeth David's recipes, they are quite complicated. You have got to read them thoroughly before you'll understand them, whereas with Delia you can take the first paragraph and go on from there.'

And in a good-natured broadside at Gary Rhodes he added: 'Don't watch it Gary! If he had any intelligence he would have switched the set off, wouldn't he?'

Rhodes later softened his criticisms by saying: 'Delia Smith is my hero. She is everybody's hero. I endorse her approach wholeheartedly.' But the can of worms had been opened. Everybody, it seemed, had an opinion *about How to Cook* and Delia's friend Prue Leith admits to finding the dispute intriguing. 'I was absolutely fascinated by that whole boiling water business,' she says. 'When people said they didn't need to be told how to boil water I would say, "Right, what's the difference between poaching and simmering water and boiling water?" And of course they didn't know.

'The fact is people DO need to be told when food should go into boiling water, when it should go into simmering water and when it should go into poaching water. Delia was talking about how to cook, assuming you couldn't cook at all.'

The legendary Egon Ronay also comes down firmly on Delia's side. 'I have the highest imaginable opinion of her because as far as I can tell she is the only one who really takes people back to basics,' he praises. 'And she does it with great patience and a basic understanding of people's ignorance. She is aiming at people who don't know how to make an omelette, or even how to break eggs properly. I think she has an extremely important role because the majority of television cookery programmes don't teach people – they are just entertainment. Sometimes they give ideas to people but they don't take people by the hand and lead them through the basics.'

He is scathing of Gary Rhodes, saying: 'I think it was a rash, silly statement he made, probably in the hope of a bit of publicity.'

Ronay, president of the British Academy of Gastronomes and the man who once famously said of Delia: 'She is the missionary position of cooks while others hope to be the karma sutra' – blames much of the criticism that has been levelled at the *How to Cook* series on envy. 'Conscious or not, there is tremendous jealousy in the cookery world,' he says. 'People who have very high book sales, like Gary Rhodes and Rick Stein, sell lots of books when their programmes are on, but Delia sells all year round so it cannot be purely attributable to the fact that she's on television. I've no doubt that it's because people find her books much more useful than any other cookery books. That's why she has such astronomical sales. She deserves to win food awards and if she doesn't have them it is because of people's jealousy.'

There is, of course, no such thing as bad publicity and the furore over *How to Cook* undoubtedly boosted sales of the book. 'The fact that people are talking about her is what makes sales,' Worrall Thompson observes. One supermarket reportedly shifted 1,000 copies in one day, and within five days of publication enough had been sold to push Delia over an important milestone: she had sold ten million in her career.

What was even more remarkable was that 78% of the sales were in hardback form, which effectively made her Britain's most successful author. While Catherine Cookson and Jeffrey Archer have sold as many units, their sales are across a far greater number of titles, over a longer period and with a lower proportion of hardbacks. Stephen Butler, research manager of the industry monitors Bookwatch, describes Delia as 'completely different to any other author, even within her field.' He explains the Delia factor as trust and power. 'No one else has anything like her clout,' he says. 'There are plenty of other successful and wealthy cookery writers, but they're not in Delia's league.'

The BBC saw *How to Cook* – billed as 'the indispensable guide to cooking for the twenty-first century' – as a 'long-game' book, predicting that as a back-to-basics guide it would sell consistently over a long period. 'It's a risk, but I decided to go back to basics,' Delia explains. 'My generation had cooking courses where we learned the basics. But although the next generation ate the food, they never learned how to cook it themselves. This book is for them.' She dedicated it to 'the young cooks of Britain' and as well as showing people how to boil an egg – complete with a colour photograph of a pan of boiling water – the book devoted a whole page to what Delia called 'the definitive recipe for perfect toast'. There followed a nine-point guide, including bossy instructions not to push down too hard on the loaf when slicing it, and to always use a toast rack.

For some it was too good an opportunity to miss. 'Now Delia Smith's going to teach you how to make toast,' wrote one incredulous newspaper critic. 'Only in the country that has turned dinner into the nation's favourite spectator sport could this occur. You don't need a millionairess with a studio in her kitchen to teach you how to boil an egg.' Nicknaming her book 'The Bleedin' Obvious Vol 1', they offered their own tip for those who couldn't tell when water is boiling: 'Stick your head in. You'll know.'

Puzzlingly, Delia also claimed that she had invented oven-roasted vegetables. 'That was a breakthrough. Now it's been copied and everyone does it,' she said, appearing to overlook the fact that people have been cooking that way for centuries.

Delia's friends, however, remain loyal. Dismissing Gary

Rhodes as 'that young man who could do with a good haircut', Delia's old boss Ken Toye sympathises with her. 'I feel very strongly about cooking and I hate the way that it has gone,' he says. 'I hate the glamour chef who has to wear a funny hat or play games to make cooking interesting. Cookery's a fascinating subject in its own right, but Delia is the only one who lets the food do the talking. She keeps to the background and lets it show itself. To me it is refreshing after all the rubbish we have to put up with.'

Delia's mentor Leo Evans also supports the philosophy of what she is trying to do. 'There is an enormous distinction between what I call method cooks and recipe cooks,' he explains. 'Either you learn how to cook, what you are doing and why you're doing it, or you read a recipe and slavishly follow it without really understanding what you're doing. Delia is teaching people the fundamental techniques which are so vital, but which so many people don't have. I know lots of cooks who have to look up a recipe every time they do it, but I can remember saying to Delia that if you are a professional pianist you don't have music in front of you, you learn.'

What there can be no denying, however, is that *How to Cook, Book One* didn't really offer anything that Delia hadn't already covered in *her Complete Cookery Course*. 'You will never have seen eggs cooking in this kind of detail before,' the BBC spokesman said about *How to Cook*, apparently forgetting the 16 pages devoted to them in the *Complete Cookery Course*. In the egg section alone the similarities between the two books are remarkable. Both go into great detail about every method of preparing them, and feature remarkably similar recipes for Egg and Lentil Curry, Eggs with Chorizo, Cheese Soufflés, and Eggs *en cocotte*.

And in the TV series she demonstrated how to tell if an egg is fresh. 'There's a little pocket of air at the top of a new-laid egg that expands when it gets stale,' Delia told us. 'A stale egg will sink, but point upwards; a very stale egg will float.' But old egg boilers knew this already, the *Sunday Telegraph* pointed out. 'They read it in Delia Smith's *Complete Cookery Course*, first published 20 years ago.

'Other things that appear in both books are recipes for lemon curd, Vegetable and Brown Rice Gratin, and Salmon and Caper fishcakes. Many of Delia's old favourites are present in *How to Cook*, albeit jazzed up versions for the nineties. Moussaka is made with parmesan and ricotta instead of the cheddar of the *Complete Cookery Course* recipe, and the rice dishes have been brought up to date with the addition of Far Eastern spices such as ginger, soy sauce and creamed coconut. Other recipes were modernised with the help of fashionable ingredients like wild mushrooms, quails eggs, and wilted rocket.

'Also like the *Complete Cookery Course*, *How to Cook* featured comprehensive sections on bread making, pizza dough, pastry, cakes, sauces and batters. As the Complete Cookery Course has never been out of print, this begs the question whether people really need another Delia book telling us the basics. The second book, due out Christmas 1999, deals with fish, meat, poultry and vegetables – topics that are already well covered in the *Complete Cookery Course*.

'The hardback version of the *Complete Cookery Course* is expensive, retailing at £22.99, but once Delia's readers have parted with £16.99 for How to Cook book one and then bought book two they could end up paying up to £34 for much the same thing.'

But Delia obviously felt the new cookery books were justified. 'I felt the basic cookery course needed to be updated to take into account all the fresh produce and ingredients available these days,' she said. 'I think we have got a bit carried away with trendy cooking in this country; it's food for kicks and it's a cul-de-sac. It seems that everything has to be wacky and buzzy these days, and we are in danger of missing out on simplicity.'

None of Delia's recent books have been without a 'key ingredient' and book one of *How to Cook* was no different. This time it was a special sauce flour that was hailed as the latest culinary breakthrough. Miller David Lines, a fan of Delia's, developed a superfine white flour that promised to take the fat – and the lumps – out of white sauces after seeing her outline the perils of making a roux in a previous television series. He wrote to her in 1997, enclosing a sample of sauce flour made from six different types of wheat, which had been individually milled before being mixed together.

'When I wrote to Delia, I expected her secretary to reply,' says David, production director at Carrs Flour Mill in Siloth, Cumbria. 'I'd sent a sample but I wasn't sure whether she would try it. I was delighted when she wrote back and said the flour worked extremely well. She then came to visit us and watched the production line and looked at the wheat from the different countries involved in the process.'

Delia hailed the 49p packet of sauce flour as a 'new and quite phenomenal way of making a white sauce' and described it as a 'huge step forward'. She was sufficiently impressed to use it in her *How to Cook* television series and as a result the company was preparing to increase production several fold. 'Supermarkets are already stocking it, but we expect a huge surge in demand next week,' said the sales director John Holmes. Sales duly soared by 405%. Supermarkets were sent a list of the items that Delia intended to feature in her programmes, including blade mace, marigold vegetable stock, Fontina cheese, Camargue red rice, and Chinese dried shrimps.

White eggs were also in vogue after Delia featured a bowl of them on the front cover of the book. Within six weeks of her television series starting, an extra 54 million eggs were sold – enough to make 27 million omelettes, 13.5 million sponge cakes and more than three million gallons of custard. The Egg

Information Service admitted the Delia effect had helped push up sales. 'We are very impressed and think Delia is great,' a spokesman said. 'She has shown that eggs are healthy and versatile. Consumers are asking for white eggs and refuse to accept that brown are just the same. If Delia uses white, they want white.'

And it was during *How to Cook* that she mentioned the 'little gem' omelette pan. The unremarkable eight-inch aluminium pan became an overnight success after she gave it her blessing on TV. It would, she said, 'serve you for a lifetime of happy omelette making'. Sales leapt from 200 a year to 90,000 in four months and its makers, Lune Metal products of Morecambe, Lancashire, had to hire extra staff to meet demand.

'It has been unbelievable,' said their shocked managing director Nick White. 'We were very proud that our product was good enough to be used by Delia on the programme. Everybody has been surprised by the result. Our forecast was that we may sell 50,000 pans because of the programme, but we are now approaching 90,000. Last May we had to make ten staff redundant and things looked a bit bleak, but I've had to hire 15 temporary staff to cope with the rush. The manufacturing industry is dead on its feet at the moment, so it's good to see Delia doing her bit.'

He said 'The omelette pan is nothing out of the ordinary. It is made of plain aluminium but won Delia's backing over more expensive non-stick ones because it allows the chef to cut inside the pan using metal utensils without causing any damage.' A spokesman for Delia said she is 'manic' in her pursuit of the perfect pan.

'It's amazing the interest she pulls in and the power she has over the cooking public,' said a BBC spokesman. 'She is the product, basically. No one has the effect she does – not to the extent that that shops run out of ingredients.' But they insisted that television guidelines on product placement were always followed and there had never been any complaints. 'She never mentions brand names or manufacturers or supermarkets,' they said.

Early in 1998 Delia received some bad news. Glyn, the brother she had not seen for ten years, had had a terrible accident and was fighting for his life. Whilst working as an engineer on a fishing boat in New Zealand, he had slipped and banged his head against a boat. He was in a coma and doctors doubted whether he would live.

Stuck many thousands of miles away on the other side of the world, Delia could only sit and pray as she waited anxiously by the telephone for news. The prognosis was grim: doctors warned her that even if Glyn did pull through he would almost certainly be paralysed. There was also brain damage, although to what extent they couldn't be sure until he woke up.

With a book to finish and a television series to film, Delia was unable to fly to her brother's bedside. But when a miracle happened and he finally regained consciousness, she immediately put plans in place to bring him home to Britain. She wanted her only brother to be where she could keep an eye on him and personally make sure that he got all the treatment he needed. In July 1998 doctors passed him fit enough to make the journey to England, and Delia paid for him to fly home.

Glyn stayed with her and Michael all summer and Delia personally looked after him at her home. She also arranged medical care and organised for a physiotherapist to come round every day to treat him. It was the first time brother and sister had seen each other for a whole decade and at times, when Glyn was in his coma, Delia must have doubted whether she would ever see him again.

Glyn admits that doctors never expected him to recover from his terrible accident. 'I fell about four metres and landed on my head,' he explains. 'I knocked myself out and was in a coma for two months or so. The accident happened at work, although at the time I wasn't actually working. I was walking up some really steep steps onto a boat and I fell and hit my head on the side of the boat. There is some permanent damage but considering that they never expected me to get out of bed again I'm doing all right.'

Although he has made an amazing recovery, Glyn's speech was badly affected by the blow to his head and he can hear only partially and in just one ear. As a result he is unable to work and Delia is helping him out financially until he is well enough to support himself. Now back at home in Nelson, New Zealand, where he is continuing to make good progress, he describes how Delia has supported him in his struggle to get well.

He explains how when he emerged from his coma he was impatient to recuperate as quickly as possible, but was frustrated when the medical help he felt he needed to get back to normal wasn't immediately forthcoming. 'There was nothing happening for me here in New Zealand,' he says. 'They hadn't arranged any speech therapy or physiotherapy and everything was taking such a long time. So my sister paid for me to go to England for some treatment. I was over there for about three months, from July to September. I hadn't seen Delia for ten years but it was more or less like old times. We've always been friends, she and I, and I've always got on with Michael – I used to play cricket with him years ago.'

Glyn was delighted with the care Delia had laid on for him. 'While I was staying with my sister I had regular speech therapy and a physiotherapist used to come round to the house most days,' he says. 'I also went to a gym which helped me get fit again physically.' Feeling significantly better after his convalescence in England, and more confident because of the speech therapy sessions, Glyn was able to convince his doctors in New Zealand to provide similar treatment.

'I came back and told them what had happened to me in England and showed them the progress I had made,' he says. 'They finally got around to organising some treatment for me and I now have a physiotherapist and a speech therapist. And Delia paid for me to have a year's membership of a gym, so on the days that I don't have physio I go to the gym.'

Glyn admits he is pushing himself hard to get well. 'I'm getting better slowly but not fast enough for me – I've always been impatient,' he says. 'The physio has more or less ended now but I'm still going to the gym three days a week. I'm trying hard. My intentions couldn't be better, I've got a strong will – always have had.' He is sufficiently well to be able to play golf again, but sadly he doesn't know if he will ever be able to work on fishing boats again. It was a job he loved. 'I'm not sure when I will be able to go back to work,' he says. 'I've always liked being at sea. Even before I became a fisherman I would rent yachts and go off sailing.

'There was a course at the Polytechnic School of Fishing, which I enrolled on in the hope of getting my skipper's licence, but I couldn't hear half of what was going on because I am still waiting for a hearing aid. I went for four days but I only heard half of the conversations so I had to leave. The course was costing thousands of dollars and I realised it was a waste of money if I couldn't hear what anyone was saying. Without a hearing aid I really don't know when I can return to work. I asked for one over a year ago but I'm still waiting. I can't just buy one either as things don't work like that over here. We have a thing called ACC, which looks after injured people and pays for their income. I have to go to my doctor every twelve weeks and get another form filled in to get my money. Each time I ask for a hearing aid and have to wait for another three months to see if I get it.'

Despite the fact that Delia helped Glyn during his hour of

need and is still assisting him financially, brother and sister are not close. Although Delia has travelled a great deal in recent years she has never visited her only brother in New Zealand and Glyn admits that she has no plans to do so. 'I've no idea when I'll see her again,' he says. 'She hasn't really got the time to come to New Zealand. She's a bit busy with the football club and writing books.' They seldom speak on the telephone and, bizarrely, did not even discuss their own father's death.

Harold Smith died from pneumonia on January 5th, 1999 at the age of 78. Delia and Michael were on holiday in the Bahamas when they heard the news and had to cut short their trip and fly home. But Delia hasn't spoken to her only brother about any grief she may feel. 'Our father was in hospital with flu and we thought he was getting better but then he died,' explains Glyn. 'I don't know if Delia was upset – I didn't really speak to her about it as she was quite busy trying to finish her latest book.'

It is a peculiar situation that shows how fragmented Delia's family became after her parents' separation. According to her brother, Delia hardly ever saw Harold and his second wife Barbara. 'I think they saw each other once a year,' he says. 'He lived in London and she lived too far away.' But the journey time between Bexley and Stowmarket is scarcely two hours and, in any event, Delia and Michael own a flat in east London – no more than ten miles from where Harold lived.

Barbara Smith has kept in touch with both of her stepchildren, but it is interesting that, shortly before Harold's funeral, it wasn't Delia who telephoned Glyn to see how he was bearing up, but Barbara's son Michael. 'Barbara writes to me now and then and just before the funeral her son Michael rang me up to ask how I was,' Glyn says. As well as not talking to her brother about her father's death, Delia did not even mention her bereavement to Father James Walsh, even though she saw the priest most weeks at Sunday evening mass in Ipswich. As far as

Father Walsh was concerned, Delia's dad had been dead for many years. He was also unaware that her brother had almost been killed. This is all the more unusual given that Delia and James Walsh are friends. He even composed the music that was used in the *How to Cook* television series.

Paul McAuley is another of Delia's friends who had no idea her father had recently passed away. He admits she can be secretive. 'There is a private side to Delia that she relishes,' he says. 'She's not necessarily all that communicative and she's got a terrific ability to know when to keep certain areas for herself. She doesn't speak about her family. We have never spoken about her father, only about her mum. It is quite difficult to get close to Delia and when you attempt to it is interesting how she buttons down. But we all have our own personal history and I think somebody in her position, who has had so much exposure – and at times the press can be superficial and bitchy – I suppose you learn to be very careful and to protect yourself.

'I think she finds it quite embarrassing to share any intimate details about herself. She is quite guarded and shy. If you are in the public eye people think you are very communicative and open, but that is not necessarily the case and I don't think Delia is particularly comfortable in many of those situations. That is where Michael does an excellent job. He makes clear ground rules about what Delia will and won't do. He's a great protector in that way.'

The *How to Cook* television series were once again shot in Delia's conservatory in Suffolk, but sadly filming on the second series in the early part of 1999 was marred by a tragic accident. Delia did not want the crew to use the toilet in her house so a portaloo was delivered for the production team to use. Unfortunately when it was lowered into position it was set down on top of one of Delia's two cats, killing it instantly.

Delia is devoted to her cats, Jo and Beau, and is featured

cuddling one of them at the back of *How to Cook*. Not only was it desperately sad for the poor creature concerned, it was also potentially life-threatening for the person who had to tell Delia what had happened. 'It was an absolutely dreadful scenario,' says an insider. 'The director Philip Bonham Carter said, 'There goes my career' and we all thought he was probably right. How do you tell someone that you have just killed their cat? Delia loves her cats and no one wanted to be the one to tell her what had happened.'

Fortunately, Delia was not at home when the accident happened but the director had to summon up all his courage and telephone her with the bad news. 'There was apparently a moment of silence at Delia's end of the phone and then she said, "Well, he was 16 years old, he's had a good life",' says an insider. 'We couldn't believe she had taken it so well.'

But the farcical situation didn't end there. 'They decided to bury the cat in a sunny spot in the garden before Delia came home and the director and Delia's husband Michael began digging a grave,' says one who witnessed the spectacle. 'But Michael was sweating like a pig and didn't look at all well. The director had to tell him to go inside before he had to ring Delia and tell her that her husband was dead too.'

Delia's two cats had been her constant companions while she wrote. Hidden away in the idyllic surroundings of what she calls her 'treehouse' at the end of her garden, she worked on her recipes while they lay curled up in a warm spot. Not actually up in a tree, but safely situated on the ground, Delia finds the wooden summerhouse a perfect place to write, surrounded by open fields and away from the distractions of the house. It's construction, complete with heating and electricity, was one of the few luxuries Delia has allowed herself. Despite her great wealth, she drove the same Volkswagon Golf for eight years and only recently traded it in for a modest Renault Clio.

Friends reveal that Michael is equally frugal. 'I've only got two suits,' he once boasted. 'No one can persuade me to buy clothes.' Pals describe how Michael – for many years defiantly casual in his choice of attire – has recently become more dapper. 'Delia always used to cut his hair – when he'd let her,' laughs Norman Hollands. 'Michael used to be quite shaggy but he's smartened up quite a lot now. I saw him a few weeks ago outside *The Magazine* offices. He had the sharp suit and briefcase and the neatly coiffeured grey hair – and the Jaguar driven by Trevor, his chauffeur.' But he still only has three suits and a friend says that his personal assistant had to grab his shoes off him when they had holes in them.'

Paul McAuley has also noticed the change in Michael. 'I find him much more dynamic, energetic and outgoing than when I first knew him years ago,' he says. 'You could say that Delia is the one who gives tremendous energy and challenge to Michael because of his very close link with her career. It is an exceptionally good partnership and they make a very powerful pair.'

Apart from the Norwich City Football Club, Delia and Michael's big extravagance is their holidays. Delia loves Barbados and they often take Etty, Hannah, Thomas and other assorted relatives with them. The couple have also been generous to their friends, most memorably on the occasion when they hosted a huge weekend party at Miller Howe and invited everyone they knew. 'Delia is very kind,' says Ken Toye fondly. 'My daughter, who is a physiotherapist, had a patient who was dying of cancer. This lady was always talking about Delia books and she had all of them except for one – the first book that Delia ever wrote. I don't like bothering Delia because she is so busy, but I forced myself and wrote and explained the situation and back came a signed copy of the book. The lady died in the summer and I know that book meant a lot to her.

'Another example was the party she held to celebrate selling her two millionth book. Everybody who had helped her along the way was invited. She remembered us all and wanted to give people something back.' When the party ended, Delia announced that she was going to visit some friends and asked Ken Toye and his wife if they wanted to go with her. What happened next had a profound effect on Ken. 'Delia took us to see some nuns who run a refuge in the Lake District,' he explains. 'It was important to her: in the midst of her celebrations she had to make that visit and let her friends share in the experience. The nuns sang some songs and gave us a blessing when we left.'

Ken firmly believes that the blessing saved his life. 'On the way home we were in a terrible traffic accident involving 50 cars,' he says. 'But we went straight through the middle of the accident and out the other side. There were cars circling and somersaulting on each side of us. I shall remember it to my dying day. It was like a dream - it was extraordinary.'

One of Delia's best friends is the chef John Tovey, whom she met in 1972 when she interviewed him at Miller Howe, the renowned hotel he owned on Lake Windermere. He is her biggest fan, not least because she helped him to rediscover Catholicism. 'It was only through her that I found my faith again,' he says. 'She is deeply religious, a true practising Christian. She has great saintly qualities.' Tovey tells how, when he came out of hospital in early 1995 after an operation, she and Michael dropped everything to go away on holiday with him. 'She helps so many people, just by being Delia,' he gushes. 'In any other country she would be Dame Delia.'

Tovey, now retired and living in Cape Town, regularly holidays with Delia and Michael. 'The three of us go away together twice a year like a family,' he says. 'We take it in turns to pick the destination. Last time it was Delia's turn and she decided we should go on a Christmas cruise to Barbados. The time before that we cruised around the Baltic and Italy. We are all three Scrabble freaks, though Delia complains I cheat, and we all like our food and wine. Often we just sit about the ship reading and saying nothing to each other, like real friends can. But we also have a lot of giggles. When I spend the weekend with them at their house we go to the pictures, watch videos, go out for fish and chips or grab a bite at McDonald's. I have loved her for a long time. I look on her and Michael as the brother and sister I never had.'

Delia admits that she has few friends. 'My work brings me into contact with a lot of people and I love people,' she says. 'But I like them more in the work context than the social context, so I don't have a big social life at all.' John Tovey is part of that select crowd. 'Delia has a very small circle of friends,' he acknowledges. 'She guards her privacy jealously because she works so hard. I don't know anyone who works so hard as Delia. In fact she gives her all to such an extent she becomes so tetchy and stressed out she is like a zombie. She needs her holidays. Being so successful has not altered that, in fact the older she gets the more she feels she has to work to rise to the challenge from younger people.'

But even on holiday Delia doesn't switch off completely. 'Once we're abroad we always make a bee-line for the markets and restaurants,' says Michael. 'A couple of years ago I bought Delia a video recorder for a birthday present and filming the local produce helps fix it in her mind. I now have more videos of local markets than you ever want to see in your life. For my birthday she bought me an editing kit but at the moment the tapes are still stacked up on the shelves of our London home.'

It was John Tovey who christened her 'Saint Delia'. He no doubt meant it as a fond pet name but after seeing it used in an average of one in three newspaper headlines, Delia is thoroughly sick of it. She says it upsets her far more than any criticism of her cooking. During her interview with the comedian David Baddiel, which rather unusually took place over a game of table football, she made a startling confession. 'I want to dive in the shower with the footballers one day and put an end to all that saintly business,' she blurted. 'I hate the saintly tag. Sometimes I think the only way to get rid of it would be to do something really wicked. In front of the press. Just for a giggle.'

Delia loves dining out, especially when she is in London. One of her friends remembers the rather surreal night when Delia took her friend Sister Wendy Beckett to dinner at Langan's Brasserie, the famous Mayfair eatery that used to be owned by the ebullient Peter Langan. 'Needless to say, Peter Langan came up, a bit the worse for wear, shouting at the top of his voice about never having seen a nun in his restaurant before,' says the friend. 'I don't think Sister Wendy had ever seen anything like it – she spends most of her time in an enclosed order – but Delia just stood there smiling serenely through it all. She treats all her friends in just the same way.'

Delia's friends find it hard to understand why she continues to attract so much criticism. It is something that puzzles photographer Max Logan: 'Some people say, "I can't stand Delia" and when I ask them why, they say, "She's so successful". I point out that she is successful because she's extremely good, but people are very stuck-up about her. Certainly all the home economists I've ever spoken to seem to find her irritating. It's an attitude that seems strange to me. Delia brought simplicity to the whole thing. Food writing was a pretty snobby set-up but she made it accessible. That is her huge advantage, she's not trying to be anything, she's just herself.'

Norman Hollands agrees: 'Years ago I said to Delia, "You're a crusader, you want to make good cooking accessible to everybody". She doesn't see herself as a crusader but she is. You've only got to look at the way she works.'

Still the sniping goes on. 'She doesn't cook Christmas lunch because she's usually in Barbados,' bitched one critic. 'For years chefs have been scornful of Delia because they see her as homely and housewifey,' says Prue Leith. 'Television cooks have always fallen into two categories. One is the helpful kind, like Delia, who actually tell you how to cook and show you how to do it. They are watched by millions more people and their books get bought. The other kind are entertainers like Keith Floyd and the Two Fat Ladies, who nobody intends to cook anything from. They are there for a completely different purpose. You don't sit taking notes when you're watching them, like you do with Delia. You sit there stuffing your face with takeaways or pot noodles while you enjoy the fact that they are entertaining you. Nobody seriously thinks you're going to cook Mendip snails on a shovel by the roadside, but it's lovely to watch somebody else do it.'

Delia is seldom seen to retaliate, safe in the knowledge that she is Britain's favourite cook. She even has a photograph of her critic Gary Rhodes on the wall of her office at *The Magazine*, although that was *before* his recent outburst. She did once allow herself a sly dig at her television rivals on the BBC's *Food and Drink* programme, but without naming anybody personally. She found it revolting, she admitted, that some TV chefs actually tasted what they had made on screen. 'I can't bear it,' she grimaced. 'It's just everything I hate. I can't bear people eating on TV, it's one thing I will never, ever do: I will never put anything in my mouth and go, "Delicious". That is just the pits, isn't it?' She also criticised *Ready, Steady Cook*, but could only accuse it of being too 'hearty'.

She admits to being wounded by what people say about her, but remains nonetheless defiant. 'The criticism does hurt,' she says. 'But I will not fall into the trap of writing books for other chefs. I write for people and that is reflected by the fact that they buy my books. Cookery lends itself to pretension more than any

240

other subject except wine and art, and I was determined to change that. Good cooking belongs to everyone. I was once signing books on a housing estate in Liverpool and an old man told me he had just made my mushroom risotto. I thought to myself, "This is what it's all about".'

Whatever her critics say, Delia's book sales speak for themselves. *How To Cook Book 2* came out in December 1999 and was an instant best-seller. And *How To Cook Book 3*, released in December 2001, sold almost 400,000 copies in just 14 weeks. Even the Naked Chef Jamie Oliver, whose books actually outsold Delia's in the year to April 2002, says of her: 'She's the guvnor.'

But as her most recent television series showed, Delia's style of presenting is undeniably dated, especially compared to that of current culinary sensation Nigella Lawson. The comely Ms Lawson, whose tendency to lick her chocolate-covered fingers inspired one reviewer to describe her Channel 4 programme as 'gastro porn', provides far more entertaining television. While Nigella was filmed in a candle-lit bath unashamedly sampling the food she had just made, Delia chose to open the television series of *How To Cook 3* with a lecture on kitchen equipment. Not even unusual kitchen equipment; but boring wooden spoons, knives and saucepans. Glamorous or interesting, it certainly wasn't.

'Delia seems intent on regarding her series as the TV equivalent of setting up a stall at the Ideal Home Exhibition and flogging saucepans by doing demonstrations,' noted the *Mirror*'s TV critic Jim Shelley. 'Like a little girl entertaining her parents' guests, Delia was determined to show us every single one of her utensils whether we liked it or not.'

At the time of writing, Delia has notched up 33 years of recipes. She has sold more than 11 million books and remains as influential as ever. She has her own website, www.deliaonline.com and is immortalised in the dictionary. So many people refer to 'doing a Delia' that the Collins English Dictionary now defines her name as 'Noun. The recipes or style of cooking of British cookery writer Delia Smith,' forever linking her with the concept of culinary excellence.

It was even announced that she is to teach that most culinary of races, the French, how to cook. A compilation of 150 of her basic recipes is to be published in France under the title *La Cuisine Facile D'aujourd'hui, par Delia* – Easy cooking for today, by Delia. 'The thought of a French person cooking an English recipe is pretty cool,' she acknowledged.

Delia remains fiercely ambitious. 'I don't think being ambitious is a bad thing,' she once said. 'We do get these incredible book sales and each time there's a new volume out, I always want it to beat the sales of the last one. It's exciting to be involved in all that. I think ambition keeps you alive. I can't conceive of not being ambitious.'

People who have known and worked with Delia over the years are well aware of this determination to succeed, which is why they refuse to believe that she will ever hang up her spatula or relinquish her culinary crown. 'I'd take any talk of her giving up cookery with a pinch of salt,' says Norman Hollands with certainty. 'I don't think she does it for the money; she really believes in it.' Betty Bealy, her friend at Look East, agrees: 'Delia was always talking about giving up cooking, that's nothing new. If you are a cookery writer I suppose you always think you're repeating yourself and you might want to do something else instead. I don't think she'll ever give up, someone would probably talk her back into it.'

She is said to be among the 50 richest women in the country – not bad for a girl who left school without a single qualification to her name. She has an honorary doctorate from Nottingham University and an OBE. The Prime Minister paid her the compliment of asking her to become a working peer and was no doubt astonished when she turned him down. But unlike many of her fans, Delia's friend Paul McAuley was not surprised that she said no.

'Delia is somebody who likes to do things well,' he explains. 'I'm sure that once Norwich have won the European Cup and are at the top of the Premiership she will sell up and go to the House of Lords, but she won't attempt it until she's got time. The day she is made a life peer she will enjoy playing the part and will make sure that she's heard and participates fully. One of the things I admire about her is her strength. Once she's focused on an idea or project she's very dogged – I would say even stubborn – about pursuing it and putting everything in, whether that be money or people or time, to make sure it is successful.'

Brother Paul appears pleased that Delia rejected the opportunity to become Baroness Smith. 'It probably says something for Delia's inner growth that she can simply take a certain distance from that,' he says. 'I don't think she's going to be taken in by titles or the glitter anymore. She gets her spiritual food from day to day living and doesn't need the extra trappings that some people consider the essentials. She has built in her own spaces for getting that spiritual resource that she needs. She's got time for prayer and is in the lucky position to be able to organise her life and decide her priorities: she doesn't have to be victim of other people's priorities.'

Brother Paul is one of the few people who know Delia well. He has watched as she has matured from an enthusiastic young Catholic into the mature and contemplative woman she is today. He believes that many of the views she expressed in her religious books have now been tempered. 'We all go through stages in our religious thinking and converts, particularly, can feel quite strongly about certain ideas,' he explains. 'But gradually people begin to see that things are not as black and white as they thought. When people appear zealous, it is usually insecurity that is behind it. Zealots basically scream out on certain issues because they believe it's a basic point that they won't give in on. It can be out of anger, almost out of panic, but as we grow older we are less hung up on things and I think Delia is probably in that situation.

'I suspect that the reason she doesn't write religious books anymore may be because she is now more circumspect and has a broader religious view than perhaps she did when she was younger. At one time she probably felt quite secure in her new-found faith in the Catholic tradition, and I think her religious books are a product of her secure time. The interesting thing is that she has probably got a much more mature, interesting faith now as an older woman but she's probably a lot less secure. There is a lot more insecurity in her ideas; they are less categoric and much more interesting. When we are young we tend to be more secure, more dogmatic, and I think a sign of religious maturity is precisely when people become less dogmatic, more understanding, more accepting of the unknown and therefore a lot more cautious about giving definite answers to things.

'We are very alike in that respect. We agree on most things and have always seen eye-to-eye. I've never come up against her and I'm not sure I want to – I think I'd lose! She's got an enquiring mind – a very critical mind – and she can be very strident when she feels there's any line she doesn't like. She's an active member of the Catholic Church but there are many things she does not go along with, particularly in terms of hierarchical teaching, and she enjoys playing her part and saying what she thinks.'

Paul thinks that Delia has finally found contentment. 'It's difficult to say whether she is happy,' he says thoughtfully. 'I would say maybe she's happy in the sense that people who are on a drive for something, who have a vision and a spiritual angst if you like, are happy. I think she realises that she is a very fortunate person to have the gifts that she does, and that she is lucky in her relationship with Michael. But I don't think she is naïve enough to imagine that you can live in perfect happiness all the time.'

And while others believe Delia will never turn her back on cooking, Paul hopes that one day she will. 'When I first met Delia she was just developing an interest in theology and religious writing,' he explains. 'She has a natural talent for communicating with people on a very straight, simple level about religious issues and I suspect there is still a part of Delia that would love to be doing that. I think part of her would be much happier involved in more spiritual issues. She's certainly got a lot of talent there, and she'd be very good doing it on television. If I had time I would love to produce her on TV, in a very light way, to make people aware of what's going on, and get them to consider certain issues; philosophical or religious. She'd be good at sparking people on that sort of common level.

'But the problem with Delia is that she's accumulated several projects that involve energy and time and the poor thing is on a wheel of time-consuming activities that block her diary out for years to come. I hope she's going to be happy to be successful enough at a certain point to be able to say "That's it" as far as cooking is concerned and dedicate herself to other things.'

Whether Delia will do this remains to be seen. Will she continue in her crusade to educate generations of young cooks? O will she decide to file her recipes away in the attic and concentrate on being a football mogul? It is more than likely she will do both. She appeared to abandon cookery once before in the eighties when she turned her attention to religious books. But just when people had started to write her off, back she came, stronger than ever. Even if she does decide to give her all to Norwich City FC it won't necessarily be the last we'll see of her.

Her old adversary Gary Rhodes has probably got it right.

'Delia is an institution,' he says. 'She will always be with us. We need Delia, in the way some people reluctantly say we need the Church of England.'